1226 - 610-7309

A HISTORY OF THE
NURSING PROFESSION

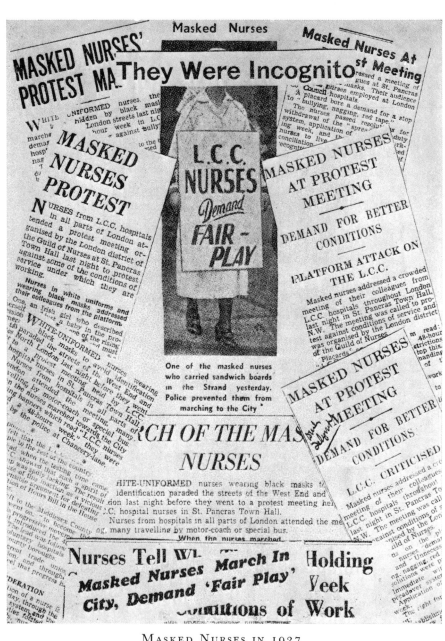

MASKED NURSES IN 1937

A HISTORY

OF THE

NURSING PROFESSION

by

BRIAN ABEL-SMITH

Professor of Social Administration
London School of Economics

HEINEMANN

LONDON

Heinemann Educational Books Ltd
22 Bedford Square, London WC1B 3HH

LONDON EDINBURGH MELBOURNE AUCKLAND
HONG KONG SINGAPORE KUALA LUMPUR NEW DELHI
IBADAN NAIROBI JOHANNESBURG
EXETER (NH) KINGSTON PORT OF SPAIN

ISBN 0 435 32004 1

Printed in Great Britain by
Biddles Ltd, Guildford, Surrey

Contents

List of Illustrations

Acknowledgements

The author and publishers wish to thank the following for their kind permission to reproduce illustrations contained in this book:

Messrs S. H. Bousfield & Co. Ltd, for Plates VII and VIII, reproduced from S. A. Tooley, *The History of Nursing in the British Empire.*

The British Journal of Nursing, for Plates XI and XII.

Messrs Cassell & Co. Ltd, for Plate XVI, reproduced from George Sims (ed.), *Living London.*

The Confederation of Health Service Employees, for the Frontispiece.

The Board of Governors of Guy's Hospital, for Plate X.

The Mansell Collection, for the illustration reproduced on the jacket and for Plate XIV.

The Matron of the Middlesex Hospital, for Plate IX.

The Norwich, Lowestoft and Great Yarmouth Hospital Management Committee, for Plate III.

Radio Times Hulton Picture Library, for Plates I, XIII, and XVII.

The Treasurer and Governors of St Thomas's Hospital, for Plates IV and V.

Victoria and Albert Museum, for Plate VI.

The Trustees of the Wellcome Historical Medical Museum, for Plates II and XV.

Abbreviations used in the Footnotes

H of L Deb.	*House of Lords Debates*
H of C Deb.	*House of Commons Debates*
STHA	*St Thomas's Hospital Archives*
COHSE	Confederation of Health Service Employees
BJN	*The British Journal of Nursing*
NT	*The Nursing Times*
NM	*Nursing Mirror*

Preface

THIS is a study of the 'politics' of general nursing from 1800 onwards. It concentrates on the structure of the profession, on recruitment, on terms and conditions of service. It describes the activities and rivalries of the professional associations and trade unions which have represented or tried to represent nurses. It analyses the main issues of public policy at different times and shows how they have been handled by the profession and by government.

The story is told against the wider background of the changing pattern of medical care, but no attempt is made to provide a history of nursing techniques or of nursing as an activity or skill. Little is said about what it was like at different times to nurse, or be trained as a nurse, or to receive nursing care. What the nurse was taught, who taught her, who examined her are all questions which are left unanswered.

Despite these substantial limitations in the approach to the subject, it has not proved possible to contain the subject in one volume without restricting the scope still further. Thus the story is focused on general nursing in the hospital setting. So much attention is paid to hospital nursing because this is where nurse training has been conducted. Mental nursing is almost entirely omitted because it has had a separate development and would justify a study of its own. The selection of general nursing for this study carries no implication that other fields of nursing practice, outside as well as inside the hospital, are any less important.

This history has been confined to England and Wales. The development and organization not only of nursing but also of medical care in general has been somewhat different in Scotland. Thus, except when otherwise stated, the statistics which are quoted cover England and Wales alone.

The book is arranged chronologically. The first chapter describes the state of nursing before reform, and the second and third deal with the introduction of training in the voluntary hospitals and workhouses respectively. The fourth chapter consolidates developments up to 1900. Chapter V describes the origin and objectives of the first professional association (the British Nurses' Association) and analyses the issues that underlay the struggle between those who favoured and those who opposed registration. Chapter VI gives the background to the Registration Act of 1919; its implementation is the subject of Chapter VII. The next three chapters are synoptic and deal with the problems of the inter-war period. In Chapter VIII an attempt is made to show the effects of registration and the changes in the profession since the beginning of the century. Chapter IX is devoted to terms and conditions of service and the rising challenge of trade unions to the professional associations. Chapter X analyses the critical problem of recruitment.

Chapter XI describes the problems of the second world war and the major changes introduced in the nursing profession— the statutory recognition of a second grade of nurse and the establishment of national negotiating machinery. In Chapter XII the later story of the war is told—a tale of continuing shortages and drastic proposals for reform. The next three chapters cover three different threads in the history of nurses under the National Health Service. Chapter XIII is concerned with the negotiation of terms and conditions of service by the new Whitley Council. Chapter XIV brings up to date the history of the recruitment and training of nurses for the general register. Chapter XV deals with the lower grades of nurse. Finally in Chapter XVI an attempt is made to explain and evaluate the events described and draw wider conclusions from them.

This study would not have been possible without assistance from many quarters. First, the King Edward's Hospital Fund for London kindly agreed in 1956 to pay the costs of research undertaken by the author under the direction of Professor Richard Titmuss into the demands for and finance of medical care. Material has been collected for a number of volumes and this is the first to reach the stage of publication. I am particularly grateful to the Trustees of the Fund for stepping outside their normal field of work to finance research of this kind.

Secondly, I would like to thank Miss Dianne Farris, who has acted as my research assistant, secretary, and public relations officer throughout the whole of the three years that the book has taken to write. She has read through masses of material looking for information on various points, handled all the correspondence, filed all the information, typed all the drafts, checked all the quotations, and marshalled all the footnotes to conform to a standard pattern. But this is not all. She has kept me constantly up to the mark by means of flattery, charm, or a good sharp shock as circumstances demanded. And last, she has been a penetrating critic of each draft as it appeared and a vigorous defender of her sex from any unjust sallies I may have been tempted to make.

This is mainly a documentary study and thus I owe much to the kind co-operation of many librarians. In particular I would like to thank Miss McInnes, the archivist of St Thomas's Hospital who, with the permission of the Treasurer and Governors, has helped us find our way around the archives of the hospital, drawn our attention to many relevant documents in her charge, and made many valuable suggestions. Secondly, Miss Thomson, the librarian of the Royal College of Nursing, has taken great trouble on our behalf and even on occasions turned a blind eye to the author's nasty habit of smoking in libraries. Thirdly, Alison Clarke, the librarian of the National Institute of Economic and Social Research, has always found us a cup of coffee and answered many queries on the layout of footnotes, on which she is an expert. Fourthly, we have been trusted by the editors with the loan of rare copies of the *Hospital* and the *Nursing Mirror*. Fifthly, we have invaded and been helped by the staff of the following additional libraries:

British Library of Economic and Political Science
British Museum, Newspaper Library Collindale
British Museum Reading Room; Manuscript Room
General Register Office Library
House of Lords Library
Ministry of Health Library
Royal College of Surgeons of England Library
Trades Union Congress Library
War Office Library
Wellcome Historical Medical Library

Much of the subject-matter of the book is, however, within living memory, and I have thus been able to check facts and discuss hypotheses with people who have helped to create what is described. I am extremely grateful to those who have given up their time by answering our letters, discussing points on the telephone, and by granting us lengthy interviews. In particular

I would like to acknowledge the help I have received from Miss Bryson of the late British College of Nurses, Miss Edwards of the King Edward's Hospital Fund for London, Miss Henry of the General Nursing Council for England and Wales, Miss Macdonald of the Royal British Nurses' Association—from the staff of the Confederation of Health Service Employees, the National Union of Local Government Officers, the National Union of Public Employees, the Queen's Institute of District Nursing, the Royal College of Nursing—from officials, who must regrettably remain nameless, of the Ministry of Health, the Inland Revenue, the Ministry of Labour and National Service, the Ministry of Pensions and National Insurance—from my colleagues on the management side of the Nurses and Midwives Whitley Council and numerous matrons, chief male nurses, other nurses and students whose brains have been picked without their knowing that I was trying to write about their profession.

An even greater debt is owed to those who have waded through the manuscript or parts of it at the different stages of its production and made valuable criticisms and suggestions, which have all been greedily incorporated in the book with this inadequate acknowledgement. From the following list some names have had to be omitted at special request: Mr H. L. Beales, Dame Elizabeth Cockayne, Miss Muriel Edwards, Mrs Forster Parsons, Miss F. G. Goodall, Miss R. A. Hone, Miss Janet Kydd, Mr Donald MacRae, Mr O. R. McGregor, Miss Dorothy Morris, Mrs Seymer, Miss Simpson, Mr and Mrs Peter Townsend, Mr Asher Tropp, Miss Doris Westmacott, Mrs Woodham-Smith.

I am grateful to Mr Denis de Marney whose skill as a photographer has restored many damaged and faded portraits to what we hope was their original state.

Finally my greatest debt is due to Professor Richard Titmuss who introduced me to this field, who has generously contributed many of its underlying themes, and who has read and commented upon the manuscript at no less than three different stages. Without the continuing encouragement and support of the Titmuss family, this book would never have been completed.

None of the above is in any way implicated in the errors or distortions that may remain. After all their kindness, any faults must be due to my own inattention or obstinacy.

London, 1960   BRIAN ABEL-SMITH

CHAPTER I

The Untrained Nurse

ILLNESS creates dependency: the sick need not only medical treatment, but personal service. The provision of this service and the administration of the treatment which the doctor prescribes are the two basic duties of the nurse. By her skilful care the sick can be restored to health.

Normally the family provides its own nursing services. But there have always been some who have had no relatives able to look after them, and others who have preferred, and could afford, to employ experienced helpers rather than to burden their relatives with the task of looking after them. From the middle of the nineteenth century there developed a body of skill and knowledge in the care of the sick which justified the division of labour—the emergence of the 'nurse', carefully selected and systematically taught. A hundred years later the untrained 'nurse' was still playing a part in the hospital service. Before 1840 she reigned supreme.

The demand for nursing services is part of the wider demand for medical care. It is influenced by national wealth; by medical skill and by the public's recognition of it; and by the extent of ill health and cultural attitudes towards it. Over the past hundred and fifty years there have been vast developments not only in national wealth but also in the potentialities of medicine. The application of science to medicine and the immense technical changes in the means of treating sickness have made ever-increasing demands on the skill of the nurse. And the public has come to regard ill health less as an imposition of the divine will which must be passively accepted and more as a product of the environment which can and should be remedied. The forces which have shaped these changes lie outside this present study but they help to determine many of the trends described—in particular the public's demand for more nurses and the nurses' demand for more skill and status.

Thus the demand for nurses, like the demand for doctors, depends on the ability of the community to pay for such services; on the family's desire to call upon outside help when faced with sickness; and on the competence of those available to provide it.[1] But there is one further influence which has played a predominant part in the last century—the increasing role of the hospital. If the patient is treated at home, other members of the family can share the nursing work between themselves and others. But if the patient is treated in hospital, the relatives can do very little: virtually all the nursing falls on people employed to do it. During the past hundred years more and more serious illnesses have been treated in hospital; this has been one of the major reasons for more nurses being employed.

In the first half of the nineteenth century, the well-to-do employed nurses in their own homes on a resident or non-resident basis to look after the 'sick-room'.[2] Working people, on the other hand, could afford to spend little on medical care —on doctors or medicines, let alone nurses. Neither group chose, as a general rule, to be treated in hospital. Not until the twentieth century were hospitals used by the rich. In the nineteenth they were for the poor, and even for them the major reasons for admission were social rather than medical: the sick poor left home because no care could be given to them there. They were faced with two possibilities. If they were fortunate they would be admitted to a voluntary hospital supported by charitable contributions. Failing this they had to enter the workhouse. The former was clearly preferable, but the number of hospital beds was extremely small. As late as 1851 there were only 7,619 patients recorded by the census enumerators as resident in hospitals, in the whole of England and Wales.[3] And many parts of the country had no voluntary hospital.

---

[1] 'Many a wife and mother has continued night and day to watch by the sick-bed, who would gladly have taken proper rest had she been able to trust the nurse.' See Charlotte Haddon: 'Nursing as a Profession for Ladies': *St Paul's Monthly Magazine*, August 1871, p. 460.

[2] The best known of this type of nurse was Mrs Gamp, described by Charles Dickens in *Martin Chuzzlewit*. She laid out the dead, delivered the babies and 'watched' the sick. Not all nurses were of this type. For example, a good and reliable midwife is described in Chapter VIII of *Lark Rise* by Flora Thompson (Oxford, 1939), which tells of life in an Oxfordshire hamlet in the eighties.

[3] *Census of England and Wales 1891, General Report*, p. 77: HMSO, 1893.

The choice between hospital and workhouse was determined not only by geography but by the policies of the hospitals themselves. There were certain types of case and certain illnesses which the voluntary hospitals would not accept. As Miss Louisa Twining[1] remarked, there were 'a large number of persons afflicted with incurable disease who are not proper objects for admission into the general hospitals'.[2] The workhouses were also used by the voluntary hospitals as dumps for the patients they had failed to cure. They were 'hospitals for those who are incurable, and who are turned out of our best London hospitals'.[3] Patients were sent 'to the workhouses to die'.[4] And a pauper funeral was greatly feared. 'The dead [were] laid in shells, the boards unplaned inside, upon a sprinkling of sawdust, perfectly naked, with a strip of calico over the body only.'[5]

The workhouses had not been designed for the care of sick people. The aged, the feeble-minded, the mentally ill, the physically sick and the able-bodied were all bundled together in the same mixed institution managed with one major aim in view —to discourage the able-bodied from seeking support from public funds. The Boards of Guardians, whose responsibility they were, did not attempt to provide a hospital service for the poor. Their task, as they saw it, was to relieve destitution, not to treat illness: and as the 'independent labourer of the lowest class' did not obtain either efficient medical treatment or skilled nursing, it would have been regarded as inconsistent with the 'less eligibility' principle to provide it for paupers.[6] As a result, no special arrangements were made for the sick people who

---

The figures given for 1851 slightly understate the true position as some of the smaller institutions were omitted.

[1] Her role in the reform of workhouse nursing is described in Chapter III. She was born in 1820. Her father was Richard Twining, the tea merchant. She was a member of the Society of Arts and Fellow of the Royal Society. She wrote and illustrated several books on religious art.

[2] Louisa Twining: *Recollections of Workhouse Visiting and Management during Twenty Five Years*, p. 37: London, 1880.

[3] Evidence to the Select Committee on Poor Relief (England) 1861— reprinted in Louisa Twining: *A Letter to the President of the Poor Law Board on Workhouse Infirmaries*, pp. 26–27: London, 1866. [4] *Ibid.*, p. 19.

[5] Quoted in Twining: *Recollections of Workhouse Visiting etc.*, p. 82.

[6] Sidney and Beatrice Webb: *English Local Government, English Poor Law History, Part II, The Last Hundred Years*, Vol. I, p. 316: London, 1929.

entered the workhouses during the first half of the nineteenth
century; even the number of paupers who were sick was neither
known nor investigated.[1] Later, when the exposures of lady
visitors and doctors led to a change in this attitude, it was discovered that out of the total of 157,740 indoor paupers in 1869
about a third were sick.[2] This total of over 50,000 patients may
be compared to the total of 19,585 patients in general and special
hospitals in 1871.[3] Thus in terms of numbers of patients, the
workhouse was found to be by far the larger of the two types of
'hospital'. This would probably have been as true of the first
half of the century as it was of the second half, if the facts had
ever been collected.

Although there had been religious orders which dedicated
themselves to the service of the sick, historically the antecedents
of the nursing profession were domestic servants. Indeed at the
beginning of the nineteenth century, nursing amounted to little
more than a specialized form of charring. Such was the background of the women employed as nurses in the voluntary
hospitals. Many of them were, or had been, married and they
brought to their work in the hospitals the experience they had
gained in looking after their own families. They were assisted
by convalescent patients working under their direction.[4] In the
workhouses, nearly all the nursing of the sick paupers was done
by such able-bodied paupers as happened to be available. There
were hardly any paid nurses until after the middle of the nineteenth century.

The nurses of this period are roundly condemned by nursing
writers. According to the standard histories, nursing had fallen
by the nineteenth century into a trough of inefficiency and

[1] Webb: *op. cit.*, Vol. I, p. 315.

[2] *Ibid.*, pp. 320, 322, and Vol. II, p. 1052.

[3] *Census of England and Wales 1891*, p. 77.

[4] One of the rules for patients at Guy's Hospital laid down in 1788 reads
as follows: 'If any patient that is able neglect or refuse to assist their fellow
Patients that are weak, or confined to their Beds, or to assist when called on
by the Sister, Nurse or Watch, in cleaning the Ward, helping down with their
Stools, fetching Coals, or any other necessary Business relating to their Ward,
or shall absent themselves at the Time they know such Business must be
done, they shall for the first offence, forfeit their next Day's Diet; and for the
second Offence, and persisting therein, they shall be discharged by the
Steward.' See H. C. Cameron: *Mr Guy's Hospital 1726–1948*, p. 75: London,
1954.

immorality.[1] This view was taken from the nursing reformers, who were not moderate in their criticisms. For example, Miss Nightingale stated that nursing was generally done by those 'who were too old, too weak, too drunken, too dirty, too stolid, or too bad to do anything else'.[2]

It is not unusual for reformers to overstate the evils they are hoping to correct.[3] It was, however, certainly unfair to condemn all the untrained nurses. There had been good nurses as well as bad before the Nightingale revolution. Indeed one of Miss Nightingale's favourite pupils, Miss Pringle, wrote after twelve years' practical experience of hospital nursing: 'Some of the nurses were of the best type of woman—clever, dutiful, cheerful, and kind, endowed above all with that motherliness of nature which is the most precious attribute of a nurse.'[4] Such evils as there were, arose largely from the system under which the old nurses were expected to work. There were features both of employment in the voluntary hospitals and in the workhouses which led to abuses.

Virtually all the existing nurses were drawn from the domestic servant class. Nor is this surprising, as domestic service was the largest field for the employment of women. One hospital favoured 'old women of the charwoman class'.[5] At St Bartholomew's Hospital Sir James Paget recalled that the nurses of 1830 were 'dull, unobservant, and untaught women; of the best it

[1] Nursing historians regard the medieval religious orders as the true antecedents of the nursing profession. Quantitative information is not available about their role, nor about the number of village women who assisted at confinements and nursed the sick at home for gain. The latter tend to be ignored.

[2] F. Nightingale: 'Suggestions on the subject of providing, training and organising nurses for the sick poor in workhouse infirmaries': *Letter to Sir Thomas Watson Bart.*, member of the committee appointed by the President of the Poor Law Board, p. 1: London, 19 January 1867: British Library of Political and Economic Science Pamphlet Collection (Coll./c/x3).

[3] One of the surgeons at St Thomas's Hospital certainly held the view that this was what the critics were doing. 'It has been latterly the fashion,' he wrote in 1856, 'for the glorification of certain amateurs of both sexes who seem suddenly to have been inspired with perfect knowledge of the conduct of hospitals of both civil and military, to descant largely on the ill-management of the nursing establishments of these institutions and the ignorance and incapability of the sisters and nurses employed.' *STHA* C56/2.

[4] 'Nurses and Doctors': *Edinburgh Medical Journal*, May 1880, p. 1049.

[5] H. C. Burdett: *Nurses' Food, Work and Recreation*, The British Hospitals Association Pamphlet No. 13, p. 5: London, 1890.

could only be said that they were kindly, and careful, and attentive in doing what they were told to do'.[1] As no unusual qualifications or experience were required, there was no shortage of recruits. All the matron of the Radcliffe Infirmary, Oxford, used to do when she wanted another nurse was to advertise for a 'careful woman' or promote one of the servants of the house.[2]

Although these women were called 'nurses', they did not always undertake the wide range of tasks which are now regarded as nursing duties. The doctor or his apprentice did more for the patients than is the case today. At least this was the practice in a number of teaching hospitals where students or 'residents' performed some of the tasks which are now left to nurses. There were junior medical posts known as 'dressers' or 'clinical clerks'. An article in a students' journal pointed out in 1877 that 'he has no greater duty than leaving each case as comfortable as circumstances permit. He should not be above arranging pillows and cushions, not only because the public will demand it afterwards, but because humanity and repair both alike call out for rest.'[3] It should be observed that hospital patients and 'the public' were two quite different groups.

In many cases nurses were on a weekly wage basis and were sacked without notice. A number were totally illiterate, signing for their wages with a cross.[4] The pay in London seems to have been between 6s. and 9s. 6d. per week with some board provided in kind.[5] Pay in the provinces was somewhat lower; the Radcliffe Infirmary paid 2s. 6d. a week.[6] The wages of women working in the cotton industry in the Manchester area were between 6s. 6d. and 9s. 6d. per week at about this period.[7] Uncertified school teachers were paid about £35 per year.[8]

Neither the pay nor the conditions of work were such as to attract any of the few women who could have been described as

---

[1] *Hospital*, 6 June 1914, p. 276.

[2] A. G. Gibson: *The Radcliffe Infirmary*, p. 235: Oxford, 1926.

[3] *Guy's Hospital Gazette*, July 1877, p. 78. See V. M. Dunbar: *The Origin and Early Development of Two English Training Schools for Nurses*, Part II, p. 23 (unpublished thesis, University of London, 1936).

[4] Burdett: *Nurses' Food, Work and Recreation*, p. 5.

[5] See Appendix III, p. 279.   [6] Gibson: *op. cit.*, p. 238.

[7] Between 1839 and 1859 for scrutchers, drawing frame tenders, bobbin fly tenders, throstle spinners, throstle reelers, bobbin winders and gassers. See A. L. Bowley: *Wages in the United Kingdom*, p. 119: Cambridge, 1900.

[8] See A. Tropp: *The School Teachers*, p. 39: London, 1957.

educated. Arrangements for the accommodation and feeding of nurses varied from hospital to hospital. In some cases nurses lived out, as in the early days of Guy's. In other hospitals 'until 1840 the day nurses always slept in the wards, having, on the male side, small rooms between the wards'.[1] In a letter written in 1854, Florence Nightingale described these small rooms as 'wooden cages on the landing places outside the doors of the wards, . . . where it was impossible for the Night Nurse taking her rest in the day to sleep at all owing to the noise, where there was not light or air'.[2] Alternatively, nurses slept in 'damp and ill ventilated rooms in the basement',[3] or in attics where the 'high temperature and excessive light' disturbed the night nurses.[4] In another dormitory the nurses complained that there were 'too many rats'.[5]

In the early days of the nineteenth century nurses 'cooked their own food (which they bought for themselves) eating it in the ward kitchens or scullery'.[6] Some hospitals issued part rations, such as bread and meat. But gradually hospitals began to provide meals for the nurses. This seemed advantageous for three reasons. First, this was the best way of ensuring that the food intended for the patients actually reached them. Secondly, it removed the need for nurses to leave the hospital daily on shopping expeditions. Thirdly, the nurses were better fed.[7]

The hospital authorities did not think it necessary to provide adequate sanitary facilities for the staff. 'One or possibly two jugs and basins and a few towels were considered sufficient for the ablutions of the staff, and nothing more potent than soap and water, possibly tinted with a dash of Condy's fluid, was used to purify their hands.'[8]

While it was not unknown for a nurse to be promoted to the rank of sister, it was more common for sisters to be separately recruited and to come from a higher social class. At St Bartholomew's Hospital we read of '. . . widows in reduced circumstances' and 'persons who have lived in a respectable rank of

[1] *The Lancet Commission on Nursing*, pp. 18–19: London, 1932.
[2] Cecil Woodham-Smith: *Florence Nightingale*, Penguin Edition, p. 51: London, 1951.   [3] Burdett: *op. cit.*, p. 5.
[4] Cameron: *op. cit.*, p. 200.   [5] *Ibid.*, p. 200.
[6] E. S. Haldane: *The British Nurse in Peace and War*, p. 85: London, 1923.
[7] Cameron: *op. cit.*, p. 195.
[8] Quoted Haldane: *op. cit.*, pp. 96–97 from the *Life of Lord Lister*, describing conditions in the Royal Infirmary, Glasgow, 1868.

life'[1]—an advantage apparently not shared by the nurses. At St Thomas's Hospital the sisters had usually been head servants in gentlemen's families. Their duties were primarily those of domestic supervisors. But in addition they were personally responsible for seeing that the doctors' orders were carried out— particularly concerning the issue of medicines. Extremely strict regulations on this subject had been laid down for many years.[2] St Thomas's was, however, certainly in advance of other hospitals in this respect.[3]

Matrons were often of a still higher class. Their main duties were administrative, and included some of the tasks at present performed by domestic supervisors, supplies officers, catering officers, hospital secretaries, and many others. With all the responsibilities of household management it is not surprising that there was little time left for the supervision of the nurses. As Miss Pringle put it, 'her time was fully occupied with her own work, she did not understand theirs'.[4] Nor were they always appointed because they had an aptitude for performing the administrative functions expected of them. At the Radcliffe Infirmary the matron apparently felt so little responsibility for nursing affairs that when empowered to employ more night nurses in 1892, she failed to take advantage of the opportunity provided for her.[5] As late as 1853 it was contended at one hospital that there was no need to have a special person to supervise the nurses.[6]

Such was the nursing hierarchy that manned the voluntary

---

[1] *Lancet Commission on Nursing*, pp. 19–20.

[2] 'You shall carefully place all the medicines for outward applications distinctly from those for internal use, and administer to the patients under your care the medicines prescribed by the physicians and surgeons of this hospital or which shall be delivered to you by the apothecary for that purpose; and, when called upon, you shall be ready to acquaint the physicians, surgeons or apothecary, with the effects of such medicine during their absence, so far as falls within your observation; and you shall punctually attend the apothecary's shop, at the appointed times, to receive the said medicines, taking great care that the labels or directions given to you therewith be not lost or misplaced.' See B. Golding: *An Historical Account of St Thomas's Hospital*, p. 207: London, 1819.

[3] Letter from John Flint South to Richard Baggallay, 11 August 1856, *STHA* C56/2.

[4] 'Nurses and Doctors': *Edinburgh Medical Journal*, May 1880, p. 1049.

[5] Gibson: *op. cit.*, p. 238.

[6] C. N. French: *The Story of St Luke's Hospital*, p. 130: London, 1951.

hospitals before reform. The matron, the sisters, and the nurses were usually separately recruited. This served to emphasize the most important fact about the early system of hospital nursing. It was not thought that any special training or experience were required to nurse the sick. It was not the matron's duty to teach the nurses. Moreover, she rarely had any qualifications for the task.

This did not mean, however, that none of the nursing staff possessed any knowledge or skill. There was one group of people in the hospitals to whom the work of the nurses mattered a great deal—the doctors. The good doctor wanted to have an assistant continuously with his patients who could be relied on to carry out his orders and report the patients' progress. Consciously or unconsciously the doctors taught the nurses. Sisters and nurses tended to stay on one ward and thus to learn what was required of them. It was the doctors who gave the nurses their orders and were consulted about new appointments.[1]

This informal system of training was haphazard but it undoubtedly produced some very good nurses. We learn that the sisters at St Bartholomew's had in 1830 'an admirable sagacity and a sort of rough practical knowledge which was nearly as good as any acquired skill'.[2] One sister was quite prepared, even at this early date, to instruct a new house surgeon. The London Hospital also had its quota of good nurses,[3] and it should not be forgotten that Mrs Roberts, the best nurse that accompanied Miss Nightingale to the Crimea, had been brought up under the old régime at St Thomas's. When the new régime came, many of the old nurses stayed on to give excellent service to the new qualified matrons.

There were also bad nurses, and drink was the major vice attributed to the profession. Drunkenness was not uncommon among the women from whom nurses were recruited. Indeed it was an era of drinking among all classes. Nor did the hospital authorities discourage the staff from taking alcohol. It was often provided to nurses as payment in kind: even nurses who were not fully boarded were provided with 'small beer'. The whole attitude to drink was totally different. Lady Palmerston did not

[1] Z. Cope: *A Hundred Years of Nursing at St Mary's Paddington*, p. 37: London, 1955.

[2] *Hospital*, 6 June 1914, p. 276.

[3] E. W. Morris: *A History of The London Hospital*, pp. 205–6: London, 1910.

think it wrong that a nurse should drink on duty.[1] Matrons who considered it their duty to supervise the recreation of their nurses could keep it under control. At the Radcliffe Infirmary every nurse had to report to the matron when she came in from an evening off duty.[2] At St Thomas's it was clearly laid down that the matron as 'superior female of the establishment' had to 'preside over their [the nurses'] morals and good behaviour'.[3]

There seems little doubt that some women of 'low character' entered employment in the hospitals. Nurses had to be alone in a ward full of men, many of whom were ambulant. It was 'not unknown for nurses of male wards to sleep in the wards with the men'.[4] But some matrons kept a sharp eye on the behaviour of their nurses. The minutes of the Radcliffe Infirmary record that 'Assistant Nurse Archer was . . . severely reprimanded for . . . permitting a patient to remain with his arm round her waist'.[5]

Historians and biographers have left us with a fairly detailed account of the operation of voluntary hospitals, but there are few records of this kind for the 'hospitals' which were administered under the poor law. The workhouses had not been intended to serve as hospitals, and no information was collected about the numbers of sick paupers or the provisions made for them. Moreover, the general public were for years prevented from visiting 'the institutions which their compulsory rates supported'.[6] For these reasons, the information available about the nursing of the sick in workhouses is of a much later date than that given for the voluntary hospitals. Not until the late fifties was public attention drawn to what had clearly been a major evil for many years.

As mentioned earlier, nearly all the nursing in the workhouses was undertaken by 'able-bodied' paupers. According to Louisa Twining, who visited all but four of the London workhouses, most of them had no paid nurses at all.[7] From the point of view

---

[1] '. . . The nurses are very good now, perhaps they do drink a little, but so do the ladies' monthly nurses, and nothing can be better than them. Poor people, it must be so tiresome sitting up all night!' This remark is attributed to Lady Palmerston by E. P. Fitzmaurice: *The Life of Granville, George Leveson-Gower, Second Earl Granville*, Vol. I, p. 136: London, 1905. The Nightingales used to dine with the Palmerstons in the early 1840's. See Woodham-Smith: *op. cit.*, p. 37.   [2] Gibson: *op. cit.*, p. 234.
[3] Golding: *op. cit.*, p. 204.   [4] Woodham-Smith: *op. cit.*, p. 51.
[5] Gibson: *op. cit.*, p. 237.   [6] Webb: *op. cit.*, pp. 317–18.
[7] Louisa Twining: *State Hospitals and Nursing in Workhouse Infirmaries*, p. 3: London, 1885.

of the Guardians, the employment of pauper nurses had advantages. First, it provided work which did not compete with trades outside the workhouses. Secondly, able-bodied paupers who were made to act as nurses were discouraged from staying in the workhouse longer than was absolutely necessary. Thirdly, and most important of all, it was economical. And even if the Guardians had wished to obtain experienced women to act as nurses, it would have been very hard to find them. Hospital nurses would not have chosen to look after the chronic sick patients in the workhouses and be employed 'in due subordination to the matron' who was totally unqualified.[1]

From the point of view of the masters and matrons of the workhouses, the system of pauper nurses was hard to administer efficiently or at least without the danger of a public scandal. It was difficult to find 'inmates' who really fitted for the work. Younger persons were not always plentiful and if available were unlikely to be resident for long periods. Thus the duty of pauper nurse tended to fall upon the older inmate. 'Such nursing as we had', wrote the medical officer of the Strand Workhouse, 'was performed by more or less infirm paupers.'[2] Of eighteen pauper nurses, fourteen were over 60 and four were over 70. Only eight of the eighteen could be relied upon to read the labels on the medicines.[3] Two of them trembled and coughed all day and their combined strength was insufficient to lift a patient up in bed.[4] Care at night was arranged by making a pauper nurse sleep in each sick ward. What annoyed the medical officer most was the fact that the pauper nurses could not be relied upon to carry out his orders. Thus when measles broke out in the children's ward, he laid down the 'most stringent regulations as regards isolation and disinfection'. Only in exceptional circumstances did the pauper women 'pay any attention to what I said'. 'I will not horrify my readers by stating the proportion of deaths to recoveries, but content myself with stating that the latter were very few.'[5]

At Shoreditch Infirmary, the average duration in office of

[1] Frances Power Cobbe: *The Workhouse as an Hospital*, p. 9: London, 1861.

[2] J. Rogers: *Reminiscences of a Workhouse Medical Officer* (ed. J. E. Thorold), p. 43: London, 1889.

[3] Poor Law Board Return: *House of Lords Papers* 1866 (372) lxi, p. 55.

[4] *Ibid.*, Copy of Statement made by Mrs Beeton, late Head Nurse of the Strand Union: *House of Lords Papers* 1866 (372) lxi, p. 46.

[5] Rogers: *op. cit.*, p. 11.

female pauper nurses was six to nine months. 'They come to
their work without knowledge; they remain without training;
they leave for other occupations, and to better themselves, for
they are unpaid,'[1] wrote the Commissioners appointed to inspect by the *Lancet*. The male nurses at Shoreditch were dirty,
uncouth, and dishonest. The female nurses were no better:
medicine was given with 'systematic irregularity; one nurse, on
her own avowal, gave it irrespective of directions, three times,
twice or once a day, according to her own opinion of the cases,
and without taking the doctor into her councils'.[2] There were
no night nurses.

Pilfering by pauper nurses, particularly of stimulants, was
frequently alleged and occasionally proved; though some of the
alleged pilfering was just part of the extensive barter system which
operated in the workhouses.[3]

A grim appraisal of the pauper nurse system was written by
Frances Cobbe, one of the early lady visitors, in 1861.

In the male wards they are usually old men, who have been
perhaps artisans or labourers, and have come to destitution by vice,
calamity, general incapacity and imbecility, or sickness and in-
firmity. The chances of a man under such circumstance turning out
a tender and skilful nurse may easily be calculated. The women's
case is worse. A nurse must possess considerable physical strength to
lift the patients, sit up all night, etc. But who are the able-bodied
women who are to be found as paupers in the Workhouse and can
obtain no remunerative employment as servants elsewhere? Alas!
there is *one* class, the most wretched of all. It is among the most
depraved and abandoned members of the community that the poor
decent woman who has come to suffer, and perhaps die, in the
Workhouse must find her sole attendant, too often her rough and
cruel tyrant. The ways in which a hard unfeeling nurse may torment

[1] The *Lancet* Sanitary Commission for Investigating the State of the
Infirmaries of Workhouses: *Reports of the Commissioners on Metropolitan Workhouses*, p. 61: London, 1866.

[2] *Ibid.*, pp. 61–62.

[3] This was the opinion of the official poor law inspector: 'Further the
statements which were made to us do not warrant a general charge to the
effect that those persons pilfer the stimulants of the patients; but there is
reason to believe that a system of barter is sometimes adopted, by which the
nurse, or indeed any inmate, exchanges one article of food or drink; and that
there are certain nurses who abuse the trust reposed in them.' Poor Law
Board Return, Metropolitan Workhouse Infirmaries and Sick Wards—
Report of Dr Edward Smith: *House of Lords Papers* 1866 (372) lxi, p. 26.

her wretched patient are beyond enumeration. She moves her roughly when every touch is agony, she neglects every little precaution which might make her bed more comfortable, she gives her food cold, she speaks brutally so as to shake her nerves to misery, she monopolizes for herself, or refuses to use for the patient, the easy chairs, cushions, or bed-rests, any kind visitor may have provided. And when the wretched sufferer has reached the last stage, and needs *every* attention in her helplessness, she refuses (as we have witnessed) to give her the cold Workhouse tea she craves for in her agony, to save herself the trouble of the needful arrangements.[1]

Such was the pauper nurse system at its worst. But there were some Guardians who had made a bad system work reasonably well. Pauper nurses were rewarded with extra rations, particularly of meat, tea, beer, or gin. In some cases, as the result of pressure from the lady visitors, they were given some sort of uniform ('a distinctive dress'). In the most progressive workhouses they were paid in cash sums varying from 5s. per quarter to 2s. per week.[2] At the Islington Workhouse the system worked remarkably well. 'Most of them', wrote the *Lancet* commissioners, 'have been in office for long terms of years; and they seem on the whole well-conducted, zealous and well managed, conscious that they are thoroughly looked after, and anxious to deserve good opinion.'[3]

The pauper nurse, like her sister in the voluntary hospitals, was given alcoholic drinks as part of the system of rewards. As an official report put it: 'Last, and perhaps most important of all, the habit of drinking strong drinks, which is so generally alleged against them, is cultivated by the allowance of one pint, or a pint and a half of strong porter daily, or at night only, with one or two glasses of gin for night duty or disagreeable work.'[4] Thus at the Strand Workhouse pauper nurses were given a glass of gin 'for laying out the dead, and for other specially repulsive duties'.[5] At this workhouse the issue of drinks interfered with the work done by the nurses as the issue was made at 7 a.m. 'As many of the inmates sold this allowance,' wrote the medical officer, 'the nurses had become partly or wholly intoxicated when I reached the House in the morning.'[6] There was one nurse who 'systematically stole the wine and brandy from the sick'.[7]

[1] Cobbe: *op. cit.*, pp. 9–10.
[2] *Workhouse Infirmaries Report 1866*, p. 24.
[3] *Lancet Sanitary Commission 1866*, p. 67.
[4] *Workhouse Infirmaries Report 1866*, p. 25.
[5] Rogers: *op. cit.*, p. 9.   [6] *Ibid.*, p. 12.   [7] *Ibid.*, p. 13.

Extremely few paid nurses were employed. According to Louisa Twining, there were only 70 in all the London workhouses in 1854[1] and the number had only increased to 111 by 1866.[2] The only qualifications prescribed for them was that they should be able 'to read written directions upon medicines'.[3] As Florence Nightingale hastened to point out, the receipt of pay was no guarantee of the quality of a nurse.[4] Paid nurses were also provided with free drink. At the Holborn Workhouse two pints of porter were issued daily, to each officer, male or female.[5]

The status of a paid nurse in a workhouse was extremely low. Paupers were third-class citizens, despised and disenfranchised; and those who cared for them were not ranked far above their charges. Nor were the conditions of work such as would attract either reliable or respectable workers. 'To be the lowest scrubber in any hospital', wrote Louisa Twining, 'is estimated a higher post than to be nurse with the sole charge of a workhouse ward, and none will fill it who can live elsewhere. . . .'[6] 'The women who are set over wards of helpless sufferers drink whenever they can obtain the means, for they come not to this, the lowest office which a worn-out woman can fill, till all other chances of subsistence are gone.'[7] There was one nurse who 'boldly stated that she had been sixteen times in the House of Correction. . . . She was a woman given to drink, and of a violent, ungovernable temper, causing great misery to the aged people under her control.'[8]

The average salary paid to fifty-three nurses employed in eleven metropolitan workhouses was £20 18s. in 1866.[9] The highest salary was £30 and the lowest was £12. The paid nurses worked from morning until night all through the year. They slept on the wards on which they worked 'whether the patients

---

[1] Louisa Twining: *A Letter to the President of the Poor Law Board on Workhouse Infirmaries*, p. 15: London, 1866.

[2] H. J. McCurrich: *The Treatment of the Sick Poor in this Country*, p. 38: Oxford, 1929.

[3] *Report of the Royal Commission on the Poor Laws and Relief of Distress*, Cd 4499, p. 240: HMSO, 1909.

[4] Nightingale: *Letter to Sir Thomas Watson Bart.*, 1867.

[5] *Workhouse Infirmaries Report 1866*, p. 108.

[6] Twining: *A Letter to the President of the Poor Law Board*, p. 16.

[7] *Ibid.*, p. 16.   [8] *Ibid.*, pp. 9–10.

[9] This figure has been calculated from information given in the *Lancet Commission 1866*, p. 24.

are men or women'.[1] They had 'not even the opportunity allowed them of attending chapel services'.[2] They ate 'only the house diet, perhaps a meat dinner daily, and an allowance of beer and gin, in many cases not even what would be valued more than anything, dry tea, but only that which is boiled in the general cauldron and served out to the inmates'.[3] Miss Twining, the daughter of a wealthy tea merchant, thought that proper supplies of 'hot tea and coffee, especially at night . . . should do away with all necessity and excuse for the stimulating, but most injurious, drink which is now thought essential to the performance of a nurse's work'.[4]

Conditions for nurses were not everywhere as bad as Miss Twining described them. For example there was a paid nurse at the Westminster Infirmary who had her own quarters and spent most of the day there. This nurse knew nothing about medicines and refused to carry out the directions she was given by the medical officer.[5] The best nurse who has survived in the literature was Mrs Beeton who obviously had some professional pride. She said in evidence given at an official inquiry: 'I never could account for paid Nurses being objected to, only for this reason, that she knows her proper Weights and Measures, and with a good feeling for her patients and Credit to herself she would expect the same; while a Pauper Nurse is not supposed to know, and at the time be content with any that is given her for the Patients.'[6] Her accommodation, while she was head nurse of the Strand Union, was pitiful. 'My room was on the same Floor as the Men's Sick Ward; only a small lobby parted us. In this Lobby was a Sink and a Dusthole; there also was all the soiled Linen washed from the Men's Sick Ward before going to the Laundry. I often got the smell so strong from the same in my Room that I could scarcely bear to remain in it.'[7]

The matrons of the workhouses had little time to spare on the nursing problems of their institutions. 'The matron's duties are varied and multiplied. She superintends the whole internal working of the establishment, the cleaning, the linen, the food, the cooking, the distribution of food, the stores &c. and in the

---

[1] Twining: *A Letter to the President of the Poor Law Board*, p. 15.
[2] *Ibid.*, p. 17.   [3] *Ibid.*, p. 16.   [4] *Ibid.*, p. 17.
[5] Rogers: *op. cit.*, pp. 113–14.
[6] Copy of Statement made by Mrs Beeton etc.: *op. cit.*, p. 45.
[7] *Ibid.*, p. 46.

discharge of these duties has as much as an active person can properly do. But in many workhouses she is expected to super-intend the nursing and bedding, and other questions relating to the sick.'[1] In the workhouses, as in the voluntary hospitals where the nursing was bad, the major cause was the same. No proper attempt was made to select, train, or supervise the nurses. The matrons were preoccupied with other duties and there were fewer doctors to supervise the nurses.

The standard of nursing in the early nineteenth century was what each hospital or workhouse chose to make it. If the accommodation and the conditions of work were such that decent women would undertake the work, decent women offered their services. Where nurses were carefully selected, adequately supervised by the matron and sufficiently controlled by the medical staff, their standard was high. But where the hospital authorities did not make proper arrangements, the standard of nursing was extremely low. *The Times* summarized the position very fairly in 1857.

Hospital nurses have been much abused—they have their faults, but most of them are due to want of proper treatment. Lectured by Committees, preached at by chaplains, scowled on by treasurers and stewards, scolded by matrons, sworn at by surgeons, bullied by dressers, grumbled at and abused by patients, insulted if old and ill-favoured, talked flippantly to if middle-aged and good-humoured, tempted and seduced if young and well-looking, they are what any woman might be under these circumstances.[2]

---

[1] *Workhouse Infirmaries Report 1866*, p. 67.
[2] *The Times*, 15 April 1857. Quoted in Haldane: *op. cit.*, pp. 85–86.

CHAPTER II

Probationers and Lady-Pupils

THE reform of hospital nursing in the second half of the
nineteenth century was focused on the introduction of
training. It involved changes in recruitment, changes in organization, and even changes in the system of hospital administration. It came as a response to wider knowledge of medical care
—the recognition by doctors and others of the importance of the
bedside care given to patients. But it took the form it did because
nursing was able to meet a social need: to provide a suitable
occupation for the daughters of the higher social classes.

Demographic factors[1] had created a pool of idle spinster
labour. Veblen and others have drawn attention to the function-
less position of the woman in the prosperous Victorian family.[2]
She was prevented by strong social pressures from engaging in
trade or competing with the superior sex in the learned professions. If she was to escape at all from the boredom of family
life, it could not be from any commercial motives. The performance of good works was already sanctioned by her class and
promoted by the High Church movement. Caring for the sick
was a logical extension of such activities, but nevertheless still
closed to the respectable girl by the 'low character' of the women
who were believed to be engaged in the work. If nursing could
be made respectable, it could provide an outlet for the social
conscience and frustrated energies of the Victorian spinster.[3]

[1] The late age of marriage, low marriage rates and migration.
[2] See T. Veblen: *The Theory of the Leisure Class*, Chapter VI: London, 1925;
and Margaret Simey: *Charitable Effort in Liverpool in the Nineteenth Century*,
pp. 62–63: Liverpool, 1951.
[3] Sir James Paget said in an address to the Abernethian Society in 1885,
that the real reason why the question of admitting young ladies to learn
nursing was never raised earlier was because none at that time wished to learn
it. 'There was less earnest love of any of the kinds of active benevolence which
you see now; much less prevalent religious zeal; very little district visiting or
teaching of the poor; very little desire for the exercise of practical knowledge

17

The Nightingale training school started in 1860, and it was not long before the potentialities of nursing as a career for gentlewomen were being enthusiastically canvassed. In 1871 the following appeared in a popular monthly:

The want of remunerative occupations suitable for gentlewomen is, in these days, painfully felt and universally acknowledged; and fresh schemes are continually being started to remedy the evil. It has been proposed to throw open the learned professions to the competition of women, and to remove the various disabilities which keep the sex in a position of inferiority. But it appears that there is one department of activity peculiarly their own, which they have hitherto failed to make the vantage-ground it might become. We refer to nursing.[1]

... Waiving the question whether women might or might not be made capable, with man's advantages of doing man's work, it surely will not be denied that a sphere of action would be preferable in which she would not have to compete with him, but in which her own peculiar endowments would give her a special advantage. And here is an opportunity for showing how a woman's work may complement man's in the true order of nature. Where does the character of the 'helpmeet' come out so strikingly as in the sick-room, where the quick eye, the soft hand, the light step, and the ready ear, second the wisdom of the physician, and execute his behests better than he himself could have imagined?[2]

The reform of nursing in Britain owes something to the example of the Protestant Institute of Deaconesses at Kaiserswerth, a few miles from Düsseldorf. It had been founded in 1833 by Pastor Theodore Fliedner as a home for discharged female convicts and had grown until it included a hospital, a lunatic asylum, an orphanage, and two schools. It was staffed by deaconesses who were bound by no religious vows and were free to leave at any time.[3] Miss Nightingale spent three months there in 1851. She admired the 'high tone' and 'pure devotion' of Kaiserswerth but she received no training in nursing. 'The nursing there was nil, and the hygiene horrible', she wrote in

anywhere but at home. And so ladies did not wish to learn nursing either for the sake of charity, or in the love of useful work, or the weariness of an unoccupied life.' See *Hospital*, 6 June 1914, p. 276.

[1] Haddon: 'Nursing as a Profession for Ladies': *St Paul's Monthly Magazine*, August 1871, p. 458.   [2] *Ibid.*, p. 461.

[3] Mrs Ross: *Women and Poor Law Administration 1857–1910*, Chapter I, pp. 7–8 (M.A. thesis).

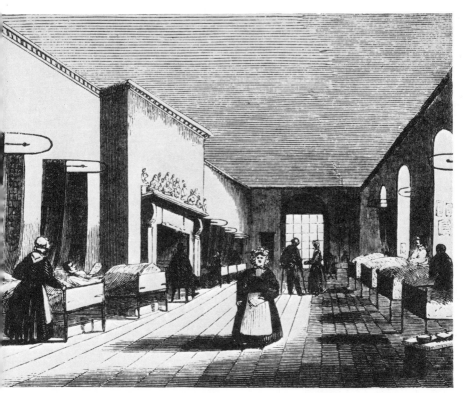

I. Interior of Rahere Ward, St Bartholomew's
(from a woodcut)

II. Pass-room, Bridewell Hospital. The Female Refuge
(drawn and engraved by Rowlandson)

III. Nurses at Norfolk and Norwich Hospital, 1864–70

IV. Mrs Green ('Nightie')
—an old nurse at St Thomas's
Hospital

V. Nurse Mary Barber
—the first probationer at St Thomas's
Hospital in 1860

1897.[1] Agnes Jones spent eight months there in 1860, and by that time the standard was apparently much higher.[2] Perhaps the greatest and most lasting contribution of Kaiserswerth to the nursing profession was the spirit of dedicated service.

It would be a mistake to attribute the nursing reform movement solely to the influence and example of Florence Nightingale[3] or to assume that the training she started at St Thomas's Hospital was the first training provided for nurses in Britain. For example, as early as 1848 St John's House began training nurses 'under the supervision of a clergyman in priest's orders'. From 1856 pupil nurses attended King's College Hospital. This connexion grew until the nursing of the hospital was undertaken by a lady superintendent, sister, associate sisters, lady-pupils, nurses, assistant nurses, probationers, and candidates on trial. The employment of this long hierarchy of nursing staff was cheap for the hospital. 'The sisters were ladies who bore their own costs and gave their services gratuitously.'[4]

Nevertheless it remains true that Florence Nightingale was the most influential of the reformers and in many ways her influence was the most wholesome. She saw the dangers of nursing falling into the hands of religious groups with all the possible rivalries which might have developed. She was afraid that the care of the body might become confused with the care of the soul, and religious loyalties come into conflict with the responsibility of the nurse to the medical and lay authorities. Her own practical experience, combined with her own aims for the nursing profession, gave her a greater insight into the problems of hospital administration than her contemporaries, even in the medical profession. Her social position gave her a vantage point from which she could thrust her ideas on the committees that controlled the voluntary hospitals. But above all she had the determination to use every weapon she possessed, including charm, social pressure, and almost blackmail to achieve the

---

[1] See Woodham-Smith: *op. cit.*, p. 72.

[2] See p. 40 below.

[3] For example Elizabeth Fry had gone to Kaiserswerth long before Florence Nightingale. Her work led to the foundation of the English Protestant Sisters of Charity, in 1840. In 1845 the High Church movement led by Pusey founded the second nursing order, the Park Village Community. The Sisters of Mercy followed in 1848 at the initiative of Priscilla Sellon. Nursing orders tended to be suspected of being non-protestant.

[4] Haldane: *op. cit.*, p. 95.

objectives she had in mind. And by force of circumstances she became the greatest publicist the profession has ever had. Her adventures in the Crimea drew public attention on an enormous scale to the problems of nursing. The special circumstances of war had focused public interest on a longstanding civil social problem. An upper-class woman had saved the British Army. This was the first step towards making nursing respectable and it enabled Miss Nightingale to play from her sofa the major role in transforming the recruitment, training, and practice of the new profession.

Her approach to nursing sprang from the changing attitude to medical care. The purpose of a hospital was to cure the sick rather than to act as a storehouse for sick persons. Miss Nightingale was well aware that the concentration of the sick in institutions could do more harm than good. Without extreme cleanliness and healthy, airy buildings, cross infection could claim more lives than medical treatment saved. To secure cleanliness alone, however, all that was needed was a more efficient and better supervised cadre of domestics. But Miss Nightingale required much more of a nurse. In the process of cure, the doctor needed a skilled auxiliary who was constantly attending the patient, and who would handle, supervise and treat each patient as he directed. The nurse also needed to be able to observe accurately the condition of the patient and report the relevant details to the doctor. For these tasks the nurse required a suitable disposition, some medical knowledge, and much supervised practice.

In essence, therefore, Miss Nightingale's solution to the problems of nursing was to find suitable girls and put them through a rigorous, though brief, training so that they would undertake thoroughly and conscientiously what she considered to be the duties of a nurse. The money subscribed to Miss Nightingale by a grateful public after the Crimean War was used to endow a training school based on these principles. Mrs Wardroper who combined the upbringing of her four children with the exacting duties of matron of St Thomas's Hospital,[1] was entrusted with the control of the new school, and she deserves much more credit for developing it than has generally been given her. It was she and not Miss Nightingale who actually trained the nurses, and it was she who was actually responsible for many of the details of the training programme.

[1] From 1854 to 1887.

The religious zeal of Kaiserswerth, the military discipline of Scutari,[1] and the cultural pattern of Miss Nightingale's prosperous Victorian home were all combined and imposed on the first recruits to the Nightingale school. The probationers were under continuous supervision during the ten hours of ward duty, were compelled to keep a diary, and were reported on weekly. Any lapse in sobriety or truthfulness meant dismissal. The training offered under these conditions was given without charge and the probationers were provided with board and lodging in the hospital, with tea, sugar, and washing, a certain amount of outer clothing and a payment of £10 for the one year's course. Supervision extended also to the periods when the probationers were off duty. Special accommodation was eventually provided in a nurses' home where the pupils could be supervised by the home sister.[2] The single bedrooms and communal sitting room, although by no means luxurious, were greatly superior to the standard of accommodation previously thought adequate for nursing staff. Living-in was made part of the training. Miss Nightingale thought it essential for moral- and character-training. It was, however, essential in these early days, if the school was to recruit from far afield. Lodgings in Lambeth would have been considered neither safe nor hygienic for a probationer nurse of the new type.

The candidates for this arduous one-year's course were carefully selected by Mrs Wardroper and meticulously vetted by Miss Nightingale. A minimum of educational attainment and a maximum of moral stature were the essential requirements for entry to the new school. As the nurses would not only need to write notes but read books on medical subjects, the field from which they could be selected was narrow. Nevertheless, the early probationers were by no means drawn exclusively from the higher social classes.

At the start it was held that 'the candidates who are best qualified for the ordinary duties of the hospital nurse appear to be daughters of small farmers who have been used to household

---

[1] The military influence has left its mark on the profession, e.g. the use of the word 'duties'.

[2] Miss Crossland, who was home sister from 1875 to 1896, played a large role in developing the actual training provided to the probationers. See Lucy Seymer's study of the Nightingale Training School to be published in 1960.

work—and well-educated domestic servants'.[1] In 1862 the Report of the Nightingale Fund Committee stated that

persons of superior manners and education, ladies in fact, are not as a rule the best qualified, but rather women of somewhat more than ordinary intelligence emanating from those classes in which women are habitually employed in earning their own livelihood. Ladies, however, are not excluded; on the contrary, where sufficient evidence is shown that they intend to pursue the calling as a business, and have those qualifications which will fit them to become superintendents their admission would be considered an advantage.[2]

More stress was laid on personal qualities than on educational achievements. High moral character was essential for a nurse.[3] There seems little doubt that Miss Nightingale, like other Victorians, believed that sexual morality preceded all other virtues. But irrespective of her private creed, expediency alone demanded that the new nurses should not only be, but should be proved to be, as chaste as the members of any religious order. Mothers of literate daughters were not in favour of their girls entering nursing, and needed some assurance that they would be protected.[4] 'One piece of indiscretion, one false step, and hopes of reforming the nursing profession and elevating its status might be set back for years.'[5]

By this system of selection the Nightingale School managed to include some of the daughters of the prosperous families of Britain, though Miss Nightingale appreciated that girls of the humblest origins could make good nurses. She specifically stated that even children brought up in the workhouse if properly educated and properly trained could make good nurses at the appropriate age.[6] Later on there were to be leaders of the

---

[1] Dunbar: *The Origin and Early Development of Two English Training Schools for Nurses*, p. 36.   [2] *Ibid.*, pp. 34–35.

[3] 'It should naturally seem impossible to the most unchaste to utter even an immodest jest in her presence.' See F. Nightingale: 'Nursing the Sick' from the *Dictionary of Medicine* (edited by Dr Quain), p. 1048: London, 1882.

[4] 'The first probationer who entered the Nightingale School for training was only permitted by her mother to do so on condition that she was never allowed to enter a male ward.' See Cope: *A Hundred Years of Nursing at St Mary's Paddington*, p. 3.   [5] Woodham-Smith: *op. cit.*, p. 267.

[6] The Poor Law Board at one time had a plan to train such girls as nurses when they had to be 'put out to places' at the age of 16 (see p. 39 below). Miss Nightingale could not see what such girls would do in the hospitals until they were 25. Even work in the civil hospitals on the female side had its

nursing profession who wanted to restrict entry to daughters of the higher social classes.[1] This was never Florence Nightingale's own intention.[2] Indeed in 1865 she had been positively opposed to 'lady' nurses who tended to be given 'to spiritual flirtations with the patients'.[3]

After the first few years of experience with the Nightingale School, there developed a more formal distinction between the 'women who were habitually employed in earning their own living' and 'the ladies'. Probably Miss Nightingale herself saw more use for ladies than when the School started. From 1867 there were two means of entry—the ordinary probationers who got free training and maintenance and the lady-pupils who paid for their maintenance during training. One advantage of this arrangement was that it made it possible to turn out more nurses from the limited funds of the Nightingale School. But it was clearly laid down that applicants for the lady class of probationer had to 'desire to qualify themselves for the superior situations'.[4] In 1881 it was stated that 'we want gentlewomen who come with settled purpose to do the work, free from all romance and affectation, but yet not wanting in some genuine enthusiasm'.[5]

At first, Miss Nightingale had reservations about lady nurses, but she soon came to appreciate the contribution they could make. The ladies came forward to take the training. In 1887, we find her regretting that the middle classes were not also offering their services.

We have not yet succeeded [she wrote to Mr Rathbone] in enlisting the better sort of women of tradesmen's families, who generally lead the most useless and uninteresting lives—unlike those of ladies, so improved in usefulness, in interest, in what public opinion allows them

---

dangers in the form of medical students. She wrote to Mary Jones, 'what excellent wholesome material there is among these Union orphan girls.' (2 May 1865, *STHA* 65/10.)   [1] See p. 63 below.

[2] 'My principle has always been', she wrote, 'that we should give the best training we could to any woman of any class, of any sect, paid or unpaid, who had the requisite qualifications, moral, intellectual, and physical, for the vocation of a Nurse. Unquestionably the educated will be more likely to rise to the post of Superintendents, *not* because they are ladies, *but* because they are educated.' See E. Cook: *The Life of Florence Nightingale*, Vol. II, p. 270: London, 1913.

[3] *Ibid.*, Vol. I, p. 252.   [4] Dunbar: *op. cit.*, p. 36.   [5] *Ibid.*, p. 37.

to do in the last thirty years while the little world of tradespeople allows them to be nothing but 'genteel', except the most energetic individuals. Tradeswomen might lead such good, active lives, like ladies, if they saw the way.[1]

The lady-pupils became Miss Nightingale's missionaries in the nursing reform movement. Between 1860 and 1903 the Nightingale School certified 1,907 nurses as having had one year's training.[2] This figure, however, does not represent the total of its influence. The new order spread by geometric progression as each trained nurse trained others. Miss Nightingale herself, who made it her business to know intimately the sisters and meet the probationers at her training school, acted as a clearing house for nursing appointments throughout the country and steered candidates of whom she approved into the key positions of the nursing world. Viewed historically, the Nightingale School became in practice more important as a training school for matrons than as a training school for nurses. Ladies were sent there 'with the special object that they should be passed on to be, first, assistant superintendents, and ultimately heads of nursing departments in hospitals'.[3] Steadily the hospitals in Britain acquired in turn matrons, nursing schools, and nurses of the new type.[4]

Miss Nightingale did not allow the 'trained' matrons whom she had engineered into the hospitals to delay in undertaking reforms. She showered them with advice both solicited and unsolicited. She coaxed them and bullied them until many of them attained the heights of uncompromising ruthlessness of which she herself was capable. The changes involved conflicts with the old nurses, the doctors, and the lay administration. For

[1] *District Nursing*, May 1958, p. 38.
[2] *Registration of Nurses, Select Committee Report; 1905* (170) vii, p. 17.
[3] *Metropolitan Hospitals, Select Committee House of Lords Third Report; 1892* (93) xiii, p. lxxxiv.
[4] 'In 1887 the following hospitals, institutions, and organizations had matrons or superintendents who had been trained at the Nightingale School: the Westminster Hospital, St Mary's Paddington, the Marylebone Infirmary, the Highgate Infirmary, the Metropolitan and National Nursing Association, the North London District Association, the Cumberland Infirmary, the Edinburgh Royal Infirmary, the Huntingdon County Hospital, the Leeds Infirmary, the Lincoln County Hospital, the Royal Infirmary, Liverpool, the Workhouse Infirmary, Liverpool, and the Southern Infirmary, Liverpool, the Royal Victoria Hospital at Netley, the Royal Hospital for Incurables, Putney, and the Salisbury Infirmary.' See Woodham-Smith: *op. cit.*, p. 410.

the introduction of trained matrons and probationer nurses meant a major change in hospital administration.

In many hospitals the matron had previously played a small role in the control of nursing affairs. Her major work had been that of a housekeeper, and in these matters she worked under the orders of the lay administration. It was she who engaged the nurses, though in some hospitals she did this in consultation with the medical staff responsible for each ward. The doctors gave them such training and knowledge as they possessed. It was not the matron's duty to tell the sisters what they ought to be doing for the doctors. Moreover, the nursing staff tended to remain continuously in the same ward.

When a hospital was run on these lines it was clear that the introduction of a matron and a training school would bring conflict. Put baldly, if the new matron was to undertake what she considered to be her duties, she had to carve out an empire of her own. She had to take over some of the responsibilities of the medical staff and some of the responsibilities of the lay administration. In addition she had to centralize the administration of nursing affairs, lowering thereby the prestige of the sisters.

Miss Nightingale was quite clear about what her new matrons had to do.

The whole reform in nursing both at home and abroad has consisted in this; [she wrote to Mary Jones in 1867] to take all power over the Nursing out of the hands of the men, and put it into the hands of *one female trained* head and make her responsible for everything (regarding internal management and discipline) being carried out. Usually it is the Medical staff who have injudiciously interfered as 'Master'. How much worse it is when it is the Chaplain. . . . Don't let the chaplain want to make himself matron. Don't let the Doctor make himself Head Nurse. *There is no worse matron than a chaplain.* It is so odd that practical Englishmen cannot see this without being told.[1]

Thus we see clashes between the old hospital staff and the new matrons with their new-fangled, interfering ways. One such battle was fought in Guy's Hospital when the new matron, Miss Burt, took over. She had no use for the existing nurses. 'They were untrained; they took money from the patients; they spent

[1] Letter from Miss Nightingale to Mary Jones, *STHA* 67/1. It must not be forgotten that some of the new nurses at this time were members of Anglican religious orders.

their evenings off in public houses and in music halls; they did not keep their patients clean and, lastly, they even wore jewellery.'[1] She asked many of the old nursing staff to leave and introduced a uniform which the nurses had to buy themselves.[2] In addition it was a firm rule that no jewellery of any kind would in future be tolerated.[3]

No longer did she allow the nurses to stay in one ward. 'If the hospital was to serve as a training school for nurses, in much the same way as it was a training school for doctors, nurses must be moved about and given the opportunity, before going out into the world to practice their calling, of acquiring experience in the different departments of the Hospital.'[4] It was this last disturbance of their settled ways which led the staff to address a letter of complaint to the Governors. The matron was accused of undermining the position of the sisters by centralizing all the nursing arrangements in her office. Moreover, the notes kept by the pupils were interpreted as a method by which the matron spied on the sisters. The Governors supported Miss Burt.

At Lincoln in 1867 these principles of the new nursing régime led to a conflict with the management. The principle 'of placing the Hospital in the hands of one qualified person trained and a lady if possible'[5] was defeated. According to Miss Nightingale's correspondent (L. Boucherett), this defeat occurred 'by the influence of the drunken doctor over his farmer friends, and thro' the anger of some of the governors whose mismanagement we had exposed'. As the result of this conflict a month's notice was given for the withdrawal of 'our nurses'.

---

[1] Cameron: *Mr Guy's Hospital 1726–1948*, p. 208.

[2] 'One cause of complaint amongst the old nursing staff was that Miss Burt ordered that a uniform should be worn. Till then they had supplied their own clothes of whatever color [*sic*] they pleased. Those who had just bought new dresses for the winter and were suddenly ordered to buy new ones of Miss Burt's pattern naturally could not afford to do so and many refused to buy new ones until they had worn out what they possessed.' See Dunbar: *op. cit.*, Part II, p. 50.

[3] 'Miss Burt too made a rule "no jewelery [*sic*] to be worn". Watch bracelets had not then been invented and every woman wore her watch on a chain . . . Sister Martha who was a most capable nurse . . . protested in vain she had no other way of wearing her watch. To avoid a quarrel she took off the chain . . . and a few days later she lost the watch.' *Ibid.*, p. 50.

[4] Cameron: *op. cit.*, p. 203.

[5] Letter from L. Boucherett to Florence Nightingale, January 1867, *STHA* V6/67.

There were many reasons why the medical staff did not welcome unanimously the new 'ladies' who came to work in the wards of the hospitals. *The Report on the Metropolitan Hospitals* (1892) spoke of 'misunderstandings' between the medical and nursing staffs. First, many of the new nurses were of a higher social class than the doctors working in the same hospitals. Secondly, the doctors feared that these educated women would undermine their authority, however much the nurses protested that they were there to carry out the doctors' instructions. A line had still to be drawn between general nursing which came under the supervision of the matron and medical treatment which remained the sole responsibility of the doctors. This line once drawn had to be carefully respected by both parties.

The Nightingale School itself was not opened without opposition from the hospital doctors. One of the surgeons (Mr South) thought that the purpose of admitting ladies was 'to place [the whole nursing establishment] in the hands of persons who will never be content till *they* become the executive of the hospitals and as they have in the military hospitals been a constant source of annoyance to the medical and surgical officers'.[1] Medical opposition lasted for many years in hospitals up and down the country. At Pendlebury Hospital a sister of the new type was held to have secured the suspension of the senior physician. This was taken as good evidence by a doctor in Manchester why it was unwise to introduce what he called 'this *imperium in imperio*'.[2] Other reasons were given by doctors for opposing the new nurses.

As mere matter of fact, ladies, as a rule, do not make first-rate nurses; and the reason is obvious. With rare exceptions they are essentially *amateurish*; or, if very much in earnest are apt to be dominated by some principle or power, not necessarily an ally to be trusted in the management of the sick. Ladies take to nursing, as a rule, from slightly morbid motive; they are 'disappointed', or they want something with which to kill *ennui*, or they have religious convictions on the subject; none of which sentiments, we may venture to say, are likely to result in producing good *staying* workers.[3]

Supporters of the new nurses on the other hand accused the

[1] Letter from John Flint South, 11 August 1856, *STHA* C56/2.
[2] Reprint from *British Medical Journal*, 17 March 1880.
[3] 'Hospital and Nursing Institutions': *British Medical Journal*, 17 March 1880.

doctors of having less creditable reasons for their opposition. Miss Lonsdale condemned the old style nurse as an ignorant and immoral drunkard and accused

the honorary staff of Guy's and other hospitals of preferring this class of woman to the highly trained lady-nurse, for three reasons: firstly, because they are able to indulge in obscene language before the patients without let or hindrance; secondly because the afore-described 'old style' of nurse is no restraint upon the students coming in and examining the patients at any hour; and thirdly, because the staff can prosecute experiments upon the bodies of their patients of such a nature that they dare not perform in the presence of a trained lady-nurse.[1]

In time a *modus vivendi* was developed. For example, Miss Pringle found that

doctors will not tolerate interference with their province and do not appreciate education and smartness if unaccompanied with loyalty and real nursing power; that they welcome and prize highly all who have proper gifts—the more refined and intelligent the better; that they help most generously, often at great sacrifice of their valuable time, and entirely without reward, in the teaching and training of the nurses; that their conduct to them is full of courtesy and con- sideration, and that they lose no opportunity of showing them kindness.[2]

In all these battles for power the new matrons had two dis- advantages. First, they were women. Secondly, they were young. On the other hand they possessed one weapon which could be kept in reserve. In the event of serious trouble they could appeal above the heads of the doctors or lay administrators to Miss Nightingale herself. She was often able to use her influence with doctors or hospital governors to ensure that the matron got her way.

In nearly all cases the new matrons triumphed. And in the voluntary hospitals they carved out for themselves positions of undisputed authority between the medical staff and the lay administration. The higher status of the matron was given formal recognition by increased pay in cash and kind. By 1892 it was accepted in the voluntary hospitals that the matron was *de*

---

[1] *British Medical Journal*, 17 March 1880.

[2] Elizabeth Pringle: 'Nurses and Doctors': *Edinburgh Medical Journal*, May 1880, p. 1050.

facto the head of an independent department. She controlled her own staff and reported direct to the hospital committee. It was a well understood arrangement that the lay administration never interfered in her department.[1]

Over the nurses themselves the matrons wielded absolute power. This power was reinforced by the para-military organization of the nursing staff and the rigid discipline imposed in the training schools. As Miss Nightingale said rather ominously 'no good ever comes of anyone interfering between the head of the nursing establishment and her nurses. It is fatal to discipline.'[2] The control of the matron over her nurses was to play a crucial role in future attempts to enrol nurses in professional organizations or trade unions.

In so far as it was the objective of the nursing reform movement to attract suitable women to the hospital this was achieved. As time went on the first trickle of timorous pupils was followed by a steady and sufficient stream of suitable candidates. Later still the stream became a torrent. Many hospitals had more applicants than they could accommodate. By the eighties and nineties nursing had established itself as a suitable and respectable career for women. It had caught the imagination of the younger generation.[3]

A number of factors contributed to the popularity of nursing. First, it appealed to the romantic or dedicated sort of girl in an age which offered few occupations for women.[4] Secondly, it was in line with the tenets of the High Church movement. Thirdly, nursing and teaching represented almost the only practicable forms of escape from the parental nest. Fourthly, private nursing

---

[1] *Third Report from the Select Committee on Metropolitan Hospitals 1892*, p. lxxxii.

[2] Quoted *ibid.*, p. lxxxiii.

[3] Burdett began his chapter on nursing in his third year book as follows: 'every boy in his teens wants to be a sailor; every girl in her teens wants to be a nurse. The boy probably outgrows the romantic period and turns to other thoughts during his college life; but the girl, unless she contracts an early marriage, casts longing eyes on the hospital world whenever her home becomes dull and dances fail to satisfy the mind.'
See *Burdett's Hospital Annual and Year Book of Philanthropy 1891–92*, p. cxxxii: London, 1892.

[4] As the *School and the Teacher* wrote in August 1856: 'the openings for females are but few. The girls in our schools have generally to choose between domestic service, dressmaking, or some occupation which we may denominate factory work.' See Tropp: *op. cit.*, p. 22n.

or a post as matron offered considerable financial rewards when compared with the few alternatives open to the sex. Fifthly, some experience of nursing became recognized as one of the 'accomplishments' which a young lady could profitably acquire. Sixthly, the development of the nursing profession represented an instalment of the emancipation of women.[1] It gave power— power over men.

Not all the young women who took up nursing had the same objectives in mind. And it would be a mistake to imagine that the Nightingale School and the training schools run by its pro-tégées were the only good training schools in Britain. Other hospitals developed schools on similar principles. On the other hand, there were hospitals that accepted ladies on less rigorous terms than the formal training schools. From the early days ladies were admitted casually to the wards of voluntary hospitals to acquire some hospital experience. They were made to pay for this privilege. One guinea per week became a typical charge for short periods, and it was accepted that some of these entrants had no intention of taking a complete training. 'They are usually exempt from the sweeping and dusting.'[2] Some hospitals quite frankly 'cashed in' on the new zeal to nurse the sick. As Miss Nightingale wrote to a friend in 1889, 'the Matrons are often compelled to take in more Probationers (who pay) than they can manage—for the sake of funds'.[3] Fees for training became a noticeable part of the income of the voluntary hospitals.[4]

Thus, St Thomas's was not the only hospital to make a distinc-tion between the lady-pupils who paid for their training and the ordinary probationers who were paid during training. Miss Hunt[5] described the system as she had known it in the following

---

[1] As Miss Dunbar remarked: 'Many of these women no doubt felt no interest in the work itself but valued it merely for the new freedom it gave them.' Dunbar: *op. cit.*, p. 32.

[2] *Burdett's Hospital Annual and Year Book of Philanthropy 1890*, p. lxxxvii.

[3] Letter from Florence Nightingale to Sister Francis, 6 November 1889, *STHA* 89/17.

[4] It represented 2½ per cent of the income of those hospitals reporting to *Burdett's Annual* in 1891.

[5] Miss Hunt was the founder and director of the Baschurch Children's Hospital at Oswestry, which has now been re-named the Robert Jones and Agnes Hunt Orthopaedic Hospital, and she helped to found the Derwen Cripples' Training College. She became a Dame of the British Empire in 1926 (*NM*, 3 July 1948, p. 274).

words: 'the difference between a probationer and a lady-pupil was that a probationer had to serve two years for a certificate, and a lady-pupil had to pay a pound a week and was given a certificate at the end of a year'.[1] It was generally accepted that the lady-pupil with her shorter period of training would get swifter promotion. 'It came to be recognized that it was from among the lady-pupils that the Sisters generally were elected.'[2] The charge for this status was substantial—a premium of fifty guineas was not an uncommon figure.[3]

The lady-pupils were carefully separated from the ordinary probationers. They were given separate sleeping accommodation[4] and even separate seats in the chapel where they were expected to engage in longer devotions.[5] They wore special uniforms. At Guy's these were 'stately black alpaca gowns'.[6] At the Middlesex Hospital they were 'arrayed in a dress of violet hue with a small train, three inches in length, which swept the floor behind them'.[7] Miss Thorold, the buxom lady superintendent of the Middlesex Hospital, honoured each lady-pupil daily with a kiss.

This system of special entry to the nursing profession gradually

[1] Agnes Hunt: *Reminiscences*, p. 64: Shrewsbury, 1935. In one case the fees paid by the lady-pupils were paid into a pension fund for nurses. See H. St C. Saunders: *The Middlesex Hospital 1745–1948*, p. 45: London, 1949.

[2] Cameron: *op. cit.*, p. 205. See also *Third Report from the Select Committee on Metropolitan Hospitals 1892*, p. lxxx.

[3] *Report from the Select Committee on Registration of Nurses 1905*, p. 9. One witness to this Committee claimed to have spent nearly £300 on her training. This included the cost of uniforms and laundry (see p. 11).

[4] Cameron: *op. cit.*, p. 265.

[5] 'I had a seat next to the aisle in the first pew devoted to the lady-pupils, with the Sisters behind on the same side. On the other side of the aisle were the maids, probationer nurses and staff nurses. For some no doubt very good reason, it has been ordained that the *élite*, as it were, of the hospital, should, after the more formal morning prayers, indulge in silent meditations after the more plebeian portion of the staff had been dismissed to their several occupations.' See Hunt: *op. cit.*, p. 64.

[6] Cameron: *op. cit.*, pp. 271–2.

[7] 'In course of time the trains became soiled and frayed and their owners, wishing to avoid the trouble and expense of renewing them, used to turn up the hems. The day inevitably came when the Lady Superintendent discovered this seemingly innocent practice. The delinquent was at once summoned to the presence. "I cannot", said Miss Thorold firmly, "and I will not allow it to be done, dear. I devised this little train so that when you lean over a bed to attend a patient your ankles will be covered and the students will not be able to see them." ' See Saunders: *op. cit.*, p. 43.

fell into decline. In 1900 the lady probationers at Guy's Hospital asked to have the same uniforms as the other probationers.[1] By this time the one year's training was considered insufficient for the best appointments.[2] One lady-pupil went back for a further two years of training.[3] No doubt the speed with which ladies could become qualified nurses contributed to the willingness of 'superior' women to undergo training.

By no means all the lady-pupils or probationers stayed to complete their training. What is now called wastage in training is no new problem in nursing.

At the outset [wrote Burdett] from some records I kept at the time, I found that out of 100 women who applied to be admitted as probationers only four became trained and certified nurses. Mrs Wardroper used to say that at the Nightingale School from 30 to 40 out of every 100 probationers would, from one cause or another, fall out of the ranks during the period of training.[4] It is desirable to remember these facts, as they illustrate how many who desire to leave home from one cause or another—very many young women regard nursing from a distance as an easy and pleasant pastime—are in practice utterly unsuited for the calling of a nurse.[5]

Wastage during training was greater among the lady probationers than among the ordinary probationers.[6]

As more hospitals accepted the Nightingale type of trainee, so the arrangements for feeding and accommodating the nurses gradually improved. The needs or demands of the new type of nurse and the payments made by some of the pupils contributed to this improvement. Separate nurses' homes of the Nightingale type were gradually provided; and though the life of the trainees remained strenuous, organized cultural activities were occasionally included in the curriculum. The nurses' home at Guy's (in 1908) possessed no less than three grand pianos.[7] Miss Haughton, the matron of Guy's before the first world war, told the nurses

[1] Dunbar: *op. cit.*, Part II, p. 62. (From the Minutes of Guy's Hospital House Committee, 28 February 1900.)

[2] In 1889, the British Nurses Association decided that three years of training were necessary. See p. 70 below.

[3] *Select Committee on Registration 1905*, p. 11.

[4] The actual figure was 40 out of every 100. See Dunbar: *op. cit.*, p. 42.

[5] Burdett: *Nurses' Food, Work and Recreation*, p. 7.

[6] Dunbar: *op. cit.*, p. 42.

[7] E. E. P. MacManus: *Matron of Guy's*, p. 39: London, 1956.

that they were 'women of England' and 'citizens of the world'. She encouraged debates, dances, swimming galas, and poetry reading.[1] The matrons were ladies with wide interests. Miss Thorold, of the Middlesex Hospital, had an exhaustive knowledge of the museums, monuments and picture galleries of Europe.[2] Miss Clarributt, of the Radcliffe Infirmary, 'knew the names of every bishop and of all the parsons within miles of Oxford'.[3]

In 1891 Burdett wrote one of his characteristic long sentences on the current arrangements for nurses.

Not only is the accommodation provided for the nurses, and the proportion of the nurses to the patients upon a basis adequate enough to meet the requirements of the day, but the public sympathy with nurses is so great that the danger of the future consists, not in any fear that the nurses will not be cared for, but rather that the comforts provided may be excessive, and so bring about results inimicable to efficient administration and demoralizing to nurses as a body.[4]

Not all hospitals had reached these standards. There were some upon which the shadow of Miss Nightingale had not yet fallen where conditions were far from good. In the West London Hospital in the 'eighties, supper still consisted of bread, cheese and beer.[5] Miss Hunt recalled conditions in a Middlesborough hospital in the 'nineties. 'We all slept in a big, bare ward, with no privacy at all, neither the bathroom nor the lavatory had a catch or bolt. The mattresses were mostly hills and valleys, and the pillows were flock, and as hard as boards. There was no sitting room, only the bare dining room, in which we had had our Barmecide feast.'[6] Unsatisfactory accommodation was not just a provincial problem. At St Bartholomew's in 1891 some nurses slept in cubicles near the diphtheria ward. Twenty-three nurses and three ward maids contracted the disease. Moreover, the imperfect sanitary arrangements gave the staff sore throats: the water closets ventilated into the ward kitchens.[7]

Conditions of work were far from good in the provincial infirmaries. Margaret Winterton wrote a vivid account of the General Infirmary at Northampton when she arrived in 1889.

[1] *Ibid.*, p. 43.
[2] Saunders: *op. cit.*, p. 40.
[3] Gibson: *op. cit.*, pp. 231–2.
[4] *Burdett's Annual 1891–92*, p. xxxix.
[5] Hunt: *op. cit.*, p. 67.
Ibid., p. 91.
[7] *Third Report from the Select Committee on Metropolitan Hospitals 1892*, p. xi.

'Our spring cleaning has just begun, and the poor nurses have it all to do, there is not a single scrubber about the place, they have pictures to clean and hang, paint to scrub, beds to repair, pillows to re-fill, in fact everything but the white-washing.'[1] She found that her suggestion that three-monthly spells on night duty should be substituted for weekly spells did not meet with approval. 'The nurses do all their washing and ironing, and this they do every alternate week when they come off night duty.' Nevertheless the existing system involved a spell on duty at the week-end of thirty hours with only a two-and-a-half-hour break for sleep.

It is hard to assess the full consequences of the movement for nursing reform. It is clear that the broad objectives were achieved. It became widely recognized by the hospital authorities that nurses required training, and training schools of varying quality were in operation throughout the country. Moreover, though there were rivalries between the training schools, these rivalries were professional rather than religious. Most important of all, the attitude of public opinion towards nursing was transformed. No longer was nursing regarded as a superior form of domestic service which did not always attract respectable members of the 'servant class'. It had become a vocation: it had become a proper occupation for daughters of the middle and upper classes. As one writer put it in 1871, it had been proved 'that love can dignify and consecrate the most repulsive tasks'.[2]

There is no reason to doubt that the medical care of the patients was greatly improved. The patients also enjoyed greater physical comfort.[3] On the other hand they must have felt a certain loss of homeliness in the wards for which the kindly intent of the new nurses did not compensate. They were kept more in bed; the prohibition of smoking and other regulations were enforced; and in general the male patients drawn primarily from the working class were forced by members of a different sex and class to conform to standards of behaviour quite foreign

---

[1] *STHA* V15/89.

[2] Haddon: *op. cit.*, p. 458.

[3] *Third Report from the Select Committee on Metropolitan Hospitals 1892*, pp. lxxvii–lxxix. For example, in the old days bed-clothes had been renewed 'about once in three weeks'. See *The Lancet Commission on Nursing*, p. 19: London, 1932.

to their normal lives. The homely, dirty, foul-mouthed nurses must sometimes have been missed.[1]

[1] The following gives us an intimate picture of New Year's Eve in the Edinburgh Infirmary in 1873:

> Kate the scrubber (forty summers,
> Stout but sportive) treads a measure,
> Grinning, in herself a ballet,
> Fixed as fate upon her audience.
>
> Stumps are shaking, crutch-supported;
> Splinted fingers tap the rhythm;
> And a head all helmed with plasters
> Wags a measured approbation.
>
> Of their mattress-life oblivious,
> All the patients, brisk and cheerful,
> Are encouraging the dancer,
> And applauding the musician.
>
> Dim the gases in the output
> Of so many ardent smokers,
> Full of shadow lurk the corners,
> And the doctor peeps and passes.
>
> There are, maybe, some suspicions
> Of an alcoholic presence . . .
> 'Tak' a sup of this, my wumman!' . . .
> New Year comes but once a twelvemonth.

See *Guy's Hospital Gazette*, pp. 124–5: London, 1925. The author of the poem was W. E. Henley who was an inmate of the Edinburgh Royal Infirmary in 1873.

CHAPTER III

Paid Nurses and Pauper Nurses

DURING the thirty years that followed the founding of the Nightingale School, the training of nurses spread throughout the voluntary hospitals. The militant, almost fanatical trained matrons fired the old nurses and trained new ones. When change came to a hospital, it was relatively swift and usually ruthless. By the end of the century, nearly all the larger voluntary hospitals in England had their own nurse training schools.

There had been opposition. In part it had been a battle of the sexes. The new ladies had had to fight the male doctors, the male lay administrators, and the male members of the hospital committees. The matrons had sought and gained a position of great power in institutions which had previously been exclusively controlled by men. The nursing reform movement was part of the wider struggle for the emancipation of women. It was relatively swift because the pressure for it came from the top of the social hierarchy: the ladies who sought power in the hospitals moved in the same social circle as the committees that ran them. Miss Nightingale and her friends could impose changes from the top. It proved much harder to reform the workhouses.

Control over the voluntary hospitals was exercised by committees of charitable intent. They saw it as their duty to aid the sick; they took from their friends and those who wished to be their friends the money to provide what the leading doctors told them was required. Control over the workhouses, on the other hand, was exercised by committees of men,[1] elected for small local areas. They were seldom drawn from the same social background as the committees that ran the voluntary hospitals, and they tended to see their duty as the protection of the ratepayer rather than the pauper. Some of the small tradesmen who volun-

[1] The first woman member of a Board of Guardians (Miss Martha Remington) was not elected until 1875.

tarily gave their services to govern the affairs of the local community found themselves rewards of a tangible character and
distributed patronage with a blatancy which their social superiors
had recently abandoned. The doctors who worked in the poor
law service were neither numerous nor persons of high standing
in their local community. Thus, in practice, Boards of Guardians
were advised or ruled by two-faced masters many of whom had
risen from humble origins. While a wide social gulf separated
the committees of the voluntary hospitals from their patients, the
distinction between management and pauper was not so clearly
marked in the workhouses. It was not unknown for a master of
a workhouse or even a chairman of a Board of Guardians to pass
his last years as an inmate of his own workhouse.

The punishing attitude of workhouse managements cannot
be wholly explained by the low standing of their professional
advisers, by the inequities of the rating system, or by the 'status
insecurity' of management itself, though all these contributed to
it. Much more important was the whole philosophy of the poor
laws which was deeply ingrained on masters, managers, and
ratepayers. As prison reformers were to learn a hundred years
later, there are severe obstacles to the improvement of curative
services in any establishment which is primarily intended to be
deterrent. Moreover, influential opinion can conveniently evade
the moral problems that any institution poses, be it a welfare
home, mental hospital, or workhouse, while that institution is
excluded from the public's gaze.

Thus the first step towards reform is public education. In the
case of the workhouses, this role was played by a number of
charitably-minded and influential persons who visited the workhouses and exposed their defects. Among the earliest visitors
was Louisa Twining. In 1853 she visited the Strand Workhouse.
She had gone to call on a respectable old woman who had been
compelled to enter it when 'strength and eyesight failed her'.
The old lady had 'begged that her friend and visitor would not
forget or forsake her when shut up from the outer world'.[1] After
a number of visits, Miss Twining planned to bring other ladies
'for the purpose of reading to the inmates, and giving comfort and instruction'.[2] The Poor Law Board objected to her
proposal, pointing out that it was 'contrary to the general practice to admit strangers into the workhouse for the purpose of

[1] Twining: *Workhouse Visiting and Management*, p. 6.   [2] *Ibid.*, p. 7.

aiding the paid and responsible officers in the performance of their duties'. It would be 'an embarrassing and inconvenient precedent'.[1]

A year later, after Miss Twining had made a personal visit to the Board, this decision was reversed provided the plan was 'quietly carried on'.[2] The ladies visited quietly, but they also assembled information on the state of the workhouses, which Miss Twining published. Her revelations led to a somewhat ineffective debate in the House of Lords in 1857 and the withdrawal of permission for ladies to visit the Strand Workhouse.[3] The ladies responded by forming, in 1858, the Workhouse Visiting Society and successfully infiltrating a number of other workhouses. By 1860, one hundred and forty members were visiting twelve metropolitan workhouses, and local branches had been established in several parts of England.[4]

The opposition to workhouse visitors had a number of causes. First, there was the natural fear of the officials that the ladies would obtain information which would be to their discredit. Secondly, there was the religious issue; if there were to be Protestant lady visitors, how could Roman Catholic ladies be kept out of the workhouses? Thirdly, there was the widespread prejudice of male Guardians against the interfering woman. One of the visitors commented sarcastically on this attitude:

We do give credit to many ridiculous stories and pity many imaginary grievances, and sometimes go to the length of bestowing unmerited tea or even indigestible lozenges and Puseyite tracts upon our proteges . . . but perhaps if the gentlemen to whom the guardianship of the poor is exclusively entrusted *never* made blunders . . . the state of our workhouses would not be precisely what it is at this moment.[5]

Among the failings of the workhouse system which the ladies exposed was the inadequate and incompetent nursing. Nor were the London ladies the only charitably disposed visitors to notice the evil. William Rathbone, the wealthy philanthropist, had come to similar conclusions from visits to the Brownlow Hill Insti-

---

[1] Twining: *Workhouse Visiting and Management*, p. 8.
[2] *Ibid.*, p. 11.   [3] *Ibid.*, p. 21.
[4] *Journal of the Workhouse Visiting Society*, May 1860, p. 197.
[5] Frances Cobbe: 'Sick in Workhouses': *Journal of the Workhouse Visiting Society*, 1861, p. 487. Quoted in Ross: *Women and Poor Law Administration*.

tution in Liverpool. And these upper-class visitors were joined in their agitation by the more enlightened of the London workhouse doctors with the tacit support of Mr Farnall, the Poor Law Inspector for the Metropolitan District. Dr Rogers in particular was so outspoken in his criticisms of conditions in the Strand Workhouse that he was suspended from his appointment. In 1866 he formed the Association of Poor Law Medical Officers as a pressure group for reform.[1]

Once it had been recognized that workhouse nursing needed to be improved, the debate began about the means by which reform should be effected. As early as 1849 it had been suggested that suitable paupers should be given training as nurses, and in 1855 this proposal was endorsed by a number of eminent doctors.[2] The plan had obvious advantages. Not only might it improve the standard of nursing in the workhouses but it might also relieve the rates of the cost of maintaining a number of able-bodied women. After their training they could be sent out to practise their newly acquired skill on the public at large.

This economical plan for reform appealed to the Poor Law Board and Boards of Guardians were instructed to carry it out, until it perished under Miss Nightingale's scorn.

Are we to expect [she wrote] that we shall find suitable women for an occupation which requires, perhaps above every other occupation, sobriety, honesty, trustworthiness, truthfulness, orderliness, cleanliness, good character, and good health, among those who, nearly all, at least in the workhouses of the large towns, are there because they have *not* been sober, *not* been honest, *not* been trustworthy or truthful, *not* been orderly or cleanly, *not* had good character or good health, because they have *not* been one or other of these things, because they have failed in one or all of these? Is it likely?[3]

By this time she had developed with Mr Rathbone a plan of her own. On 31 January 1864, he wrote asking her for a staff of trained nurses and a matron to be sent to staff the Brownlow Hill Workhouse Infirmary in Liverpool. He offered to pay the cost of the experiment for three years. The Vestry which controlled the Workhouse Infirmary needed lengthy persuasion to

---

[1] Rogers: *Reminiscences of a Workhouse Medical Officer*, pp. 50–51.

[2] Twining: *Workhouse Visiting and Management*, p. 17.

[3] Nightingale: 'Suggestions on the subject of providing, training and organising nurses for the sick poor in workhouse infirmaries': *Letter to Sir Thomas Watson Bart.*, 1867, p. 3.

accept this novel idea, but a year later permission was obtained. Accordingly Miss Nightingale sent 'her best and dearest pupil' Miss Agnes Jones,[1] at the age of 32, to become matron of the Brownlow Hill Institution. She arrived with a staff of twelve trained nurses and within a month sacked thirty-five of the old pauper nurses for drunkenness.[2] She attempted to train other able-bodied women as pauper nurses, giving them a small wage and the title of 'Assistant Nurse', but most proved unsatisfactory.[3] The standards Miss Jones demanded were very high and the material unpromising.

This experiment could do no more than demonstrate the value of paid nurses who were properly selected and properly trained. It is, however, one thing to prove the advantages of reform by local demonstration and quite another to secure its adoption all over the country within any reasonable period of time. It takes more than clear empirical evidence to defeat vested interests, to overcome public prejudice and to drive to action a timid administration. All this had been learnt by Miss Nightingale during her attempts to reform the medical administration of the army

[1] Agnes Jones was born of Irish parents in 1832. Her father was a colonel in the army. In 1853, while travelling abroad, she visited Kaiserswerth and decided to stay there for a week. On returning home she did some voluntary home nursing among the poor and other social work, and looked after her mother who by this time had become widowed. In 1860, when her sister relieved her of her domestic ties, she returned to Kaiserswerth and was trained for eight months. It was here that she learned 'the habit of implicit obedience'. While in Kaiserswerth she was invited to take over the superintendency of the Liverpool Infirmary after further training in London. Her mother at first refused to allow her to live in a hospital, but within a year Agnes Jones overcame this opposition, and escaped from her family to enter St Thomas's Hospital for a year of further training. Though Miss Jones judged the caps at St Thomas's 'too round and coquettish for Sisters' she used to say afterwards: 'Without a regular hard London hospital training I should have been nowhere.' According to Miss Nightingale 'she went through all the work of a soldier; and she thereby fitted herself for being the best general we ever had'. See Margaret Tabor: *Pioneer Women*, Second series, pp. 95–123: London, 1927.

[2] Conditions in the Infirmary reminded Miss Nightingale of Scutari. 'Immorality was universal. Filth was universal. The patients wore the same shirts for seven weeks; bedding was only changed and washed once a month; food was at starvation level; spirits entered the Infirmary freely. The number of patients was very large, 1,350, rising at times to 1,500.' See Woodham-Smith: *op. cit.*, p. 350.

[3] W. M. Frazer: *A History of English Public Health*, pp. 86–87: London, 1950.

and the sanitary policies of the British administration in India. Workhouse nursing would not be altered all over the country without far-reaching changes in the whole system of workhouse administration. Thus she evolved a comprehensive pilot scheme for London. Miss Twining had suggested in 1861 the provision of separate institutions for the different categories of 'inmate'. Miss Nightingale saw that this was unlikely to be achieved without a separate administration for London financed by one general system of rates. Small authorities could not afford separate institutions nor would they see the importance of appointing qualified nurses let alone qualified matrons. She sent her plan straight to the top of the Poor Law Board and induced the President, Mr Villiers, to visit her at home. Judging that he lacked the necessary energy to secure the legislation she wanted, she went up to Cabinet level and sold her ideas to Lord Palmerston. Everything seemed to be going well, when her hopes were dashed to the ground by the death of Lord Palmerston in 1865 and the fall of the Government a year later.[1]

A similar, though less far-reaching scheme was devised by the Association for Improving Metropolitan Workhouse Infirmaries, which was founded in February 1886. London was to be divided into six administrative 'unions' for the treatment of the sick poor, governed by elected ratepayers and financed by a general infirmary rate equalized over the metropolitan area. Each union was to build an infirmary for the care of 1,000 acute cases. Miss Nightingale supported the scheme.[2]

Although Miss Nightingale's attempts to secure a complete reform of workhouse administration failed, the pilot nursing scheme at Liverpool proved eventually a spectacular success. At first there was friction between Miss Jones and the governor of the Infirmary. She complained of his 'want of refinement' to Miss Nightingale who managed to pacify both parties.[3] But the improvement in the care of the patients was dramatic. More remarkable, the cost of maintaining the sick was far less than

---

[1] See Woodham-Smith: *op. cit.*, pp. 348–53.

[2] See Ross: *op. cit.*, Chapter VIII, pp. 9–10.

[3] She wrote to the Governor telling him that the eyes of the world were upon him as the leader in a great reform. Miss Jones reported that he seemed 'so gratified and flattered by your letter'. See Cook: *The Life of Florence Nightingale*, p. 128.

before. Although the managers of the workhouse were converted to the principle of trained nurses, the conflict between the new nurses and the Vestry probably convinced the Poor Law Board that reform on the Nightingale lines involved too great an upheaval.[1]

The Liverpool experiment was repeated at the new Highgate Infirmary in 1869. Again there were difficulties. Miss Nightingale was 'transfixed with horror' to receive a letter of complaint saying that the nurses she had sent were being insubordinate to the patients. They had said that the food was 'good enough for paupers' and that the patients 'required a great deal of waiting on'. She paid great attention to the letter because it was 'very fairly written and signed by two men patients'.[2]

Despite these teething troubles, she was convinced that trained nurses had to be introduced into the infirmaries. There needed, however, to be a team of nurses. One trained nurse alone would be wasted in a large infirmary. Indeed she considered, with Henry Bonham Carter, whether it would be wise to try to get the Poor Law Board to recommend to Boards of Guardians the establishment of training schools. At least this might mean that government grants would be provided for the erection of nurses' homes. On the other hand Poor Law Guardians would be unwilling to finance nurse training, and even if they could be persuaded to do this, they would probably insist on selecting the probationers, which would be highly undesirable. Bonham Carter thought it wiser to infiltrate new matrons with teams of nurses into the larger workhouses, and fight out the battles with the Guardians if this proved necessary.[3]

Meanwhile, in December 1864, widespread public attention had been called to the problem of workhouse nursing, by the death in the Holborn Workhouse of a pauper named Timothy Daly from filthiness caused by gross neglect. The newspapers took up the case, and Thomas Wakley, the owner of the *Lancet*, commissioned three doctors to visit all the Metropolitan Workhouses and write 'reports for his journal, of the way in which the sick were treated'.[4] The revelations thus published in the *Lancet* led to an official inspection and an official report. 'I was so much

---

[1] Woodham-Smith: *op. cit.*, p. 355.   [2] *Ibid.*, p. 362.
[3] Letter from Henry Bonham Carter to Florence Nightingale, 26 June 1871, *STHA* 22/71.
[4] Webb: *op. cit.*, pp. 317-18.

obliged to that poor man for dying', wrote Miss Nightingale to Sir John McNeill.[1]

One consequence of these revelations was the Metropolitan Poor Act of 1867. Miss Nightingale's plan for a metropolitan authority was applied only to the treatment of the insane and infectious for whom separate institutions were erected. For the non-infectious sick, a greatly modified version of the proposals of the Association for Improving Metropolitan Workhouse Infirmaries was implemented. Some of the smaller unions and parishes were grouped together to form sick asylum districts, while the larger unions were encouraged to provide separate infirmaries for the sick. Thus from 1867 onwards were built the infirmaries of London which came to be called hospitals at various dates between 1931 and 1948 and were to be found, with few exceptions, still in active service ninety years later.

An administrative structure had been developed in London under which the nursing of the sick poor could be improved. For the rest of the country, one positive result of the 1866 inquiry was that the Local Government Board advised Guardians to employ a sufficient number of competent paid nurses 'with a year's experience in some institution for the sick'. The Board did not mention the question of training, so the advice was easily bypassed. Thus a scrubber or laundress was frequently 'appointed to the responsible position of nurse to perhaps twenty or thirty persons suffering from complaints, for the treatment of which laundry work or scrubbing affords certainly no preparatory training'.[2]

Increasingly, Boards of Guardians became aware that they needed to employ more paid nurses, and some were beginning to recognize the need for trained nurses. There was, however, a great lack of trained nurses. The voluntary hospitals were not turning out enough to meet all demands even if the nurses would have been offered, and willing to accept, employment in the workhouse infirmaries. Thus, probationary nurses were admitted for training to suitable sick asylums under Section 29 of the Metropolitan Poor Act. In 1873, the Central London Sick Asylum District was empowered 'to receive single women or widows between 25 and 35 years of age as probationers who were to

[1] Woodham-Smith: *op. cit.*, p. 348.
[2] S. Lane-Poole: 'Workhouse Infirmaries': *Macmillan's Magazine*, July 1881, p. 223.

remain as such for at least a year and were to be employed under the control of the medical officer and matron'.[1] In 1875 the Local Government Board expressed the hope that 'the system of training and supplying its own nurses would extend to each of the new infirmaries being built in the metropolis'.[2]

In 1887–89 the Local Government Board reported that 'in all the sick asylums and separate infirmaries' the system of employing pauper inmates as nurses had been 'entirely superseded by the employment of paid nurses', and in 1891–92 further progress, more especially in the metropolis and some of the larger provincial towns, was again reported 'both as regards the number of nurses employed and their qualifications for the office'.[3] These statements were untrue. First, there was in 1885 a suburban workhouse with 300 sick and infirm inmates and no trained nurse on day duty. Secondly, only by the narrowest definition of 'nursing' could it be said that paupers were not doing such work. 'Almost all provincial infirmaries', wrote a contributor to a contemporary monthly magazine, 'are nursed by paupers under the control—or not under the control—of one paid nurse, who is herself under the authority of the ignorant matron of the workhouse.'[4] There was an infirmary in London where the matron stated that she did 'not expect nurses to do the nursing themselves, but only to superintend the paupers'.[5]

Where it operated, the system of pauper nurses in 1881 had changed little from that of twenty years earlier. 'Pauper women are selected for nursing by the matron, and all the pay they receive is some beer, and occasionally a half-a-crown a week. The master observes that he can manage this sort of woman much better than trained nurses, as they are wholly dependent on his will, and his power over them is despotic.'[6] And some of the pauper nurses exercised despotic power over the pauper patients: 'the bed will not be made without a fee',[7] wrote a contemporary observer. Some of the paid nurses were not much better. 'When friends visit the patients on visiting day, the nurses take care that some share of the things that are brought for the inmates shall go to themselves.'[8] As one enlightened Guardian

---

[1] Ross: *op. cit.*, Chapter VIII, p. 19.   [2] *Ibid.*, p. 19.
[3] *Report of the Royal Commission on the Poor Laws and Relief of Distress* Cd. 4499, p. 241: HMSO, 1909.
[4] Lane-Poole: *op. cit.*, p. 224.   [5] *Ibid.*, p. 223.
[6] *Ibid.*, p. 224.   [7] *Ibid.*, p. 223.   [8] *Ibid.*, p. 223.

remarked 'you can see how absolutely miserable, in a quiet way, an unkind nurse can make her patients; and it is very difficult for us, as guardians, to ascertain from the poor people what their sufferings can be. They won't complain until they are safe out of it and not coming back again.'[1]

Though these evils still remained, progress was certainly being made all over the country. The Local Government Board was being diligently watched and prodded on to greater efforts not only by Miss Nightingale but also by Miss Twining and her fellow lady visitors. In 1879, the ladies had formed the Association for Promoting Trained Nursing in Workhouse Infirmaries at a meeting held 'at the house of Constance, Marchioness of Lothian'[2] and by 1885 the Association was paying for the training of nurses, and was itself employing 53 one-year trained nurses to work in the workhouses.[3] By 1898, it had trained and secured appointment for over 800 nurses.[4]

The key to the whole situation was the matron. One good nurse, the Association argued, could 'reform the whole nursing arrangements'.[5] But it knew of only 'one Board of Guardians which has had the sense and boldness to elect a lady'.[6] It was 'a difficult reform to effect, owing to the jealousy of many masters and matrons'.[7] The Association wanted to see the post of matron in the hands 'of educated and refined women (with practical knowledge obtained in some well-regulated institution)' instead of 'the usual type of matron whom alas! the guardian mind is still prone to elect'.[8] She should be 'the controlling and purifying influence in the sick wards, the protector not the persecutor of the sick, the director, not the accomplice of the nurses, and the cordial co-operator, not the opponent, of the medical officer'.[9]

In 1897 the Local Government Board issued an order defining more closely the work that could be done by 'pauper inmates'.

---

[1] *Ibid.*, pp. 223–4.
[2] Twining: *State Hospitals or Nursing in Workhouse Infirmaries*, p. 6.
[3] *Ibid.*, p. 7. In addition to their pay, the probationers received a third-class railway ticket to the training school and an indoor uniform. After two years of good service, their nurses were given a medal. They were expected to 'make some provision for the future by placing a sum quarterly in the Post Office Savings Bank' (p. 15).
[4] Louisa Twining: *Workhouses and Pauperism*, p. 36: London, 1898.
[5] Twining: *State Hospitals*, etc., p. 7.   [6] *Ibid.*, p. 10.
[7] *Ibid.*, p. 10.   [8] *Ibid.*, p. 9.
[9] Lane-Poole: *op. cit.*, p. 225.

They were not to undertake the duties of a nurse 'in the sick or lying-in wards of the workhouse'—but they could be employed as attendants as long as they worked under the supervision of a paid officer and had been approved by the medical officer. For the paid nurses themselves the only qualification prescribed was 'practical experience in nursing'. But the order required 'in every workhouse having a nursing staff of three or more persons, the appointment of a superintendent nurse with a qualification of at least three years' training in a recognized school'.[1]

The minority report of the Royal Commission on the Poor Laws (1909) drew attention to the large role still played by paupers.

In spite of all the efforts of the Local Government Board, which have, in the past two decades, effected great improvements, there are still many rural workhouses without even one trained nurse; there are still scores in which there is absolutely no nurse, trained or untrained, available for night duty; there are even some, so far as we can ascertain, in which there is no sort of salaried nurse at all. Everywhere the Master and Matron have still to employ pauper assistants to help in attending the sick. In spite of all that has been done the Reports of the Local Government Board Inspectors . . . show very clearly that this deplorable system of pauper assistants is far from decreasing in as rapid a manner as may have been hoped after the issue of the Nursing Order of 1897.[2]

In one part of the country (Wiltshire and Worcestershire) in 1902, 3,117 patients were cared for by 210 paid nurses and 222 paupers. Even at night the paid staff of 57 were 'assisted' by 33 paupers.[3] Similarly 34 sane paupers 'assisted' 66 paid attendants in the care of 1,124 imbeciles and epileptics.[4] Not all the paid nurses had received training.[5] Of 133 nurses, 23 were untrained and 21 had been trained for less than one year.

---

[1] *Poor Law Commission 1909*, p. 241.

[2] H. Russell Wakefield, F. Chandler, G. Lansbury, B. Webb; *Separate Report, Report of the Royal Commission on the Poor Laws and Relief of Distress* Cd. 4499, p. 861: HMSO, 1909.

[3] *Workhouse Nursing, Departmental Committee Report, Part II Minutes of Evidence:* 1902 Cd. 1367, p. 166.

[4] *Ibid.*, p. 167. These figures apply to the counties of Gloucestershire, Herefordshire, Somerset, Staffordshire, Wiltshire and Worcestershire.

[5] Apart from the training provided in poor law institutions, the London Hospital ran a six months' course for 'institution nurses'. See *Third Report from the Select Committee on Metropolitan Hospitals 1892* (93) xiii, p. lxxxviii.

In short, a third of the nurses had clearly inadequate formal qualifications.

This was the worst of workhouse nursing at the beginning of the twentieth century. The richer and more progressive authorities, on the other hand, without any direction from the centre, had started nurse training schools in the larger infirmaries. Some of them were of a high standard.[1] There was no shortage of applicants to take the training in the infirmaries that maintained a resident medical officer, while those without a resident medical officer had a dearth of applicants.[2] Between 31 and 32 per cent of probationers left before they had completed the three years' training.[3]

The workhouse probationer was not of the same social class as the probationer at the voluntary hospitals. One matron told the Departmental Committee on Workhouse Nursing in 1902, 'I do not like the type who are applying now. They are too often of the servant class, and the servant class have not yet learned how to command the kind of people we get as patients. . . . I have had one or two nice probationers, but the others are very different.'[4] It should be noted that the nurse was expected to 'command' the patient.

There was a similar difficulty in finding trained nurses to work in the workhouses. Those who were prepared to apply for jobs tended to be those who had failed in their work in the voluntary hospitals. The Workhouse Nursing Association not only organized nurse-training but acted as an employment agency for nurses seeking jobs in the workhouses. In one year, out of 41 trained nurses who applied to the Association for posts, only 18 were considered suitable for acceptance, and only 4 of them were ultimately appointed.[5] And most of those who had been trained at the cost of the Association left for other jobs as soon as they had served the period which they had promised before they took the training. They wrote to Miss Twining complaining of the cramped accommodation, the long hours of duty, the wretched diet, the lack of privacy outside working hours and the

---

[1] *Select Committee on Registration 1905. Committee on Workhouse Nursing 1902,* Part I, p. 7. Haldane: *The British Nurse in Peace and War,* p. 149.
[2] *Committee on Workhouse Nursing 1902,* Part I, p. 8.
[3] *Ibid.,* p. 5.
[4] *Ibid.,* Part II, p. 90.
[5] Twining: *Workhouses and Pauperism,* p. 213.

rigid control of workhouse officials. 'I am compelled to admit', wrote one nurse, 'the utter uselessness of nurses fighting for proper administration under untrained management . . . we stand so often entirely unsupported.'[1]

There were further reasons for workhouse nursing being unattractive to trained nurses. Most of the patients were chronic and bedridden; many were classed as 'incurable'. There was less opportunity for the exercise of skill or at least there was less visible reward when skill was exercised. Workhouses were places of custodial care and lacked all the variety and interest of the voluntary hospitals. Moreover, the central authority refused to allow medical students to be admitted.

Miss Nightingale had laid great stress upon the position of the matron in the hospital hierarchy. Only if she were supreme in her own sphere could the system of nursing be changed. The nursing superintendents in the workhouses were seldom granted this status. Thus we find as late as 1914 the *British Journal of Nursing* complaining not without traces of feminism and snobbery that 'the Department of Nursing in workhouses [is] not under the authority of the trained Superintendent Nurse, but under the authority of the usually ill-educated Master—a man whose social experience in no way fits him for the unbridled authority he is often permitted by the male Guardians to wield'.[2]

The knowledge and social position of those in charge of the voluntary hospitals had led to the appointment of lady matrons and the granting to them of a high status in the hospitals. The Guardians were not equally enlightened and their chief officials resisted the challenge to their own position which the appointment of a lady matron would inevitably have become. Moreover, the motives of the ladies who were entering nursing were not always those of the great pioneers. Agnes Jones had been called by God as well as sent by Miss Nightingale to work in the Liverpool Infirmary. In 1900 the ladies tended either to make their careers in the high status voluntary hospitals or to work privately for those who could afford to pay. Vocation had become tinged with professionalism. Thus in 1900 there were still sharp contrasts between the nursing standards provided in the voluntary hospitals and those provided in the workhouses. At the root of this dichotomy lay the philosophy on which the

[1] Twining: *Workhouses and Pauperism*, pp. 191–2.
[2] *BJN*, 26 September 1914, p. 237.

whole system of the administration of the poor laws was ostensibly based. The provision of a high standard of medical care would have been in conflict with the principle of less eligibility. The philosophical battle between the duties of discouraging pauperism and the duties of treating illness, between the relief of the rates and the relief of the sick, which was fought within the 1909 Royal Commission on the Poor Laws, had been joined forty years before. Louisa Twining had seen from the start that much pauperism was caused by sickness rather than wickedness. She had advocated the break up of the poor laws and the establishment of public hospitals supported by taxation to run parallel to the voluntary hospitals supported by subscriptions. Florence Nightingale had devised the administrative structure within which the plan could have been put into immediate operation.

The two ladies shared the same values: 'So long as a sick man, woman, or child', wrote Miss Nightingale, 'is considered administratively to be a pauper to be repressed and not a fellow creature to be nursed into health, so long will these shameful disclosures have to be made'.[1] Mrs Woodham-Smith sums up her attitude in these words: 'Suffering lifts its victims above normal values. While suffering endures there is neither good nor bad, valuable nor invaluable, enemy nor friend. The victim has passed to a region beyond human classification or moral judgements, and his suffering is a sufficient claim.'[2] Eighty years later, what had been the philosophy of a few pioneer women of the upper class became the rationale of the National Health Service Act introduced by a Labour government.

---

[1] Woodham-Smith: *op. cit.*, pp. 351–2.   [2] *Ibid.*, pp. 351–2.

CHAPTER IV

Nursing at the Turn of the Century

THE second half of the nineteenth century was a period of rapid growth in the number of nurses employed both in the workhouses and in the hospitals. Not only were more women taking up nursing but more nurses were demanded. The system of medical care was developing and the more complex medical techniques became, the more nurses were required. Most important of all, more patients were being looked after away from home.

More beds were provided in voluntary hospitals. The census enumerators had found only 7,619 patients in hospitals in England and Wales in 1851. By 1901, the total had increased to 39,184.[1] The charity hospitals were no longer confined to large towns: a battery of small cottage hospitals had been established.[2] All these extra beds led to a demand for more nurses. In addition, staffing standards were improved. For example, between 1878 and 1898, the number of nurses per occupied bed in four London teaching hospitals increased by about 70 per cent.[3] The number of probationers increased about three-and-a-half times, but the number of qualified nurses, including lady-pupils and sisters, remained about the same. By the turn of the century, probationers represented over half the nursing staff of the large hospitals. The whole of this increase in probationers was not achieved by an increase in the number of recruits; the new 'professional' lady matrons extended the period of training so that it lasted for three years.[4]

In its early days the introduction of formal training for nurses

[1] See the *Census of England and Wales 1901 General Report*, p. 136: HMSO, 1905.

[2] Between 1855 and 1895, 294 cottage hospitals were established. See H. C. Burdett: *Cottage Hospitals, General, Fever and Convalescent*, p. 17: London, 1896.

[3] St George's, King's College, Guy's and Westminster. See *Burdett's Hospital Annual and Year Book of Philanthropy 1903*, pp. 57–58.

[4] Cope: *A Hundred Years of Nursing at St Mary's Paddington*, p. 95; and see p. 70 below.

VI. Miss Nightingale

VII.
MISS AGNES E. JONES

VIII. MRS WARDROPER
Matron of St Thomas's
Hospital

placed no financial burden on the voluntary hospitals; probationers were cheap labour. But even though the expansion of the nursing departments was achieved by a steady growth in the number of probationers, in time the cost of nursing a patient rose sharply. The sheer increase in the number of nurses and the development of costly nurses' homes added more to hospital expenditure than was saved by using cheap labour. On the other hand lady-pupils contributed to their income. In addition hospitals were not averse to 'exploiting' nurses by hiring them out for private work at substantially higher fees than the nurses were paid. As Burdett put it in 1890, 'the hospitals are making large sums by their private nursing institutions, and this manner of maintaining charities is rather hard on the nurses; it is taking from them with both hands'.[1] In 1901 these activities raised £3,957 for those London hospitals reporting to *Burdett's Annual* (0·9 per cent of their income).

The number of patients in the workhouses also increased. Patients were becoming more willing to enter the infirmaries and Boards of Guardians were tending to restrict medical relief given to people in their own homes.[2] In 1869 there had been estimated to be about 50,000 sick paupers in the workhouses. By 1911 this number had increased to over 100,000.[3] This led to a need for more nurses. Even more important was the substitution of paid nurses for pauper nurses.[4]

The expansion of the paid nursing staff was very large after 1866. The metropolitan nursing staff increased from 111 in 1866 to 784 in 1883–84, and 1,246 in 1901. In the last year, 1,924 paid nurses were employed in the rest of England and Wales. This total paid staff of 3,170 was supplemented by about 2,000 probationers.[5] Such was the paid staff responsible for the

[1] *Burdett's Hospital Annual and Year Book of Philanthropy 1890*, p. lxxxvii.
[2] Webb: *op. cit.*, Vol. I, pp. 329, 333; and Vol. II, p. 519.
[3] *Ibid.*, p. 322n.
[4] 'We find neat and becommingly [*sic*] dressed young women in a suitable uniform, in place of the wretched old creatures who, in pauper dress and black caps, prowled about the beds of our sick poor.' Quoted by Jeanne L. Brand: *The British Medical Profession and State Intervention in Public Health 1870–1911*, p. 272 (Ph.D. thesis, University of London, 1953) from a paper of the Workhouse Nursing Association, April 1889, Local Government Board Miscellaneous Correspondence No. 42722/89.
[5] *Report of the Royal Commission on the Poor Laws and Relief of Distress* Cd. 4499, p. 242: HMSO, 1909.

care of some 100,000 patients. One nurse to twenty patients was the average standard in the workhouses at a time when one nurse to two or three patients was the standard for the large London teaching hospitals. This extension of paid nursing contributed to the rising cost of the poor law infirmaries.

It is estimated in Appendix I that there were in 1901 about 63,500 female nurses and 5,700 male nurses in England and Wales including both those working in institutions and those working in the homes of the patients. Nursing was mainly a female occupation. The men worked mainly in the mental hospitals, where about 3,900 were employed.[1] There were therefore nearly 2,000 male nurses at work outside the mental hospitals[2]—most of them as mental nurses employed in the patient's own home. The voluntary hospital would not admit men to the nurse training schools. Indeed a great prejudice existed against male nurses in general. One reason given for this was that the male more than the female nurse was believed to be liable to 'usurp the functions of the doctor'.[3] A second reason was that there were no male nurses whose social origin was comparable to that of the ladies who controlled the large voluntary hospitals. There were, however, as a representative of male nurses pointed out in 1904, some cases which female nurses absolutely refused to look after.[4]

Out of the total of about 69,200 nurses and midwives in England and Wales not many more than 16,000 worked in the hospitals and other institutions,[5] and over 10,000 worked in the mental hospitals and related institutions. Thus over half of the nurses worked in the homes of patients. For this there were four reasons. First, it was still the case at the end of the nineteenth century, as it had been at the beginning, that the more prosperous classes saw no need for hospital care. Secondly, there had developed under charitable auspices a system of district nursing for the poor. Thirdly, the well-to-do had become conscious of

---

[1] See Appendix I, p. 255.

[2] *Select Committee on Registration 1905*, p. 4.

[3] Registration of Nurses, *Select Committee Report; 1904* (281) vi, p. 60.

[4] Such as that of a young man who had been circumcised. See *Select Committee on Registration 1904*, p. 64.

[5] From returns collected in 1905, Burdett calculated that the nursing staff of 554 hospitals and institutions in England and Wales consisted of 9,669 nurses and 6,285 probationers. See his evidence to the *Select Committee on Registration 1905*, p. 184.

the value of skilled nursing services and readily employed a nurse at home even for minor ailments. Fourthly, trained nurses found work in the home more attractive than work in hospital. Hospitals did not enjoy the place in public esteem which they occupy today. In general they were institutions which cared for the poorer members of society if not as paupers then as deserving subjects of public charity. More patients were going into hospital, but there was still a fear among working people of care away from home. It was still believed that admission to hospital was the precursor of death, and this belief was not without statistical foundation. The rich entered the hospitals only to visit, inspect, or govern. There was, moreover, little that was done in hospital which could not equally well be done inside a prosperous household away from the risks of cross-infection. Antiseptics and anaesthetics were in their infancy; blood transfusion was unknown and the activities of surgeons were closely confined. Nevertheless, the major developments in medical and surgical techniques took place in hospital with working-class patients.

By 1900 the greater recognition of the value of skilled nursing had led to a greater demand for the services of nurses in the home to care for both rich and poor. The renewed interest in the condition of the poor in the second half of the nineteenth century had led not only to friendly visiting and moral instruction but also to the provision of nursing services in the home by a variety of charitable bodies. From the modest beginnings in Liverpool in 1859, when William Rathbone had paid the nurse who had looked after his wife to go and 'nurse certain poor patients in their homes',[1] charitable bodies providing district nurses had spread throughout the country. The administration of the system was 'deliberately based on the existence of a class of leisured women and constituted a challenge to [the] organizing of the poor into institutions'.[2] Such services could with advantage have been provided by Boards of Guardians, but they hardly ever were.[3]

The growing provisions of skilled lady nurses to look after the poor not only in hospital but also in their own homes did

[1] Margaret B. Simey: *Charitable Effort in Liverpool in the Nineteenth Century*, p. 70: Liverpool, 1951.

[2] *Ibid.*, p. 70.

[3] Webb: *op. cit.*, Vol. I, p. 337.

not go unnoticed by those anxious to find opportunities for the employment of ladies. 'There is no reason', wrote one observer, 'why the rich should not obtain for money services which are freely bestowed upon the poor. Ladies will now take fees as doctors, but they will nurse only for charity. Why is this?' [1] She went on to make the case for lady nurses being provided on a paying basis for those who could afford it. She saw advantages for doctors and patients, and also for gentlewomen in search of suitable remunerative occupations.

Doctors, especially those whose large practice obliges their visits to be limited in time and infrequent, do feel the want of efficient and intelligent help in the sick-room; indeed physicians say that the science of medicine will not be perfected until accurate and constant observations of all the stages of a disease are made and reported by some qualified individual. Who could do this so well as a trained nurse, whose general culture and education had quickened her powers of accurate observation and correct description? Invalids of the upper classes would soon feel the advantage of being tended by a lady of refinement and scientific training, and would be willing to remunerate her services at such a rate as would in time repay the expenses of her preparatory study. . . .[2] Nurses might well become rich.[3]

Though riches came to organizers of domiciliary nursing rather than to the nurses themselves, the rest of Charlotte Haddon's words proved to be prophetic. Many more 'invalids of the upper classes' employed nurses, and many a wife and mother was able to take proper rest because she could trust the nurse. The urge among the upper classes to nurse the poor in the second half of the nineteenth century was accompanied by an urge to be attended by nurses when they themselves were sick. As an apothecary remarked in 1905, 'I remember when I was a boy I never saw such a thing as a nurse inside my house. Now my boy has hardly anything the matter with him before in comes a nurse the first thing, before we can say "Jack Robinson".'[4] From the nurse's point of view, work in a private house was more attractive than hospital nursing, partly because the pay was

---

[1] Haddon: *op. cit.*, p. 458.
[2] *Ibid.*, pp. 458–9.   [3] *Ibid.*, p. 461.
[4] *Select Committee on Registration 1905*, p. 48. Dr Fenwick had made the same point the year before when he said: 'Everybody has a nurse, even for the measles child.' See *Select Committee on Registration 1904*, p. 4.

better and partly because the work was pleasanter and less strenuous. In 1901 the workhouses were paying probationers about £13 a year, on the average.[1] In the voluntary hospitals a few years before the average pay of a probationer was about £14 a year. Nurses (i.e. persons with practical experience of nursing) in the workhouses were paid about £17 a year. In London, salaries paid to nurses in the three years after qualification averaged just over £26 10s. a year.

In attempting to make comparisons with the domiciliary nurses, it should be remembered that hospital nurses received more in kind than they received in cash. If expenditure on nursing salaries in thirteen hospitals in 1902 is divided by the number of nurses, the average annual salary of a nurse is found to be £19. The cost of maintenance, laundry, and uniforms for nurses in these same hospitals amounted to over £25 per head. Allowing for all costs attributable to nurses' board and lodging, £30 per head might be a more realistic figure.[2] Thus we can take £57 per year to be the total remuneration (in cash and kind) of the trained nurse in hospital at the turn of the century. At this time a female certified teacher earned about £80 per year.[3]

For domiciliary work, two guineas per week with meals provided was quite a common charge for the services of a nurse. Even allowing for spells of unemployment and the margins charged by the organizers of private nursing,[4] it is clear that private nursing was more remunerative. If the nurse chose to go on a salaried basis she would receive £30 to £50 a year with all found.[5]

Not only was the pay better but the work was normally less arduous. In the voluntary hospitals the hours of work were very long. 'A hospital nurse generally works twelve hours a day,' wrote Burdett in 1890.[6]

At St Bartholomew's Hospital on three days in each week, and sometimes for four days in each week, the nurses are kept on duty fourteen hours in each day, with no intermission, except at meal

---

[1] The figures given in this chapter for the pay of nurses are summarized from the details given in Appendix III.

[2] These figures are taken from *Burdett's Annual* for this year. See also *Select Committee on Registration 1905*, p. 185.

[3] See Tropp: *op. cit.*, p. 273.

[4] See p. 58 below.   [5] See Appendix III.

[6] *Burdett's Hospital Annual and Year Book of Philanthropy 1890*, p. lxxxv.

times . . . after deducting the time allowed for meals, and the hours off duty, a Bart's nurse is kept continuously at work for nearly twelve hours on every day throughout the year, with the exception of fourteen days, when she is away on her annual holiday.[1]

This 84-hour week was an extreme case. At the Nightingale School the nurses worked 10 hours a day. And in the workhouses the nurses had about 70 hours a week on duty with a fortnight's holiday once a year. Moreover, the workhouse nurse lived a life akin to that of a prisoner: she was not allowed visitors and was granted one late pass a year (after ten o'clock). She was allowed a short period of free time in the evening. In 1892, it was suggested that this should be altered to the afternoon 'on moral and hygienic grounds'.[2] The life of a private nurse was obviously less restrictive and strenuous. The continuous care of one patient could hardly be as exhausting as work in hospital. Moreover, the trained nurse could often insist that the domestic staff in a private household did much of the heavy work.

Both voluntary hospitals and workhouses suffered from the competition of the private sector. There was no shortage of probationers in the voluntary hospitals; but once trained many young ladies went off to nurse the class from which they had come.[3] The loss of newly trained nurses was worse in the workhouses than in the voluntary hospitals, though in 1901 we read of one voluntary hospital having to close a ward for lack of experienced nurses.[4] The Departmental Committee considered that a large percentage of prospective nurses became poor law probationers 'with the sole object of obtaining valuable training at no cost to themselves and with no idea of remaining in the Poor Law Service any longer than is necessary to qualify themselves for the more remunerative positions which are to be obtained elsewhere'.[5] One matron of a workhouse infirmary suggested that the low status of workhouse nursing hindered the recruitment of trained personnel.[6] As a result she could only get the cast-offs from the fever hospitals. Nurses looking down the advertising columns would say 'not that, that is an infirmary'.

[1] Burdett: *Nurses' Food, Work and Recreation*, pp. 15–16.
[2] *Lancet*, 6 February 1892, p. 327.
[3] *Select Committee on Registration 1904*, p. 48.
[4] A. Cleveland: *Norfolk and Norwich Hospital*, pp. 98–99: London, 1948.
[5] *Committee on Workhouse Nursing 1902*, Part I, Cd. 1367, p. 7.
[6] *Ibid.*, pp. 89–90.

There was a national shortage of trained nurses. The hospitals, the doctors, and the general public were broadly aware that training was important. Of the total number of female nurses in England and Wales (63,500) about 25,000 could be described as trained in the widest sense.[1] About one-half of these worked in the hospitals. These 25,000 women covered a wide range of skills and came from a variety of social backgrounds. In addition to the large London voluntary hospitals there were children's hospitals and fever hospitals where the skill of their nurses was confined to these special fields of work. There were small provincial voluntary hospitals and workhouses where the training was little more than nominal. At least, the products of such training schools did not satisfy the matrons of the London teaching hospitals. When they came, as apparently was common, to get their London certificates, it was found that they had not benefited from their previous training. 'They have something to unlearn'[2] was the verdict of the London Hospital.

The trained nurses included among their number daughters of the higher social classes who seem to have entered the hospitals largely as lady-pupils. At the other end of the scale there were the girls of 'servant class' who were admitted to nursing in the workhouse. It is unlikely that in 1901 there were more than 10,000 nurses whose training would have satisfied Florence Nightingale. The number who were both 'ladies' and trained was probably less than 5,000. The new 'young ladies' were a small minority of the profession.

When professional organization started, controversy centred on the problems of domiciliary nurses. Nearly three-quarters of these had had no hospital training at all. There were many girls who could not afford the long period on low pay while training in a voluntary hospital and did not choose to train in a workhouse. Such girls could join the various charitable associations who sent them out with their district nurses for a period of from six months to a year, paid for their training and offered them employment when they had completed their apprenticeship.

It is significant that out of the over 67,000 female nurses and midwives recorded in the 1901 census, over 27,000 (42 per cent)

---

[1] Burdett estimated that there were between 25,000 and 30,000 trained nurses out of the 74,000 nurses in Great Britain. See *Select Committee on Registration 1905*, p. 102.

[2] *Ibid.*, p. 25.

were over the age of 45 and over 6,000 were aged 65 or more. Nearly 45 per cent were married, widowed, or divorced. By 1931 this percentage was to fall to about 12 per cent.[1] The elderly widows must have comprised a very high proportion of the untrained.

The great demand for nurses to work in the home led to abuses. There simply were not enough of them to go round. In London the wealthy could hire the best nurses from the voluntary hospitals. But not all of these private-duty nurses had completed their training. The London Hospital sent out 160 nurses, including probationers in their second year, to work unsupervised in private houses. The hospital earned £4,000 a year from this arrangement, making a net profit of £1,700 for the hospital. For the not so rich in London, and all classes in most other parts of the country, qualified nurses were few and far between. There were, however, some nursing associations which did provide trained nurses.

The voluntary hospitals were not the only people to see the financial opportunities created by the strong demand for private nurses. Anyone could start a private agency. There were some who entered the field solely for commercial motives. They were not reluctant to charge what the market would bear and underpay the nurses they employed. Burdett had heard of the owner of such a 'private adventure home' leaving £27,000 on her death.[2] It was claimed that some of these private enterprises took 25 per cent to 40 per cent of the nurses' earnings.[3] Miss Lückes, the matron of the London Hospital, called these small agencies 'mere private speculations'.[4] One free-lance nurse described the system as 'a great and crying evil', 'sweating is hardly too strong a term'.[5]

The intervention of the grasping middleman was only one evil of the system. The agencies were not providing qualified nurses. Any woman could be called a nurse and sent out to the public. Girls were employed with incomplete training or no training at all.[6] And in many cases the same charge (two or three guineas a

---

[1] See Appendix I, Table 4.

[2] *Select Committee on Registration 1905*, p. 103.

[3] *Lancet*, 17 February 1894, p. 426.

[4] *Select Committee on Registration 1905*, p. 27.   [5] *Ibid.*, p. 93.

[6] Sir James Crichton Browne gives a case of this: 'I came across a nurse who was attending on a patient of mine in a mental case. I asked her whether she was a trained nurse, and she said she was. Then I asked her what her

week) was made for both trained and untrained. A representative of the British Medical Association summed up the position as follows: 'as a rule they do receive the same remuneration, because the very fact of their charging the same as a fully-trained nurse they think stamps them as being fully trained, and that is their only claim very often'.[1] The public did not know what it was getting and often did not ask. As Burdett pointed out, in the crisis of sickness, the stricken family did not stop to check a qualification; the problem as they saw it was to get a nurse as quickly as possible.

There were, however, a number of reputable nurse-supply agencies. Nurses could, of course, be hired for domiciliary work from the voluntary hospitals. While this involved exploitation of the nurses for the financial benefit of the hospital, there was some guarantee about the quality of the women who were supplied. In addition, Burdett, of the British Hospitals Association, had started a Nurses' Co-operative which employed 500 nurses, had a turnover of from £45,000 to £50,000 a year and only took 5 per cent of the nurses' earnings to pay for expenses. The Royal British Nurses' Association[2] set up in 1896 its own co-operative, the Chartered Nurses' Association, employing 120 nurses in 1905 and taking $7\frac{1}{2}$ per cent of earnings. The object of the Society was to protect nurses 'against being exploited by private agencies'.[3]

Although there was some exploitation of nurses and although the middle classes were being deceitfully provided with unqualified nurses when they thought they were hiring qualified ones, this did not mean that the unqualified were uniformly bad and had no function in the system of medical care at the end of the nineteenth century. There were many simple women who catered for the needs of the poorer sections of the community. Such were the nurses who were employed by charitable bodies. They were paid about 15s. a week and provided a homely service which did not pretend to rival the skilled attention of the

---

training had consisted in, and she told me her late husband was a policeman. I suppose that in the police cells she had perhaps seen cases of *delirium tremens*.' See *ibid.*, p. 57.

[1] *Ibid.*, p. 67.

[2] See p. 69 below.

[3] S. A. Tooley: *The History of Nursing in the British Empire*, p. 378: London, 1906,

qualified nurses.[1] But in addition to these provisions by charitable bodies, there was an even simpler service provided on a casual basis for the poorer patient all over the country. The village woman who needed employment, the widow or the married woman, turned her hand to nursing as readily as to charring or taking in washing as opportunities occurred.

A picture of this pattern of nursing emerges in Charles Booth's inquiry into the condition of the aged poor in 1894. He published reports on 353 areas (excluding London)[2] and in 46 of these nursing was reported as a typical occupation of the aged woman, usually bracketed with charring and earning the same pay: 4s. or 5s. a week.[3] In one area it was reported that the Guardians employed aged women to nurse paupers at 1s. a week.[4] This latter work was only accepted reluctantly, which was held to indicate that the old women of the area were sufficiently well off to do without employment.[5] This casual system of nursing was tending to be superseded by the nursing institutions.

Working people needed a simple and homely service. They wanted 'the sort of woman who would go to a village and help clean up the cottage, put things generally straight, and see the children go to school all right, and so on'.[6] Many of the patients attended were senile or chronic cases. Even Miss Lückes, matron of the London Hospital and intimate friend of Miss Nightingale,[7] remarked that 'for a number of cases a very little training goes a long way'.[8] One general practitioner stated that if only the qualified ladies were available he could not see how the poorer people would be nursed at all.[9] The practical nurses were meeting a real need.

---

[1] The East London Nursing Society had, in July 1891, 27 nurses at work for a salary of 15s. per week. 'The Nurses are not ladies.' (*Third Report from the Select Committee on Metropolitan Hospitals 1892* (93) xiii, p. lxxxix.)

[2] Usually an area was a union or part of a union. In some cases the report covered only a parish.

[3] C. Booth: *The Aged Poor in England and Wales—Condition*, pp. 120, 158, 282: London, 1894.   [4] *Ibid.*, p. 156.   [5] *Ibid.*, p. 120.

[6] *Select Committee on Registration 1905*, p. 100.

[7] Miss Lückes was trained at Westminster Hospital and after experience as a night sister at the London Hospital and as matron of Pendlebury's Children's Hospital in Manchester, was appointed matron of the London Hospital in 1880 at the age of 24. She held this post for thirty-nine years. See *NT*, 27 February 1919, p. 166.

[8] *Select Committee on Registration 1905*, p. 23.   [9] *Ibid.*, p. 76.

CHAPTER V

The Battle for Registration

WITH the introduction of training, an extremely varied group of people were engaged in the practice of nursing. Ladies with excellent instruction and servant girls with a minimum of training belonged to the same occupation, and there was little by which the general public could judge their professional competence. To remedy this situation, a group of ex-lady-pupils, urged on by feelings of insecurity about their own status, banded together to introduce a firm distinction between the trained and the untrained by establishing a register of nurses.

Persons practising as nurses included girls who had been probationers for three or even four years, one-year-trained lady-pupils, district nurses who had served an apprenticeship of six months, and those whose skills had been acquired on the hedge-row of experience. The standard of the training schools themselves varied widely between the high quality of most of the large London hospitals and the low quality of those smaller and poorer establishments which could not provide adequate training but made use of probationers as a form of cheap labour. The new matrons were able to discard unsatisfactory nurses from the hospitals and infirmaries which they had taken over but they had no means of controlling the small hospitals and the wide field of domiciliary practice.

The establishment of a register for practising nurses would have made it possible to remove the name of any nurse who had discredited her profession. But the militant qualified nurses demanded more from registration than this. They wanted to draw a firm line between those who were fitted to practise as nurses and those who were not. But how was a qualified nurse to be defined? Training alone was not held to be a sufficient test: the training hospitals were issuing certificates but the quality of the training given varied widely. Thus some central body was to be set up which would decide which hospitals were providing adequate training and which were not. In addition, there was to be a national examination to ascertain whether each individual trainee had benefited sufficiently from her course. Only those who had passed this examination were to be admitted to the register.

Miss Nightingale's training had been no more than a means of creating competent nurses. Hers was essentially a practical course and was within the capacity of the country girl. The probationer was disciplined to handle competently and effectively all the situations she encountered in the hospital ward. And from this discipline came the strength and confidence needed to meet the heavy emotional and physical demands of nursing work. The militant lady-pupils on the other hand saw training in a different light. It was an apprenticeship, a period of trial, almost an initiation ritual, to test who was fit to bear the title 'nurse'. The greater its severity, the higher its intellectual demands, the longer its duration, the greater the status of the profession. The very fact that every woman thought she could nurse made it the more necessary to emphasize and exaggerate training requirements.

The first move to form a professional association (the British Nurses' Association) with these objectives in mind came from the lady-pupils. The leader was Miss Ethel Gordon Manson. She came from a prosperous and influential family; her father was a doctor who died when she was three, her stepfather was a Member of Parliament. She entered the Children's Hospital, Nottingham, as a paying probationer in 1878 at the age of 21. After one year she went on to the Manchester Royal Infirmary.[1] From there she was appointed sister of Charlotte Ward at the London Hospital where 'she was always complimented on the apple-pie order of her cupboards and on the freshness of the lovely flowers in her care'.[2] Early in 1881, three years after starting training in a children's hospital, she was appointed matron of St Bartholomew's Hospital at the age of 24.[3] In 1887

[1] The Manchester Royal Infirmary has records going back to 1871. There is, however, 'absolutely no trace' of Miss Manson's name either in the nursing register or in the salaries and wages records. It has not, therefore, been possible to ascertain how long she spent at the Manchester Royal Infirmary.

[2] BJN, April 1947, p. 37.

[3] 'One evening she read that St Bartholomew's Hospital in the City of London required a Matron. Here was her chance. She decided that she

she married Dr Bedford Fenwick who played an active part in medical politics, and she retired from nursing to devote her energies, for the next sixty years, to the organization of the profession. She was a great admirer of Mrs Pankhurst.

Mrs Bedford Fenwick 'adored smart clothes, beautiful colours, classical music, good books, and she had a flair for exquisite furniture and china, both modern and antique'.[1] She was a very forceful personality. She pressed her views persistently and without compromise throughout her long career in nursing politics. She demanded the highest possible standard of nursing and she believed that this could be secured by confining entry to the profession to the daughters of the higher social classes. Nurses should 'come from a class of women who had been trusted for so many years that the failures would be the exceptions'.[2] Firm educational and financial barriers should be erected in training schools to keep out undesirable recruits. Thus her husband laid great stress on the technical knowledge required by a nurse,[3] and argued that nurses undergoing training should be paid no salary at all and be charged a total fee of five guineas for examination and registration.[4]

The obvious objection to this approach was that it would restrict the field for recruitment to such an extent that there would be a great shortage of nurses. But the supporters of registration argued that the abuses of the present system were preventing many desirable girls from undertaking training. As Sir James Crichton Browne put it in 1905, 'nurses are so uncertain in character; there are many miserable specimens among them, that I can understand some educated women having diffidence about joining the ranks'.[5] A list of scandals and crimes was compiled with which persons describing themselves as nurses were associated. Dr Fenwick emphasized that

---

would become that Matron. Early next morning she dressed with utmost care and laid a little emphasis on her "great age" (she was 24 years old) and armed with particulars of her experience and glowing testimonials, she presented herself at the astonished Secretary's office at 9 a.m. punctually, and revealed the reason for her early visit. . . . After promising to help her in her ambition, he made the necessary inquiries and a week later she was summoned to the Board meeting and informed that her application had been successful.' See *ibid.*, April 1947, p. 38.

[1] *Ibid.*, p. 38.   [2] *Select Committee on Registration 1905*, p. 33.
[3] *Select Committee on Registration 1904*, p. 8.
[4] *Ibid.*, p. 11.   [5] *Select Committee on Registration 1905*, p. 51.

'a good many women feel very strongly the great discredit that is brought upon them by so-called nurses who commit crime'.[1]

There were other reasons why the alleged crimes of nurses played a large part in the case put by Mrs Bedford Fenwick and her allies. Such examples were used to show the advantage to the public of control over domiciliary nursing. The wealthy in particular would be benefited.

The public at present is helpless. It is an important point that this matter does not affect the poorer classes; they are excellently looked after. They have the Queen's Jubilee Institution which looks after them in their own homes. If they go into the infirmaries they have well-trained nurses; if they go to the hospitals they have excellent trained nurses supervised day and night, but the richer classes are perfectly helpless.[2]

Steps needed to be taken to protect them from criminal nurses as at present there was not 'any sort of discipline or control over these women. They go to prison, they come out again, and they go on nursing.'[3] Registration would 'improve the character of the women who went in for nursing'.[4]

But concern for the public interest and the welfare of patients, particularly rich patients, were not the only motives that lay behind the movement for state registration. The new lady nurses were seeking to enhance their own status.[5] In part this search for status was related to the wider feminist movement. 'The nurse question is the woman question', said Mrs Fenwick.[6] There was also a desire for parity with the medical profession and greater prestige in the eyes of hospital managements. 'A committee of businessmen', Mrs Fenwick stated, ' . . . will often select a woman with [housekeeping] experience rather than one who has the qualifications which would make her the best head of a nurse training school. In their view it is often of more importance that she should know the price of mutton.'[7] The nurse

---

[1] *Select Committee on Registration 1905*, p. 11.

[2] *Select Committee on Registration 1904*, p. 12.

[3] *Select Committee on Registration 1905*, p. 34.

[4] L. L. Dock and I. M. Stewart: *A Short History of Nursing*, p. 254: New York, 4th edition, 1938.

[5] As an ex-lady-pupil, Miss Wortabet, put it, 'nursing ought to be a dignified profession. . . . I do not think nursing ought to be in the hands of ignorant women at all.' (*Select Committee on Registration 1905*, p. 14.)

[6] Dock and Stewart: *op. cit.*, p. 254.

[7] *Select Committee on Registration 1905*, p. 31.

must be recognized as 'an individual of some importance in the state'.[1]

Mrs Fenwick's views were by no means shared by all the leaders of the nursing profession. In particular, Miss Nightingale firmly opposed registration; she felt it would do great damage to the cause of nursing. 'Seeking a nurse from a Register', she wrote in a private note, 'is very much like seeking a wife from a Register, as is done in some countries.'[2] Her principle objection was that registration would involve the introduction of examinations for nurses: the professional competence of a nurse could not be judged in this way. All an examination could test was knowledge, and a nurse could acquire all the knowledge she needed in six months.[3] 'The idea of the new-fangled people seems to be to put nurses on the level of dictionaries—a dictionary can answer questions.'[4] She laid great stress upon the personal qualities required by nurses. If a public examination were to take the place of assessment by the individual hospital, she feared that less attention would be given to personal qualities in the selection and training of nurses.

Miss Nightingale's views were influential. Not only had she many close friends in the nursing world with whom she engaged in continuous correspondence, but she also had many friends in politics and some contact with the Palace. Moreover, she was connected with the management of several hospitals and was able to impose her views on the matrons and thus on the nurses of those hospitals. For in such matters the matron's word was law.[5] As Sir James Crichton Browne told the Select Committee of 1905, 'the moment the matron of a hospital is opposed to us [the Royal British Nurses' Association] . . . no nurse from that

[1] *Select Committee on Registration 1904*, p. 75.

[2] British Museum, Nightingale Papers.

[3] *Select Committee on Registration 1904*, p. 52. Some support for her view can be found in a follow-up study of a small sample of successful candidates in the Final State Examination held in April 1945. The quality of the nurses was assessed by senior nursing staff one year after the examination and compared with the marks in the examination. There was no significant relationship. See *Working Party on the Recruitment and Training of Nurses: Minority Report*, p. 44: HMSO, 1948.

[4] From a letter of Miss Nightingale's quoted in the House of Lords on 27 May 1919. See *H of L Deb.*, col. 836.

[5] So much so that an unfortunate probationer, having dressed a doll for an exhibition arranged by Mrs Fenwick, was forbidden by her matron to enter it.

hospital would join our Association; and then if a change takes place, and a matron comes in who is favourable to us, the nurses come in'.[1]

The most vigorous opposition to registration came from the two hospitals in which Mrs Fenwick had worked; from Sydney Holland of the London Hospital[2] and from Dr Moore of St Bartholomew's. They were firmly opposed to any measure which would narrow the field of recruitment to the nursing profession. 'The numbers of women in the upper classes are comparatively small who wish to nurse. We have exhausted the numbers of Florence Nightingales in the world . . . registration would not add one single person.'[3] The proposed fee was prohibitive and would exclude 'many women who would make excellent nurses'.[4] The educational standard of a nurse should not be raised too high. 'Some domestic servants ultimately become admirable nurses; others are quite unfitted for it. Some people with higher education become excellent nurses; some are absolutely unfitted for it.' 'It is very important' that the door to nursing should be as widely open as possible.'[5] Registration would lead to 'a diminution in the number of nurses and the supply would be more difficult to keep up'.[6]

Sydney Holland did not sympathize with the nurses' claim for professional status. 'We want to stop nurses thinking themselves anything more than they are, namely, the faithful carriers out of the doctor's orders. The other side are always talking about nursing being a profession and "graduates" in nursing, just as they do in America.'[7] The superior nurses upset the households 'of what are called gentlefolk'. 'Some nurses consider that they ought to have fourteen footmen to wait upon them.'[8]

Support for nurses of humbler origin also came from the nursing associations. Miss Hughes said that the best nurses were from the servant class.

I would suggest nowadays that the general education is of much

---

[1] *Select Committee on Registration 1905*, p. 59.

[2] Miss Nightingale was also a governor of this hospital.

[3] Sydney Holland in evidence to the *Select Committee on Registration 1904* (see p. 39).

[4] *Ibid.*, p. 47. See also *Select Committee on Registration 1905*, p. 105.

[5] *Select Committee on Registration 1905*, p. 41.

[6] *Ibid.*, p. 50.   [7] *Ibid.*, p. 37.   [8] *Ibid.*, p. 56.

higher level than it used to be some years ago, and from my own experience of the Nurses' Co-operation, I know that some of the most successful medical nurses were those who had been upper servants —that they fitted into the households and caused less jar and less friction than many of those who considered themselves superior in station, who could not adapt themselves so well.[1]

The argument about the registration of nurses was not just a battle of principle, there were also vested interests and personal feuds. Some provincial hospital matrons favoured registration as they thought that this would place the certificates they issued on a parity with those issued by the smart London hospitals.[2] Their own status would thus be enhanced and more of 'the best type of girl' might come to them for training instead of going to the London hospitals. At other small provincial hospitals registration was opposed through fear that the training they were giving might be found wanting and they would be denied approval as nurse training schools. If their certificates of training were to lose their value, they would no longer be able to get probationers. Without probationers it would be extremely difficult and costly to get the nursing done at all.

There may in addition have been a few matrons who were opposed to registration, seeing it as a challenge to their own position. We have already noted the supremacy of the matron in governing the nursing affairs of her own hospital. They may have feared the interference of an external authority which would attempt to control the training they were providing.[3]

Such were the real issues that lay beneath what one nursing writer called 'the thirty years' war'—a battle for status conducted against a background of rampant snobbery and militant feminism. These issues became obscured by all the personal quarrels and procedural debates of the struggle for registration.

The first steps towards the organization of the nursing profession were taken in conjunction with the management of the voluntary hospitals. Burdett, the spokesman of the Hospitals' Association, saw the benefits which a register of nurses could

[1] *Select Committee on Registration 1904*, p. 84. Miss Hughes was superintendent of a nursing association.

[2] See Mrs Hobhouse's evidence: *Select Committee on Registration 1905*, p. 81.

[3] See the evidence on behalf of the British Medical Association: *ibid.*, p. 71.

provide.[1] But the type of register he envisaged was very different from that which Mrs Bedford Fenwick had in mind. His register was not intended to be selective. It was simply needed 'so that the Lady Superintendent and medical men may write from the country to the Association, and have a reasonable assurance that they will thus be able to ascertain the character of a nurse with reasonable certainty, and so protect themselves from risks to which they are at present exposed'.[2] It was not surprising that Mrs Fenwick dismissed this idea as a 'central registry office similar to that in vogue for domestic servants'.[3]

Thus in 1887 the Hospitals' Association, at the request of Miss Wood,[4] held a meeting at Burdett's house in Porchester Square to discuss the formation of a nursing section of the Hospitals' Association. A number of leading nurses attended including Mrs Fenwick and Miss Thorold.[5] No contemporary record seems to have survived describing the meeting in detail. It is clear, however, judging by the consequences, that it was stormy. According to one account the meeting at Burdett's home ended with Mrs Fenwick inviting 'the ladies who had been interested in forming a nursing section' to her house where the British Nurses' Association was born.[6] The nurses 'determined to protect their calling from the interference of outsiders'.[7] Both Burdett and Mrs Fenwick were uncompromising and opinionated people, but beneath this clash of personalities there was an irreconcilable difference of approach.

From that time relations between Mrs Bedford Fenwick and

---

[1] Burdett played an outstanding role in the hospital world for half a century. He was born in 1847, the son of a parson. His first job was in a bank in Birmingham. Next he became secretary of the Queen's Hospital, Birmingham, and resigned from this to take a job in the share and loan department of the Stock Exchange. In London he joined the committee of the Seamen's Hospital and was elected vice-president.

The publications he started include *Burdett's Hospital Annual*, the *Nursing Mirror* and *Hospital*. For many years he was spokesman for the management of the voluntary hospitals. He laid down the system of standardized accounting for voluntary hospitals which, with modifications, was in use until the beginning of the National Health Service. He also played a role in the foundation of King Edward's Hospital Fund for London.

[2] *Nursing Record*, 2 March 1893, p. 110.   [3] *Ibid.*, p. 110.

[4] Superintendent of the Great Ormond Street Hospital for Children.

[5] Matron of the Middlesex Hospital. See pp. 62–63 and 31 above.

[6] Tooley: *op. cit.*, p. 371.

[7] *Nursing Record*, 2 March 1893, p. 110.

Burdett were extremely embittered. Not long after this meeting Mrs Bedford Fenwick had her lawyer dispatch a letter to Burdett threatening him with legal action if he libelled her in the *Hospital*. And during the next six years, in Mrs Fenwick's view, Burdett 'prudently confined [himself] to abuse and misrepresentation of every scheme with which [she had] been identified'.[1] Abuse did not only come from Burdett's side. In 1893 Mrs Bedford Fenwick wrote in the *Nursing Record*, 'it is notorious how this official of the Stock Exchange meddles with matters with which he has no concern'.[2]

After the meeting in 1887 each group proceeded with its own plan. The Hospitals' Association under the leadership of Burdett established a register of trained nurses and issued a badge. The register was open to those who proved that they had 'worked for at least one year on the staff of a hospital or infirmary', and 'had been trained in the duties of a nurse'.[3] A testimonial of good character and entrance fee of 2s. 6d. and a payment of 1s. a year thereafter were also required. The Registration Committee consisted of fifteen, of whom three were distinguished matrons (Mrs Wardroper, Miss Lückes, and Miss Vincent) and three were doctors from London teaching hospitals.[4] But little use was made of this register either by nurses or hospitals.

The militant lady nurses, on the other hand, proceeded to form the British Nurses' Association with Mrs Bedford Fenwick as permanent president and the other nurse founders as permanent vice-presidents. It was 'a union of nurses for professional objects'[5] which, according to its supporters, contained the '*élite* of the profession'.[6] The affairs of the Association were governed by a General Council consisting of the President and Vice-presidents, a hundred medical men, a hundred matrons and a hundred sisters or nurses. Day-to-day business was conducted by a smaller executive committee which consisted of the President, the matrons of the London teaching hospitals, fourteen doctors, and fifteen other nurses of whom twelve had to be matrons.[7] Thus the constitution laid it down that power should

---

[1] *Ibid.*, 16 March 1893, p. 140. [2] *Ibid.*, 9 February 1893, p. 74.
[3] *Hospital*, 21 May 1887, p. 129. [4] *Ibid.*, 17 December 1887, p. 202.
[5] Dr Fenwick before the *Select Committee on Registration 1904* (see p. 2).
[6] Sir James Crichton Browne before the *Select Committee on Registration 1905* (see p. 50).
[7] *Hospital*, 10 March 1888, p. 397.

rest in the hands of the doctors and the London hospital matrons. The infirmary matrons, the provincial matrons, and the ordinary working nurses were 'kept out in the cold'.[1]

Under the leadership of those lady nurses who were not influenced by Florence Nightingale, the British Nurses' Association, became a pressure group for state registration, and while awaiting official action, took steps in this direction on a voluntary basis. It started a register to which were admitted, up to 1 January 1889, those nurses who produced 'satisfactory evidence of professional attainment and personal character and of having been engaged three years in nursing'.[2] Thus lady-pupils who had received only one year's training were admitted; but for future applicants (from 1889 onwards) it was decided that three years' training was required.

This decision was important. Burdett thought one year of training sufficient and Miss Nightingale still favoured one year of training with a proviso that two years were needed for those who were going to train others,[3] but the British Nurses' Association insisted that training should last for three years. Unfortunately, there is no record of the considerations which led to this conclusion. But when a Select Committee of the House of Lords was appointed to investigate the management and conditions of the Metropolitan Hospitals, the Association succeeded in persuading the Committee to adopt its own recommendations on nurse training rather than those of Miss Nightingale. The report of the Select Committee influenced training schools and a three-year training became standard practice. In 1897, it was officially laid down for superintendent nurses in workhouses.[4]

Not only did the Association want the training to last for three years, it also wanted national standards of training to be laid down. In 1889, every hospital in the United Kingdom was approached and asked to form a board to organize nursing education. The response was disappointing; the vast majority of the hospitals replied that it was 'out of their province' to do so, or did not reply at all.[5] Miss Nightingale, however, was not surprised that hospital managements did not welcome the sug-

---

[1] Letter to *Hospital*, 31 March 1888, p. 438.

[2] *Ibid.*, 10 March 1888, p. 397.

[3] *Third Report from the Select Committee on Metropolitan Hospitals 1892*, p. lxxix.

[4] See p. 46 above.   [5] *Select Committee on Registration 1904*, p. 6.

gestion. She wrote to Sir Henry Acland in March 1894: 'The Hospital Managers are not yet imbued with the perception of what is requisite for the proper conduct of a Training School. Their regulations and arrangements will not teach them.'[1]

Meanwhile the British Nurses' Association agitated for an official register of nurses. In 1889 a mass meeting was held in the Mansion House.[2] And in the same year Dr Fenwick proposed, and got the General Medical Council of the British Medical Association to pass, a resolution in the following terms: 'That an Act of Parliament should as soon as possible be passed for providing for the registration . . . of . . . nurses.'[3]

For the reasons stated earlier in this chapter, opposition to the British Nurses' Association concentrated on this aspect of its activities. Early on, the Association managed to approach Princess Christian (daughter of Queen Victoria) who consented to become its patron. As Miss Nightingale put it 'they are trying to make a Nurses' Republic with a Princess at its head'.[4] This royal patronage proved a great asset to the Association as it made the opponents of registration hesitant about pressing their views in public.[5] Miss Nightingale in particular was restrained from public controversy, but her major reason for lying low was fear of dividing the profession into two camps. It was for this reason that her opposition to registration was subversive. It was none the less effective while she lived to conduct it. She felt very strongly about registration right from the start. In a private letter to 'Little Sister' (the name by which she called her dear friend Miss Pringle) she spoke as early as 1889 of the mischief which the Association was doing to the 'quiet progress' of nurse training.[6] But she refused to ally herself with Burdett who was never inhibited from plain speaking.

Registration could be achieved in two ways. First, there could be an Act of Parliament. To prevent this Miss Nightingale got her friend Mr Rathbone to prepare a very confidential brief for the Duke of Westminster and organized a memorandum signed by influential nurses.[7] When the BNA saw that it was making

[1] In the Nightingale Papers, *STHA* 94/2.
[2] *Nursing Record*, 13 April 1919, p. 181. See also the Nightingale Papers as above. [3] *Select Committee on Registration 1904*, p. 6.
[4] BM, Nightingale Papers.
[5] See the correspondence between Florence Nightingale and Henry Acland, July 1889, *STHA*. [6] 12 July 1889, *STHA* 89/8.
[7] 8 June 1891, *STHA* 91/7.

little headway by this approach it turned to the less satisfactory alternative method which was to apply for a Royal Charter by which it would be entitled to register nurses.

This application led to an inquiry held by the Privy Council in 1893 and a Charter was granted for the following purposes:

(1) The founding and maintenance of schemes for the benefit of nurses in the practice of their profession and in times of adversity, sickness and old age.

(2) The maintenance of an office or offices for supplying information to persons seeking for nurses and to persons seeking employment as nurses.

(3) The maintenance and publication of a list of persons who may have applied to the Corporation to have their names entered therein as nurses, and whom the Corporation may think fit to enter therein from time to time, coupled with such information about each person so entered as to the corporation may from time to time seem desirable.

(4) The promotion of conferences, public meetings and lectures in connexion with the general work of the Corporation.

(5) The doing of anything incidental or conducive to carrying into effect the foregoing purposes.[1]

The power asked for included the word 'register'. In the power granted the word 'list' had been carefully substituted. Miss Nightingale and her allies were largely responsible for this change,[2] and they came out into the open to the extent of pointing out in a letter to *The Times* that 'the list will have nothing in common with legal registers of the medical or other professions, but will simply be a list of nurses published by the Association'.[3]

According to the *Lancet* these were 'baseless and pointless allegations'.[4] Miss Nightingale was attacked personally. 'She has long looked upon the active world from the distance which a sick room imposes between the sufferer and those who toil.' But it was not many years before the Royal British Nurses' Association was itself pressing for a register to be established under an Act of Parliament. Its powers under the Charter were

---

[1] *Lancet*, 17 June 1893, p. 1459.

[2] A note she made on 7 August 1892 reads: 'Stop it at the Privy Council. But if not try again at the House of Commons.' BM, Nightingale Papers.

[3] *The Times*, 3 July 1893, p. 7. The letter was signed by Florence Nightingale, the Duke of Westminster and eight leading matrons.

[4] *Lancet*, 8 July 1893, p. 101.

found wanting. It had no control over the training schools and very few nurses bothered to have their names entered on the 'list'.[1]

The substitution of the word 'list' for the word 'register' was not the only change that occurred when the RBNA was granted its Royal Charter. Under the old constitution Mrs Bedford Fenwick and the other ladies who founded the Association were permanent members of the General Council while other council members had to stand for election every three years. Under the new constitution all members of the General Council had to face triennial elections. Moreover, the Charter was granted 'to an equal number of representatives of the medical and nursing professions'.[2] Thus the activities of the Association depended upon medical support.

Soon after the Charter was granted dissension arose between the Fenwicks and their friends and the rest of the Association.[3] It is not clear how far these quarrels were due to disagreements about policy (the Fenwicks certainly favoured more militant action than the other members of the Association) or clashes of personality (Mrs Fenwick was not pleased to lose the permanent presidency of the Association). Whatever the cause, Dr Fenwick resigned from the Treasurership in 1894 and Mrs Fenwick was unwillingly retired from the General Council at the end of the same year. For the next few years, the Fenwicks did their best to damage the Association. Mrs Fenwick attempted to form a splinter group of the Association into a private nurses' society and together they conducted the Barlow case which caused the Association no little embarrassment.

Nurse Barlow had gone to the Association's office to ask for a voting paper to which she was entitled. When the paper was not immediately given to her, she wrote a letter to a newspaper complaining that the Association was badly organized. When the Association reacted to this adverse publicity by threatening to remove her name from their list, she went to court and won her case by arguing that her livelihood as a nurse was at stake, for if she was struck off the register she would be at a professional disadvantage. Princess Christian called an emergency meeting

---

[1] See p. 78 below.   [2] Tooley: *op. cit.*, p. 375.
[3] The May issue of the *Nurses' Journal*, the official organ of the Royal British Nurses' Association, published an appeal for unity under Her Royal Highness Princess Christian.

of the Association, which resolved that the conduct of Miss Barlow was disloyal and unjustifiable.[1] Princess Christian herself sent a message to a meeting in February 1896 which included these strong words: 'I cannot conceal my disapproval or the pain I experience at the disloyal course adopted by Miss Barlow and her advisers.'[2] Dr Fenwick stated that Miss Barlow's letter had appeared because 'faith was being broken with the ladies who formed the Association. Those ladies were promised a permanent seat on the governing body of the Association.'[3]

Dr Fenwick continued his campaign against the Association. He objected to informal voting,[4] to the treasurer's reports,[5] to the chairman's rulings[6] and even to a vote of thanks to officials.[7] The *Hospital*'s reporter commented in April 1896 that 'by this time Dr Fenwick's interruptions and objections had exhausted the patience of the meeting. . . . Sir James Crichton Browne finally remarked that Dr Bedford Fenwick was really taking a little too much upon himself in undertaking, as he appeared to do, to speak for the whole of the medical profession.'[8] Beneath all these manœuvres there were important issues at stake. Since the Royal Charter, there had been changes in the general council of the Royal British Nurses' Association. How far Miss Nightingale may have been behind these changes is not clear, but the climax came in 1896 when the Association passed a resolution opposing state registration. The doctors who had now such a large say in the affairs of the Association were blamed for this 'betrayal'.[9]

The doctors were organized in two groups. The largest organization was the British Medical Association with about 20,000 members. It considered itself 'the only voice of the medical profession'.[10] But in the view of its rival the Incorporated

[1] *Hospital Nursing Supplement*, 18 June 1895, p. cxxvii.
[2] *Ibid.*, 1 February 1896, pp. cli–cliv.
[3] *Ibid.*, p. clii.   [4] *Ibid.*, 1 February 1896, p. cliv.
[5] *Nurses' Journal*, August 1896, p. 77. He said the Association was 'now on the verge of bankruptcy'; see *Hospital Nursing Supplement*, 25 July 1896, p. cxliv. When he had resigned from the treasurership in 1894 the treasury had been empty 'owing to the heavy expenses in procuring the Royal Charter'. (*Ibid.*, 28 April 1894, p. xxxii.)
[6] *Hospital Nursing Supplement*, 18 January 1896, p. cxxx.
[7] *Ibid.*, 25 July 1896, p. cxliv.
[8] *Ibid.*, 8 April 1896, p. xxiv.
[9] Dock and Stewart: *op. cit.*, p. 255.
[10] *Select Committee on Registration 1905*, p. 61.

Medical Practitioners' Association, the BMA was 'very largely officered by the West End consultants in London, and the consultants in the big towns'.[1] The Incorporated Medical Practitioners' Association claimed to represent 'the general man of the profession'. It put the case of the humble general practitioner.

It was not hard to see why the doctors were not unanimously in favour of the registration of nurses. The West End consultants could support Mrs Fenwick and her allies in the belief that registration would lead to more good nurses and this would serve the interests of their patients both in hospital and at home. Moreover, the relation between doctor and trained nurse was clearly established in London teaching hospitals. The supremacy of the medical profession on medical matters had been conceded; its position was unassailable. The consultant depended very heavily upon good nursing in his domiciliary practice. As one doctor put it as tactfully as he could, 'the consulting man is not able to watch the case quite so thoroughly as a general practitioner would do, I mean to say as thoroughly, but not so closely'.[2]

The position was different in the provinces, particularly in rural districts, where general practitioners did not enjoy the same status nor the same incomes as the London consultants. A director of district nursing said, 'I have found in the country that many of the doctors fear competition by nurses . . . when he is starting he wishes to take the simple cases as well as the more acute work, and, . . . people are very apt to send for the nurses when they might otherwise send for the doctor.'[3] The doctors feared that the nurses might become serious rivals and undercut the fees they charged for professional services. Nurses might flourish their certificates in front of the patients and try to make out that they 'knew more than the doctor',[4] while the patients might be tempted to use the nurse as a substitute for the doctor as 'you can get a nurse for very little . . . while the doctor's fee is higher'.[5] Mrs Fenwick dismissed all this as 'ignorance of social relations and etiquette'.[6] The suggestion that nurses would, if registered, compete with the doctors was 'very mischievous'.

This difference of view among the doctors came into the open before the Select Committee of 1905. How far these differences

[1] Ibid., p. 78   [2] Ibid., p. 79.
[3] Ibid., p. 82.   [4] Ibid., p. 78.
[5] Ibid., p. 83.   [6] Ibid., p. 32.

underlay the break between the doctors and nurses in the nineties is not clear. Whatever the cause, Mrs Bedford Fenwick and her allies temporarily lost control of the Royal British Nurses' Association. She had, however, other irons in the fire. In 1894 she had started the Matrons' Council of Great Britain and Ireland for all those matrons who wanted state registration. In 1902 the Society for the State Registration of Nurses was formed. And in 1904 these two bodies came together[1] to form the National Council of Nurses which represented British nurses at the International Council of Nurses which Mrs Bedford Fenwick had helped to form five years earlier. The National Council was also pledged to secure state registration. These bodies were founded partly because the Royal British Nurses' Association had failed to secure the purpose of registration.

The 'list' organized by the Association had never really caught on in the way Mrs Fenwick had hoped it would. There were never more than two or three thousand names entered on it. The certificate it provided on payment of a fee of one guinea added nothing to the certificates which could be obtained from most of the hospitals in which training had been taken. Nor was the list well maintained.

The Association professes to require evidence of character (by the production of recent testimonials) before it will put a nurse on its register, and to register only women who have had three years' hospital training, but it appears that women are registered who have not completed their full period of training at any one hospital, and of whom it is not known whether they have proved themselves competent or otherwise.[2]

The movement for the registration of nurses was given encouragement by the registers set up for other professions. Within two years of the register of doctors being set up in 1858, a movement had started for the registration of teachers. As in the case of nurses, the overt reason given by those who wanted a register was to protect the public and the profession from private schoolmasters, 'who, by reason of their often total lack of either learning or professional skill, were bringing *bona fide* practitioners into

[1] The other founder associations were the League of St Bartholomew's Hospital Nurses and the Leicester Royal Infirmary Nurses' League.

[2] *Third Report from the Select Committee on Metropolitan Hospitals 1892*, p. xc.

disrepute'.[1] Powers were needed to strike off teachers 'judged to have been guilty of infamous conduct in any professional respect'.[2] By the 1890's the secondary school teachers were seeking a register from which the elementary school teachers should be excluded.[3] But in 1899 it was enacted that a register should be set up which should be open to all teachers irrespective of the type of school in which they taught.

A more important precedent for the nurses was the Midwives Act of 1902 which introduced a register for midwives. The first bill presented to Parliament on this subject had been in 1878, and by 1891 both the General Medical Council and the Royal College of Physicians supported registration. In both 1892 and 1893 Select Committees had reported in favour of the regulation of the practice of midwifery[4] because 'a large number of maternal and particularly infant deaths as well as a serious amount of suffering and permanent injury to women and children is caused from the inefficiency and want of skill of many of the women practising as midwives, without proper training and qualification'.[5] Evidence had been presented that there were unqualified midwives who did not use antiseptics or even soap and water,[6] who deliberately suffocated the child[7] and who dosed the mother with gin 'and many a woman has been a drunkard simply from that cause'.[8] Moreover, unqualified midwives were reluctant to send for the doctor.[9] Thus the Committee held that the registration of midwives would lead to more rather than less calls on the medical profession. There was, therefore, little cause for 'the apprehension expressed by certain witnesses belonging to the medical profession, lest their interests might be injuriously affected by the improvement in the status of midwives'.[10]

The Act of 1902 was far-reaching. The 'name or title of midwife' was reserved for those certified under the Act, and it was laid down that 'no woman shall, habitually and for gain, attend women in childbirth otherwise than under the direction

---

[1] G. Baron: 'The Teachers' Registration Movement': *British Journal of Educational Studies*, May 1954, p. 133. The references on the registration of teachers have been kindly supplied by Mr Asher Tropp.

[2] *Report of the Schools' Inquiry Commission 1868*, pp. 204–5.

[3] Baron: *op. cit.*, pp. 134–5.   [4] *H of C Deb.*, 26 February 1902, col. 1152.

[5] *Midwives' Registration, Select Committee Report 1893–4* (367) xiii, p. iii.

[6] *Ibid.*, p. 27.   [7] *Ibid.*, p. 3.

[8] *Ibid.*, p. 29.   [9] *Ibid.*, p. 22.   [10] *Ibid.*, p. iv.

of a qualified medical practitioner, unless she be certified under this Act'.[1] A Central Midwives Board was set up consisting of four doctors and five other persons one of whom was to be appointed by the Royal British Nurses' Association.[2] The interests of existing midwives were protected by enacting that any woman should be certified by the Board who produced satisfactory evidence 'that, at the passing of this Act, she had been for at least one year in *bona fide* practice as a midwife and that she bears a good character'.[3]

The registration of midwives was interpreted as an important precedent by those who sought the registration of nurses, and by the turn of the century, the Royal British Nurses' Association was again loyal to the cause of registration. In 1903 a bill it had drafted was debated and rejected by Parliament. In 1904 another bill from the Society for State Registration suffered the same fate but it did lead to the appointment, in June of that year, of a Select Committee 'to consider the expediency of providing for the registration of nurses'.[4]

The British Medical Association was heartily in favour of registration. It even argued, on the lines of the Midwives Act, that it should be made a penal offence for unqualified women to practice as nurses.[5] But it did not make clear how this measure was to be enforced. The Incorporated Medical Practitioners' Association was opposed to registration and expressed the fears of rural general practitioners.

It was clearly impossible to forbid unqualified women from engaging in nursing. There were far too few qualified nurses. There were only 2,500 on the list organized by the Royal British Nurses' Association and only 1,500 members of the society which wanted state registration. Many names were duplicated in the two sets of figures. As we have seen, Burdett thought there were only about 20,000 to 25,000 nurses in England and Wales who could claim to have any sort of training out of the 64,000 engaged in practice.

From the viewpoint of the smart London hospitals there seemed no statistical difficulty about having all the nursing in the country done by suitable ladies. They were flooded with appli-

---

[1] *Midwives Act 1902*, 2 Edw. 7, Chapter 17, Section 1.
[2] *Ibid.*, Section 2.
[3] *Ibid.*, Section 2.
[4] *Select Committee on Registration 1905*, p. iii.   [5] *Ibid.*, p. 68.

cants and probably assumed that this position held throughout the country. Sir James Crichton Browne said that there were ten times more applicants than places;[1] Burdett, though more cautious, held the view that many more nurses could be trained if the London hospitals were expanded.[2] The large number of applicants in London, however, gave no real indication of the potential number of probationers. Many women applied to more than one hospital, not all the applicants were suitable, and the capacity of the London hospitals was small.[3] Moreover, if the Royal British Nurses' Association had its way, any hospital with less than fifty beds would not be approved for training purposes.[4] This would reduce the output of trained nurses.

Even if the supply were sufficient to meet the demand within reasonable time, there remained the economic difficulty. How could the poor pay the ladies at the salaries they would expect? Would the ladies be willing to do the many and varied nursing tasks in the villages and scattered rural communities? Might not working people prefer less skilled assistance from women of their own class?

The Select Committee decided in favour of registration. 'It is desirable that a Register of Nurses should be kept by a Central Body appointed by the state, and that, while it is not desirable to prohibit unregistered persons from nursing for gain, no person should be entitled to assume the designation of "Registered Nurse" whose name is not upon the Register.'[5] The central body was to approve training schools and admit to the Register those who had had appropriate training, were equipped with requisite knowledge and experience and were of good character. Existing nurses were to be admitted to the Register solely on evidence of efficiency and character.

These registered nurses were not necessarily to be the only persons engaged in nursing work. Four years after the passing of any registration act, the central body should 'submit a report to the Privy Council on the advisability of instituting a separate Register of Nurses whose training is of a lower standard than that

---

[1] *Ibid.*, p. 58.   [2] *Ibid.*, p. 109.
[3] According to Burdett's figures which include the London infirmaries there were less than 700 vacancies each year. See *Select Committee on Registration 1905*, p. 184.
[4] *Select Committee on Registration 1904*, p. 72.
[5] *Select Committee on Registration 1905*, p. iv.

laid down for "Registered nurses" '.[1] It was nearly forty years before such a register of assistant nurses envisaged with such foresight by the Select Committee of 1905 was in fact established.[2]

[1] *Select Committee on Registration 1905*, p. v. The report was claimed as a great personal victory for Mrs Bedford Fenwick. She was, however, firmly opposed to the possibility of there being two classes of nurse. 'It would do away with the value of registration altogether . . . [it] would simply confuse the public.' See *ibid.*, p. 33.

[2] See Chapter X below.

CHAPTER VI

The Profession Comes to Power

ONCE an official committee had reported in favour of registration the nursing organizations demanded action. Bills
to register nurses became a regular feature of the parliamentary
session. Each year from 1904 to 1914 a registration bill lay before
Parliament. Mrs Bedford Fenwick spent hours in the lobby of
the House of Commons 'instructing, persuading, pleading'.[1]
Delegations favouring registration and delegations opposed to
registration were received by Ministers of the Crown.

The Government was courteous and evasive. Those who
favoured registration were reminded that there were forces
opposed to it, and those who were opposed to it were reminded
that there were many in favour whose opinion could not be
ignored. Moreover, serious difficulties stood in the way of any
system that was proposed. But in 1908 a registration bill passed
the House of Lords with unenthusiastic support from the Government.[2] Progress in the House of Commons was more difficult to
achieve. Mr Asquith, with a heavy legislative programme, was
unwilling to give facilities for the bill. Moreover there were no
less than three rival bills in the field.

The organizations that favoured state registration hastened to
call a conference and negotiate an agreed bill. Lord Ampthill,
who had steered the bill through the House of Lords, presided.
The conference reached agreement, and a permanent committee—the Central Committee for the State Registration of
Nurses—was established. Represented on this committee was the
Royal British Nurses' Association, the Matrons' Council for
Great Britain and Ireland, the Society for the State Registration
of Nurses, the Fever Nurses' Association, the Association for

[1] *BJN*, 25 November 1922, p. 336.
[2] *Lancet*, 25 July 1908, p. 280. The Earl of Crewe speaking for the Government 'considered it unlikely that the measure . . . would create a revolution
either within or without the nursing profession'.

Promoting the Registration of Nurses in Scotland, the Scottish Nurses' Association, the Infirmary Nurses' Association and the British Medical Association. Later the National Union of Trained Nurses joined the team.

The number of practising nurses represented by this impressive coalition is not known. Nurses belonged to more than one organization, and retired nurses like Mrs Bedford Fenwick played a prominent role. An enormous total of supporters (30,000) could be calculated if every member of the BMA was included,[1] but this sort of arithmetic did more harm than good to the Central Committee's case. Moreover the representative character of some organizations was disputed. The Matrons' Council was accused of being a self-elected body.[2] In 1914, 457 matrons were opposed to registration, and yet it was claimed that 500 were in favour. The total of matrons suggested by these figures greatly exceeded the number of matrons in Britain.[3] The Royal British Nurses' Association itself was also criticized: the system of election it employed was to circulate a list of thirty people willing to serve. Members could of course delete names and substitute others, but this seldom occurred.[4]

Thus each year, up to the outbreak of war, the Central Committee's agreed bill was presented to the House of Commons: and each year, the Government refused to give it facilities. But when war began, the agitation temporarily subsided as the nurses dispersed to play their part in a united war effort. In 1914, there were still many hospitals and many nurses who were opposed to registration. Nor had the nurses much of a following among the general public. There was nothing to be gained politically by satisfying one section of a minor professional group which would not be lost by antagonizing other nurses and influential members of hospital committees.

This balance of political interest was completely changed by the impact of the war. First, the introduction of more untrained women to work in the hospitals united the professional nurses in a desire for registration. Secondly, widespread public sympathy

---

[1] The membership of the British Medical Association was 23,000. See *Hospital*, 7 June 1919, p. 247.

[2] *Select Committee on Registration 1904*, p. 29.

[3] *Hospital*, 18 July 1914, p. 431.

[4] In 1918, 454 voting papers were sent in unaltered and twelve were amended. *Ibid.*, 22 June 1918, p. 259.

and admiration were enlisted for the nurses' cause. Thirdly, women earned the vote.

The war involved an upheaval for the nursing profession. Never before nor since were so many patients provided with residential care away from their homes: the higher social classes were included among the patients.[1] Nurses were needed on an unprecedented scale, and the demand seems to have been met by increased recruitment, by reducing the provision for the civilian sick, and by admitting large numbers of the untrained and partially trained to hospital work in Voluntary Aid Detachments.[2]

Soon after the outbreak of war, nurses left the civilian hospitals to look after the armed forces. By the middle of 1915, 276 territorial nurses had gone abroad. Moreover, the 23 territorial general hospitals which each contained 520 beds at the outbreak of war were expanded to 1,000, 2,000, or even 3,000 beds. Additional nurses were recruited to staff them. At first the nursing was done, as was the traditional army practice, by trained nurses and experienced male orderlies. But it soon became clear that this system was making exorbitant demands on skilled personnel. The proportions of trained nurses and male orderlies were reduced and their places taken by selected probationers and VADs.

The staffs of civilian hospitals were depleted as nurses left their posts to care for the wounded servicemen. The mental hospitals suffered for the further reason that about half the nursing staff was male and a large number of male nurses volunteered for active service. Female nurses undertook more nursing in the male wards, but nursing standards were substantially lower than before the war.[3] In addition there were fewer beds available for the civilian sick as both the voluntary hospitals and the infirmaries admitted war casualties. It was suggested early on in the war that the test for admission to poor law infirmaries should be medical need: destitution alone was not enough.[4]

[1] The wounded officers accustomed the middle classes to the idea of hospital care which in turn contributed to the widespread demand for 'pay beds' after the war.

[2] There is remarkably little published information about the organization of nursing during the first world war. The twelve-volume official history of the medical services of the war is singularly silent on the problems of nursing. Full statistical information is not available. For much of our account we have had to draw inferences from the opinions expressed in periodicals at the time.

[3] *Lancet*, 26 February 1916, p. 477.

[4] *Hospital*, 15 August 1914, p. 538.

There were reductions in the number of nurses working out-side the hospitals. When the position was reviewed at the beginning of 1917 it was found that the number of school nurses in Great Britain had fallen from 663 before the war to 539 at the beginning of 1917 and some of this number were engaged in war work. The number of health visitors in 1917 was 1,117, while 1,600 or 1,700 were certainly required. There was even a fear in the autumn of 1915 that private patients might suffer owing to a shortage of private duty nurses.[1]

The enormous demand for nurses did lead in the first world war, as in the second, to a large increase in the supply, though the supply was never sufficient to meet the demand at peacetime standards of staffing. More ladies came to take the formal hospital training. In one hospital, the average monthly number of applicants for training increased from 35 to 150. Matrons were able 'to weed out with a drastic hand, and to choose the educated women to train as nurses'.[2] Accommodation became so short that resident pupils were no longer admitted for short periods of training.

By the summer of 1916 the War Office had become concerned about the supply of nurses for the armed forces. A committee was set up 'to consider the existing system of obtaining nurses for the hospitals for sick and wounded soldiers at home and abroad, and to make such recommendations as they may consider necessary for augmenting the supply'. The committee included no representative of the nursing profession. Lord Knutsford was a member of the committee, who, as chairman of the London Hospital, had been the most outspoken critic of the nursing organizations and their objectives. It is not surprising that the appointment of this committee was not welcomed by the nursing profession.

In September 1916 the committee was reconstituted with eight nursing representatives including four matrons of London teaching hospitals. Lord Knutsford resigned. The new terms of reference were to ascertain 'the resources of the country in trained nurses and those partially trained in nursing, so as to enable it to suggest the most economical method of utilizing their services for civil and military purposes'.

The committee collected statistics showing roughly the distribution of trained nurses. The figures showed that military

[1] *Hospital*, 4 September 1915, p. 1065.
[2] *Ibid.*, 4 March 1916, p. 502.

hospitals at home were employing nearly 8,000 nurses to staff about 126,000 beds. In addition there were a further number of nearly 4,000 trained nurses manning about 93,000 beds in hospitals abroad. There were also about 800 beds for officers under private management,[1] staffed by about 192 trained nurses. In total, therefore, they collected information covering about 220,000 beds staffed by about 12,000 trained nurses. The returns covering the civilian sick were obviously incomplete. In the case of England and Wales, poor law institutions which were not recognized as training schools for nurses were omitted. It seems likely, however, that in the whole of the United Kingdom there were not more than 6,000 trained nurses looking after all the physically sick civilians receiving institutional care.

In military hospitals at home there was about one trained nurse for sixteen beds. In the voluntary hospitals there was about one trained nurse for nineteen beds. In the poor law institutions with training schools in England and Wales there was one trained nurse for forty-four beds. In the hospitals for officers under private management there was one trained nurse for every four beds. The standards of staffing of military hospitals by trained nurses were higher than those of civilian hospitals. The small hospitals for officers established 'by persons laudably anxious to assist the work of tending the sick and wounded' had an extremely high ratio of trained staff. The only change in the ratios of trained staff recommended by the committee concerned these private officers' hospitals. 'An appeal might be made . . . to reduce the present proportion of trained nurses from one to four to that of one to six.'

The largest addition to the stock of regular nurses during the war came from the Voluntary Aid Detachments. The VAD scheme originated in 1909.[2] It was organized by a Joint Committee of the British Red Cross Society and the Order of St John of Jerusalem. At the outbreak of war there were about 80,000 members, and at the end of the war there were 120,000 members. Of this last total, there were 12,000 Voluntary Aid Detachment

[1] Lady Diana Cooper describes in her autobiography how her mother's house in Arlington Street was converted into such a hospital. 'The golden drawing room became a ward for ten patients. The ballroom held another twelve. The centre skylit saloon was the dining and club room. The walls were hung with glazed linen, the floor covered by linoleum.' See Diana Cooper: *The Rainbow Comes and Goes*, p. 135: London, 1958.

[2] *Hospital*, 16 November 1918, p. 144.

nursing members working in military hospitals and 60,000 members working in auxiliary hospitals. The latter were unpaid.

The hospitals were thus flooded with an army of volunteers at the beginning of the war, who were drawn to a considerable extent from the higher social classes. They helped to man the existing hospitals and they staffed the temporary hospitals and convalescent homes that were opened in the great houses of Britain by their owners. Some VADs had had full hospital training, others had had more limited nursing experience, and the remainder were totally unqualified. To fit all the unpaid volunteers into positions which accorded with their training and their social position faced the organizers with an impossible task. Moreover, the VADs and the regular nursing staffs did not work together without friction.

Short courses of training were provided for VAD recruits.[1] But the training given only added to the suspicions of the VADs entertained by regular nursing staffs.[2] These suspicions were fanned by the Royal British Nurses' Association in the *British Journal of Nursing*. And even the *Nursing Times* expressed concern lest these 'unprofessional women', 'these ignorant amateurs' would pose as nurses after the war on the strength of brief experience in a military hospital.[3] Already these young women, with their 'express training', were 'assuming full nurses' uniforms, with the addition of a large red cross, and being called and treated as trained nurses by medical men and society people connected with the British Red Cross Society'.[4] Moreover, some of the VADs had found their way to the bedsides of the wounded soldiers on the Continent, leaving behind them 'the injured feelings of the many trained nurses' who were eager to go.[5]

One VAD member was reported to have said that nursing civilians was not sufficiently interesting.[6] And, in general, the voluntary workers had a snobbish attitude towards 'the paid

---

[1] St Thomas's Hospital, for example, gave the emergency probationers no certificate and kept them 'quite distinct from the ordinary probationers whom they do not even meet'. See *NT*, 24 April 1915, p. 486.

[2] Lady Diana Cooper states that within a few weeks of entering Guy's as a VAD, she was 'giving injections intravenous and saline, preparing for operations, cutting abscesses and once even saying prayers in Sister's absence'. See Cooper: *op. cit.*, pp. 127–8.   [3] *NT*, 10 April 1915, p. 427.

[4] *BJN*, 4 July 1914, p. 22.

[5] *Nursing Notes*, January 1915, pp. 3–4.

[6] *NT*, 4 September 1915, p. 1065.

nurse'. A sister of ten years' standing, working in a Red Cross hospital, wrote to complain that 'the untrained commandant —a girl young enough to be my daughter—insists upon all the "volunteers" being called "sister" whether titled dames or domestics'.[1]

In the national emergency, many nurses with good training returned to the hospital wards. Nurses with certificates for one year's general training, nurses with three years' general training and no certificates, nurses trained to work in fever hospitals, nurses trained only in children's nursing, nurses with years of experience and no training, women with first aid certificates, women without either training or experience all had to be fitted into old hospitals and new hospitals in a matter of months. There was no time to check all the credentials. And even if all the information had been available, there were no unambiguous rules of precedence which fitted everyone correctly into the disciplined and rank-conscious hospital world. Mistakes were inevitably made. And the British Red Cross Society itself was faced with the delicate task of resolving disputes in its volunteer army.

It was therefore not surprising that the British Red Cross Society became keen to develop some order in the nursing profession. The matrons and hospital managements were facing similar problems, and were therefore less opposed to some form of organization. And the regular nurses, fearing competition from the VADs, were more anxious than before that their superior status should be given formal recognition. Moreover, Miss Nightingale had died: she was no longer in the background wielding her great authority. But these reasons alone do not explain the developments in the organization of the nursing profession that occurred during the war. Above all else there was the unity of purpose and the willingness to accept change which were the products of the war effort itself.

The new initiative came from Sir Cooper Perry (a member of the Army Medical Board and Medical Superintendent of Guy's Hospital), Dame Sarah Swift (Chief Matron of the British Red Cross Society and formerly matron of Guy's Hospital), and the Honourable Arthur Stanley (Chairman of the Joint War Committee of the British Red Cross Society and Order of St. John, and from 1917 Treasurer of St. Thomas's Hospital). At the

[1] *BJN*, 2 October 1915, p. 282.

beginning of 1916 Stanley addressed a skilful letter to the nurse-training schools proposing the formation of a College of Nursing. He drew attention to the total lack of co-ordinated organization among the nurses themselves, but stated that there was no unanimous feeling in favour of any system of state registration.

> Nevertheless [he continued] I am convinced that something should be done at once to co-ordinate the various interests involved, and, without prejudice to ultimate developments, whether by legislation or otherwise, my own view is that for the time at least we must rely upon a voluntary scheme of cooperation amongst the nurse training schools throughout the country. . . . Just as the Royal College of Physicians and Surgeons through the conjoint Board organise the teaching and examination of medical students, as the chartered institutes of accountants, of surveyors, engineers and other bodies, as barristers and solicitors organise the teaching and examination of candidates for entrance to their respective professions, so do I feel most strongly that now is the right time for some such movement in the nursing profession. . . . The promoters, having obtained the sanction of the Board of Trade to the registration of the college with its memorandum and articles of association, should appoint the first council of management, two-thirds of whom should be Matrons of Hospitals or Superintendents of Nursing, or Sisters or Nurses still engaged in the active practice of their profession.[1]

The letter itself shows why Stanley achieved so much more than Mrs Bedford Fenwick. The letter came from a distinguished layman who had previously played no part in the controversies of the profession and who was associated with a hospital (St Thomas's) whose nurse-training school commanded universal respect and whose matron (Miss Lloyd Still) was highly regarded in the nursing world. Secondly, it suggested an organization of supreme status on a level with the Royal Colleges of the medical profession. Thirdly, it offered initial control of that organization to those to whom the letter was addressed. Fourthly, it side-stepped the controversial issue of registration. Most important of all, the time was propitious.

The letter immediately received a very favourable response and a conference was called at St Thomas's Hospital. The training schools supported the idea of a College of Nursing. It was left to Mrs Bedford Fenwick to strike a discordant note. She complained at the conference that the organizations with which

[1] *Hospital*, 15 January 1916, p. 355.

she was connected had not been approached. Arthur Stanley explained charmingly that this omission was solely due to the rush with which the arrangements had been made. It seems possible, however, that it was thought more likely that the support of the training schools could be gained if the Central Committee was not associated with the project.

The new college was formed and registered with the Board of Trade, and a council had to be appointed to control the affairs of the College of Nursing Limited. There was a danger that the selection of some training schools to serve on the council might antagonize other schools which were not given this representation. This difficulty was avoided by creating a consultative committee on which places were allotted to prominent training schools. In this way, the full support of the training schools was retained.

By the end of March 1916, the College had formally come into existence. The principal objects were:

(1) To promote the better education and training of nurses and the advancement of nursing as a profession in all or any of its branches.

(2) To promote uniformity of curriculum.

(3) To recognize approved Nursing Schools.

(4) To make and maintain a register of persons to whom certificates of proficiency or of training and proficiency had been granted.

(5) To promote Bills in Parliament for any object connected with the interests of the Nursing Profession, and, in particular, with their education, organization, protection or for their recognition by the State.

The articles of association specifically prevented the College from imposing on its members or supporting with its funds 'any regulation which, if an object of the College, would make it a Trade Union'.

For the purpose of admitting nurses to its own register, the College recognized for training civil hospitals and infirmaries with at least 250 beds. There had to be a resident medical or surgical officer, at least one course of lectures a year, and an examination for qualification.[1] Male nurses and mental nurses were tacitly excluded from membership of the College.

[1] *Ibid*, 15 January 1916, p. 355.

Once the support of the training schools had been firmly established, the College started to woo the Royal British Nurses' Association. It wanted an amalgamation because this would unite the profession and bring in both funds and members. It would also bring the College a Royal Charter and make it possible to delete the invidious word 'Limited' from its title. From the early days Mr Comyns Berkeley, the treasurer of the Royal British Nurses' Association, had been associated with the College,[1] and in February Burdett had appealed in the columns of *Hospital* for the support of 'the broader-minded registrationists'.[2] When the registrationists did not respond enthusiastically, Burdett scolded them.[3] Mr Stanley, the chairman of the College, was more diplomatic. The Central Committee was offered equal representation to that of the College on the first Nursing Council in the College's draft bill. 'It would be very unfair', Stanley said, 'that they should not have a voice in the first council appointed under the Bill, which their efforts have done so much to gain.'[4]

Princess Christian indicated that 'should a satisfactory scheme of union between the College of Nursing and the Royal British Nurses' Association be formulated, she would be disposed to accept a position of honour in the conjoint Society'.[5] Mrs Bedford Fenwick, on the other hand, was less responsive. She objected to the excessive lay control of the College of Nursing Ltd.[6] But Mr Stanley continued to be conciliatory. 'I cannot but feel', he wrote to her in November, 'that the differences between us are matters rather of expediency and policy than of fundamental principles.'[7] But the Central Committee attacked the College's Bill in public. From this action the Royal British Nurses' Association disassociated itself.

Seeing the enemy divided, Burdett launched a vicious attack

---

[1] *Hospital*, 8 April 1916, p. 76.   [2] *Ibid.*, 26 February 1916, p. 479.

[3] 'It is widely recognized throughout the nursing world that the extreme partisans and advocates of State Registration by demanding the Bill, the whole Bill and nothing but the Bill, have it in their power to break away from agreement and the College of Nursing by refusing all compromise and any modification of the proposals as they stand in the Bill. . . . In this connection it is well to keep this truth in mind, that had the advocates of nurse registration from the earliest days exhibited a spirit of compromise and a sole desire to benefit the nurses by registration, State Registration would have been sanctioned by Parliament long ago on the only practical and sufficient basis.' *Ibid.*, 10 June 1916, p. 241.   [4] *Ibid.*, 24 June 1916 p. 310.

[5] *Ibid*, 24 June 1916, p. 309.   [6] *BJN*, 30 September 1916, p. 282.

[7] *Hospital*, 18 November 1916, p. 145.

on Mrs Bedford Fenwick—'the one woman, who wishes to keep everything in her own hands and to hold that position by denouncing much that is self-respecting and worthy in the nursing world'.[1] His first editorial for the *Hospital* in the year 1917 compared the war being waged within the nursing profession to the wider war on which the country was engaged. 'Demonstrably both wars had their origin in the overmastering desire for supreme power, possessed, in each case, by a single individual.'[2]

As a result of, or in spite of, Burdett's onslaught on Mrs Fenwick, the Royal British Nurses' Association definitely decided on amalgamation with the College. Princess Christian stated that 'the fusion of the two bodies can and will be of great advantage to both the nursing profession at large and the public generally'.[3] All that was now needed was a revision by the Privy Council of the Royal Charter of 1893. At this brief moment of unity, the editor of the *Nursing Mirror* day-dreamed about an 'architecturally beautiful building' inscribed 'The Royal College of British Nurses'.[4] Mrs Bedford Fenwick continued her attacks on the principle of admitting the laity to official control of the nursing profession.

In the months that followed, the Central Committee re-formed its ranks. Negotiations on the bill were reopened with the College, but no agreement was reached. Meanwhile the Royal British Nurses' Association conducted dilatory negotiations with the Privy Council on its new charter. By November 1917 the College of Nursing had become impatient and an arrogant letter was dispatched to the RBNA.

It was undoubtedly of some importance to the College in its early days to seek to ally itself with your Association, just as it was of importance for your Association to obtain enlarged powers, the new infusion of energy, and increased membership, which would have come about by the establishment of the amalgamated bodies as the Royal British College of Nursing; but as the College of Nursing has now become well known, and as an appeal for funds made by the British Women's Hospital on its behalf has met with the widest sympathetic reception by the press and public, the advantage to the College of amalgamation becomes less obvious.[5]

The registrationists were now firmly divided into two camps

---

[1] *Ibid*, 2 December 1916, p. 187.   [2] *Ibid.*, 6 January 1917, p. 285.
[3] *Ibid.*, 27 January 1917, p. 351.   [4] *NM*, 24 February 1917, p. 401.
[5] *Hospital*, 17 November 1917, p. 142.

and the position remained unchanged throughout 1918. The *Hospital* and the *British Journal of Nursing* resumed their bitter attacks: the brief moment of unity was over. Meanwhile the College of Nursing was growing from strength to strength. The membership on 31 March 1917 had been 2,553. A year later it amounted to 8,000. By 1919 the membership was up to 13,047. By then, the College could afford to ignore the Central Committee.

Even at this late hour, when so many nurses favoured registration, there remained a number of hospital governors and matrons who were still opposed. The Marquess of Dufferin and Ava explained the reasons in the House of Lords. They 'feared that the standardisation by the State of qualifications of nurses would tend to make nurses independent of the Hospital School by reducing the great amount of competition from unskilled nursing workers, which would tend to raise the salaries not only outside the hospitals but in the hospitals themselves. Registration really meant the abolition of cheap nursing labour.'[1] It was considered that the bill 'in effect [would give them] a monopoly in the organisation and the union of all trained nurses'.[2] That the peer quoted above could claim some accuracy for his views was confirmed by Lord Knutsford, who continued to oppose registration, and was quoted as having said 'you would never have got your Bill unless someone had bribed away my matrons'.[3]

Once the profession had closed its ranks on the broad issue of registration, it became more probable that Parliament would act. Parliament was now well disposed towards women in general and nurses in particular. Fifteen years before, the suffragettes had been dismissed as the 'shrieking sisterhood'.[4] Now the shriekers had proved their worth. They had nursed the wounded, manned munition factories and replaced men in a variety of essential jobs. In short, women had made a crucial contribution to the war effort. They had earned the vote.

If women were to have the vote, then the demands of some hundred thousand electors belonging to the nursing profession could not be ignored. The House of Lords even seemed in awe of the opposite sex. 'Women now have the vote; they have to be

---

[1] *H of L Deb.*, 27 May 1919, col. 844.
[2] Lord Ampthill: *ibid.*, 27 May 1919, col. 824.
[3] *Ibid.*, 27 May 1919, col. 824.
[4] *H of C Deb.*, 16 March 1904, col. 1339.

considered more than they used to be. .... Women are now likely to get what they insist on having.'[1] The major political parties in the Commons had more mundane, political fears. 'If you force nurses [by opposing registration] to form trade unions in order to secure that which they regard, and rightly regard, as a measure of justice and a right to them, you will simply throw them into the arms of the Labour Party.'[2]

So we find generous tributes to the nursing profession in both Houses of Parliament. In the House of Commons, a Labour member spoke of 'the debt we owe them for the sacrifices they have made during the progress of the last horrible war'.[3] As another member put it, 'Parliament and the whole Empire [are] under a deep debt of gratitude to the nurses for the work which they have performed'.[4] There was no further cause for doubt. The nurses were to have registration.

The Government accepted registration 'in principle'. What was not agreed was the exact form which registration should take. For while the different sections of the nursing world had united on the principle, there was still no agreement on the detail. Indeed, the fundamental agreement on the main issue was disguised by bitter controversy on what must have seemed to be minor procedural matters.

It was agreed that in the long run control of the training schools and the machinery of registration should be vested in a body about two-thirds of whose members were nurses. And eventually these nursing representatives would be elected by registered nurses. Meanwhile, there had to be some caretaker body to organize registration and thus create the electoral roll which would select the nursing members of the proposed council. The battle centred on the composition of this caretaker council which would be able to influence who was registered and who was not, which would in turn affect the ultimate council with its wide powers over the whole nursing profession. There were historical reasons and personal reasons why the battle between the College of Nursing and the Central Council had to be fought to the finish. But beneath all the sparring on points of detail, what was really going on was a duel which would yield to the

---

[1] Earl Russell: *H of L Deb.*, 27 May 1919, col. 846.
[2] Lord Ampthill: *ibid.*, col. 827.
[3] Mr Roberts: *H of C Deb.*, 28 March 1919, col. 797.
[4] Lt-Col. Raw: *ibid.*, 28 March 1919, col. 793.

victor the cherished position of major spokesman for the nursing profession.

The Royal British Nurses' Association stood for high professional standards irrespective of the staffing needs of the hospitals. It was allied with the British Medical Association in the hope that the medical profession would allow no compromise with nursing standards just as it had allowed none with the standards of medical education. The College of Nursing, on the other hand, was allied with hospital managements and was prepared to pay some attention to the staffing needs of the hospitals in the standards it laid down for the nursing profession.

Each organization presented its own bill to Parliament. The Royal British Nurses' Association's bill was introduced in the House of Commons in June 1919. It provided that out of the eighteen female nurses on the first council, four were to be nominated by the Royal British Nurses' Association, four by the College of Nursing Ltd, and ten by other nursing organizations. Seven of these last ten seats were allocated to organizations which were also on the Central Committee for State Registration and were thus allies of the RBNA against the College of Nursing. The eight doctors, four of whom were to be appointed by the British Medical Association, were also likely to support the Royal British Nurses' Association. So although the bill gave equal representation to the RBNA and the College of Nursing, this fairness was only superficial: the bill made sure that the allies of the Royal British Nurses' Association had a majority of the seats on the council.

The bill sponsored by the College of Nursing Ltd was presented to the House of Lords in May 1919. The fact that the College found its sponsors among the peerage was in itself significant. For the peerage were then, as now, strongly represented among the chairmen of London teaching hospitals. The proposals under the Lords bill for the composition of the provisional council were also superficially fair to the two rival professional bodies. The College was to have twelve representatives and the RBNA and its allies were also to have twelve representatives. In addition the British Medical Association was to have three representatives, who might be expected to favour the Royal British Nurses' Association's case. But managers of hospitals were to have six places, three for the British Hospitals' Association, and three for the Poor Law Unions.

The debates on the bills in the two Houses of Parliament consisted to a considerable extent of shadow boxing. Each side naturally claimed that its own proposals were the more democratic. The RBNA camp argued that the doctors must have 'if not a predominant influence, at any rate a very great influence in any body framed to conduct the affairs of the nursing profession'.[1] The Lords bill was dubbed 'a hospital governors' and matrons' bill'.[2]

Sinister motives were attributed to the College of Nursing, and the sources of its finances were sharply criticized. Not only did the bill intend to make the College of Nursing the centre of the new body that controlled nursing, but also the new council was actually to make itself responsible for the College. The College at that time had 14,000 members. The bill provided that when this number reached 30,000 the permanent council could then be set up. One peer was very alarmed by this: 'Do your lordships not see what will happen? There are between 70,000 and 80,000 trained nurses in this country. The College of Nursing have 14,000 already. Within a few weeks they can get another 16,000 and make up the 30,000, and then, having got the electorate entirely under their control, they will be able to settle everything. The other 40,000 or 50,000 nurses will not have a say.'[3] The College had also promised these 14,000 on their register that they would not be required to pay a further fee for registration. They had also the sum of £40,000 which was to be used for running the register. They proposed to provide ready-made machinery for the state registration of their profession.

The bill sponsored by the Royal British Nurses' Association found a wide measure of support in the House of Commons. But just as the College of Nursing was criticized in the Lords, so the Royal British Nurses' Association was criticized in the Commons. Some members had decided views on what control by the Royal British Nurses' Association really meant.

We have got to see that the avenue into the nursing profession is kept open for the daughters of the working classes as much as any other class. I observe that we are putting the whole future of the nursing profession outside the control of Parliament. . . . I am not at all certain in this handing over to a body which must necessarily become, to a certain extent at least, an aristocratic and autocratic

---

[1] The Marquess of Crewe: *H of L Deb.*, 27 May 1919, col. 840.

[2] The Marquess of Dufferin and Ava: *ibid.*, 27 May 1919, col. 843.

[3] Lord Ampthill: *ibid.*, 27 May 1919, col. 833.

body. . . . Quite naturally they desire to keep the profession preserved to those particular people and their friends.[1]

So Parliament witnessed the ugly spectacle of two professional organizations airing their private feuds before the forum of public opinion. Nor were Members unaware of what was going on. Behind the scenes the new Minister of Health (Dr Addison) was trying to negotiate between the two nursing empires. He tried to give every organization of nurses a fair say in the provisional council. But the consequence was to enlarge the membership until it became hopelessly unwieldy.

The Minister eventually gave up the attempt to bring the two camps together. He told the House of Commons that he had been convinced against his will that agreement was not attainable.[2] 'The controversy appears to have been unfortunately mixed up with personal and sectional interests which cannot be reconciled.'[3] The Government decided to bring in its own bill. Under it, the Minister of Health was himself to appoint the provisional council. Major Barnett, the proposer of the Royal British Nurses' Association bill, congratulated the Minister on his skill and courage.[4] 'It is a courageous act for my right hon. Friend will have to select the ladies to sit on this Council.'[5] He obviously did not envy the Minister his task.

By December 1919 the Minister's bill had received the royal assent. The Register set up under the Act consisted of four or more separate parts. In the words of the Act

the register shall consist of the following parts:

(a) a general part containing the names of all nurses who satisfy the conditions of admission to that part of the register;

---

[1] Col. Wedgwood: *H of C Deb.*, 28 March 1919, col. 811.

[2] *Ibid.*, 27 June 1919, cols. 557–8.

[3] *Ibid.*, col. 558.

[4] *Ibid.*, 18 November 1919, col. 870. Major Barnett was rewarded for his part in securing the Registration of nurses in the election campaign three years later. In his constituency the nurses organized a 'picturesque procession of nurses in uniform . . . led by Miss Isabel Macdonald upholding the splendid banner of the Royal British Nurses' Association. The procession marched briskly, to the delight of dancing children, lovely little creatures who promised Daddy's vote for Barnett "to please the nurses". . . . The nurses' slogan "vote for Major Barnett, the champion of skilled nursing for the breadwinner, and mother and babe" won instant and sympathetic response.' See *BJN*, 25 November 1922, pp. 333–4.

[5] *H of C Deb.*, 18 November 1919, col. 871.

(b) a supplementary part containing the names of male nurses;

(c) a supplementary part containing the names of nurses trained in the nursing and care of persons suffering from mental diseases;

(d) a supplementary part containing the names of nurses trained in the nursing of sick children;

(e) any other prescribed part.[1]

Persons without formal training were to be admitted to the Register at the outset. The Council was to admit persons

on producing evidence to the satisfaction of the Council that they are of good character, are of the prescribed age, are persons who were for at least three years before the first day of November 1919 *bona fide* engaged in practice as nurses in attendance on the sick under conditions which appear to the Council to be satisfactory for the purposes of this provision and have adequate knowledge and experience of the nursing of the sick.[2]

The maximum registration fee for these 'existing nurses' was to be one guinea.

It was also the duty of the Council to approve training schools. But any school aggrieved by not being approved, could appeal to the Minister of Health.

While existing practical nurses were able to acquire the title 'registered nurse', there was no provision for nurses with a lower standard of training to be registered in the future.[3] Some Members of Parliament championed the cause of the practical nurses in the debates of 1919. It was suggested that a supplementary part should be added to the Register so that separate rules could be made for this class of nurse. It was suggested that registered nurses would be too grand to do the proper work of the district nurse,[4] and thus the effect of the Act would be to narrow the entry to the profession and create a shortage of nurses.[5]

[1] *Nurses Registration Act, 1919*, 9 & 10 Geo. 5, Chapter 94.

[2] *Ibid.*, Chapter 94 S. 3 (2) (c).

[3] The Select Committee of 1905 had recommended a separate register for 'nurses whose training is of a lower standard than that laid down for Registered Nurses'. See *Select Committee on Registration 1905*, p. v.

[4] 'It is absolutely imperative if the woman in the cottage is the patient, that someone who is nursing her should be prepared to do the housework. . . . Cottage nurses . . . will feel slighted if they are not given equal recognition. The result will be that you will get no more cottage nurses.' See Capt. Bowyer: *H of C Deb.*, 18 November 1919, col. 876.

[5] 'Whenever I see a Friday afternoon Bill, I always look to see who is to be put in prison, because it is my experience that these Bills which meet with

Another Member, Sir Courtenay Warner, championed the cause of the probationers: 'what are called probationers in hospitals are practically in the position of the slaves of the nurses'. He summed up by saying 'the voice of the untrained nurse or the nurse who has not been completely trained is absolutely unheard and absolutely unrepresented in either of these Bills'.[1] This was as true of the Act that ultimately reached the Statute Book as of the two bills that preceded it.

---

the universal support of all hon. Members in this House, inevitably contain, wrapped up somewhere, a penal clause punishing somebody. . . . We have got to consider here, not only the setting up of a registration system for nurses, but to some extent—I dare say justifiably—the narrowing of the field of supply of nurses and the closing of the nursing profession. I dare say it may be justified, but for myself I always dislike to see any legislation passed into law which closes a profession or narrows down the avenue through which people can approach that profession.' See Col. Wedgwood: *H of C Deb.*, 28 March 1919, col. 810.

[1] *Ibid.*, 4 July 1919, col. 1351.

CHAPTER VII

Parliament Intervenes

NURSING had been officially recognized as a profession. It had been granted what the law and the church had never felt it necessary to seek: a statutory register. It had followed the path of the doctors, the teachers and midwives, and achieved its objective two years before the dentists. With its military heritage showing in its language, its religious tradition conveyed in its sentiment and its humble ancestry revealed in its uniform, the profession had come of age.

The Nurses' Registration Act was passed at a unique moment in the history of the nursing profession. Though the situation changed rapidly, immediately after the war there did not seem to be a shortage of nurses. Indeed, it was believed that the number of nurses awaiting registration amounted to about 70,000 or 80,000. The demands made by the war on nurses had been tremendous. They had gone to work for the armed services at home and overseas, they had manned the temporary hospitals and nursing homes. There had been acute shortages in the mental hospitals and in the small infirmaries, but London matrons had had so many applicants for training that they had been able to weed out candidates 'with a drastic hand'.

In 1919, as more and more nurses were released from the armed forces,[1] there was a fear in nursing circles that there would not be enough jobs to go round. This fear had contributed to the united demand for a Register. Indeed one of the principal aims of registration was to secure that the limited number of appointments went to the best qualified. On no account must VADs be allowed to 'pose as nurses', and usurp the positions which should properly go to fully trained nurses. The Act laid down that the General Nursing Council should admit to the Register persons who for three years before 1 November 1919

---

[1] 'In the House of Commons, Mr Churchill stated that out of 23,931 Army nurses, 3,790 had been demobilized.' See *NT*, 8 March 1919, p. 211.

had been '*bona fide* engaged in practice' and 'had adequate knowledge and experience of the nursing of the sick'. The leaders of the profession were determined not to admit VADs under this section. They were determined, too, that no special register should be created which would allow them to be called nurses on the basis of a shorter period of training. The profession insisted above all else upon what it called the 'one portal' entry.

The Royal British Nurses' Association and the College of Nursing were agreed that untrained VADs should be kept off the Register. But Sir Arthur Stanley[1] was not only chairman of the College of Nursing but also still actively connected with the British Red Cross Society which had the responsibility of looking after the VADs it had recruited. For this reason there had always been a suspicion in the minds of its opponents that the College might allow VADs to become members of the College and then later smuggle them on to the statutory Register. Such was the implication of the statement made by Mr Paterson, a fellow of the Royal College of Surgeons, at a meeting of the Royal British Nurses' Association early in 1918: 'When the College was first started it was clearly the intention of its promoters to introduce the VAD workers within its folds in some way or other.'[2] The charge was repeated even though three months earlier Sir Arthur Stanley had stated the College's position in this matter. 'Our endeavour will be to draw a clear line between trained nurses and VADs, and to encourage such of the latter as are suitable to obtain three years' certificate from a general hospital, which will enable them to become members of the College of Nursing.'[3]

The Government was assisting VADs to get trained. The Ministry of Labour had formed the Nurses' Demobilization and Resettlement Committee, 'to help demobilize and resettle in civilian life'[4] those who had worked as nurses for the armed services. Advice was given about further training. There were fears in the nursing world that the Government planned special privileges for VADs. A statement by the president of the Local

---

[1] He was knighted in 1917.   [2] *Hospital*, 16 February 1918, p. 425.
[3] *Ibid.*, 17 November 1917, p. 146.
[4] In its report the Committee stated that it could not 'undertake to supply (1) a sort of upper domestic servant at a salary of £20 a year "all found" which some people offer; (2) a children's nurse in a private family'. See *Lancet*, 21 June 1919, p. 1090.

Government Board, Dr Addison, had encouraged these suspicions: 'we shall need very many more nurses than we have ever
had before' he told *The Times* correspondent, 'and we are fortunate in having ready to hand at this time thousands of women
who have gained invaluable experience in VAD work'.[1]

The plan which the British Red Cross Society eventually
devised for the VADs, under Sir Arthur Stanley's leadership, was
to provide a niche for them in the nursing world which would
be acceptable to the trained nurses. 'What one would like to see',
he said, 'in every village is a proper system under which VADs
trained in home nursing and first-aid could work. They could
perfectly well do all the small things such as attending to cuts
and the like.'[2] 'A regular service of properly trained nurses with
three-year certificates would be undesirable, as in many cases
the nurses would be wasting most of their time.' Even this
modest plan was described by Mrs Bedford Fenwick as 'pushing VADs into positions which should be reserved for trained
nurses'.[3]

Thus the leaders of the nursing profession feared that the
Government intended to give professional status to the VADs. In
addition, the organizations opposed to the College of Nursing
feared that Sir Arthur Stanley would use his association with the
College to give them some preferment. These fears embittered
relationships between the rival nursing organizations and dominated the attitude of the profession as a whole while the General
Nursing Council devised the detailed regulations needed .to
implement the Registration Act.

The first General Nursing Council was appointed early in
1920. It was its duty under the Act to start the Register and thus
create the electorate which would select the nursing members
of the second council two years later. It consisted of nine lay
members and sixteen nurse members. Of the nine lay members,
two were appointed by the Privy Council to represent the public
and two by the Board of Education 'to provide experience of
educational work in the more general sense'.[4] The remaining
five members appointed by the Minister of Health gave 'the only

[1] *NT*, 18 January 1919, p. 48.   [2] *Ibid.*, 9 October 1920, p. 1171.
[3] *BJN*, 25 September 1920, p. 172.
[4] Evidence given by Mr Brock for the Ministry of Health to the Select
Committee on the General Nursing Council. See General Nursing Council:
Select Committee Report 1924–5, (167) vii, p. 1.

opportunity of appointing to the Council medical men, either concerned in general medical practice, or with the special types of practice represented by the supplementary parts of the register'.

The long and bitter disputes about the appointment of the first nursing members of the General Nursing Council had ended with the Minister of Health deciding to make the appointments himself. In practice, out of the sixteen nursing members appointed, eleven were matrons or ex-matrons and five were nurses. Only two poor law infirmaries were represented. And most significant of all, the College of Nursing had nine members on the Council,[1] and the Royal British Nurses' Association had only four or five. The College of Nursing had become indisputably the major spokesman for the profession. The Minister's decision did broadly correspond to the strength of the organizations concerned.[2]

The Registration Act did not create any greater unity among the professional organizations than had existed before. The first Council was deeply divided into two groups.[3] There was the majority of sixteen which included the non-nursing members and those nurses (nearly all matrons) who favoured the point of view which was shared by the College of Nursing and the Association of Hospital Matrons.[4] There was a minority of six, of whom Mrs Bedford Fenwick was the most outspoken, who broadly favoured the point of view of the old Central Committee for the Registration of Nurses, or, as Mrs Bedford Fenwick grandilo-

[1] Including four members of its council and one ex-member (Miss Seymour Yapp). One member of the College of Nursing was also secretary of the Professional Union of Trained Nurses (Miss MacCullum). See *NT*, 1 May 1920, p. 509.

[2] By 1925, about 24,000 nurses had joined the College of Nursing. In the same year the RBNA had about 5,000 and the Professional Union of Trained Nurses had 600 paid-up members. The Society of State Registration for Nurses, which had changed its name to the Registered Nurses' Parliamentary Council, had about 4,000 members.

[3] See the evidence given by Miss MacCullum to the *Select Committee on the General Nursing Council 1925*, p. 66.

[4] This body had been formed in 1919 as an organization of matrons with which Mrs Fenwick was not associated. It soon became a power in the nursing world and gained the active support of Princess Marie Louise, the daughter of Princess Christian. By 1928 it had 467 members. The Matrons' Council had only 125 members and a subscription income of under £15 in 1926.

quently put it, 'what we call the Free Nurses' Organizations'.[1] When the minority were defeated in the Council, they appealed to the Minister of Health. As Mr Brock, the Ministry's spokesman, said with some understatement, 'they are not slow in putting their views before us'.[2]

In practice the minority fought for the most searching examination of the credentials of any candidate for admission to the Register. Irrespective of the intentions of Parliament, the Register must be kept select. Only thus, it was held, would the profession attain the appropriate place in public esteem and only thus would the best type of woman wish to take up nursing. This view, sincerely held and vehemently advocated, led to a restrictive attitude towards the admission of existing nurses and a desire to impose upon new entrants an extremely rigorous examination.

The Council decided that it needed to devise rules for the admission to the Register of three different categories of nurses. There were 'existing nurses' who had been in the profession before the Registration Act was passed, nurses with intermediate qualifications who had completed their training after the Act but before the examination system was introduced, and nurses who could be admitted to the Register by examination. The rules for the existing nurses were the most urgent and the most controversial.

By the Registration Act, Parliament had handed over to the General Nursing Council the problem of determining the exact criteria for the admission of existing nurses to the Registers. The Council had to decide what were satisfactory conditions for a nurse to be engaged in '*bona fide*' practice. The Council had to devise some means of ascertaining whether the applicant had 'adequate knowledge and experience of the nursing of the sick'. The conditions devised by the Council were very strict and remained strict irrespective of the wider public interest.

It was decided, after many months of debate, to make one year's training an essential qualification for admission to the Register as an 'existing nurse'. If more than one year had been laid down, the lady-pupils, including Mrs Bedford Fenwick herself, would have been excluded not only from the Register but also from membership of the General Nursing Council. By

[1] *Select Committee on the General Nursing Council 1925*, p. 30.
[2] *Ibid.*, p. 11.

drawing a line at one year, the Council intended to keep off the Register many of the practical district nurses as well as the VADs. A registration sub-committee under the chairmanship of Mrs Bedford Fenwick was set up to vet the applications. On this basis the Register was opened in November 1921.

With good will on all sides this procedure could have worked well. The Council had appointed a registrar and it would seem natural that the real work of handling applications would be done by the officials and that the sub-committee of the Council would do no more than ratify the recommendations of its chief officer and decide questions of policy as they arose. In practice, however, the procedure proved cumbrous and unworkable. The chairman of the registration sub-committee insisted on going into long details about every certificate and cross-examined the registrar on every case.[1] There were personal frictions. Mrs Bedford Fenwick resented the fact that the staff of the Council were members of the College of Nursing.[2] As a result, in the first four months, 3,235 cases were received and only 984 completed. Sixteen members of the Council (including the chairman) re-signed, leaving the minority of six unable to form a quorum.

The Minister of Health had to intervene. Under the Act the existing council was due to come to an end in November 1922 and the nurse members of the new council were to be elected by nurses who had been admitted to the Register. It would be intolerable for the Council to be elected by only a tiny fraction of the profession. If the present procedure continued 'many of the nurses would be dead and buried before they got on the register'.[3]

The Minister persuaded the members of the Nursing Council to withdraw their resignations with a promise that he would sup-port them in reorganizing the procedure of the Council. The

[1] *H of C Deb.*, 22 March 1922, col. 626.

[2] This even led to a question in the House of Commons. 'Mr Griffiths asked the Minister of Health whether, as all the nurses who are heads of the General Nursing Council office staff are members of the College of Nursing Ltd, he can state if it is intended that all the highly paid posts shall, with his approval, be kept exclusively for membership of that limited liability com-pany, or whether other registered nurses who do not belong to it are to be allowed to participate in the work of the Council in some of the remunerative posts created from time to time?' (*Ibid.*, 27 March 1923, col. 321.)

[3] Sir Alfred Mond, Minister of Health: *ibid.*, 22 March 1922, cols. 625–6.

majority went back to work and changed the membership of the registration sub-committee. For the future, only doubtful applications for admission to the Register were to be brought before the Registration Sub-Committee, and nurses were to be allowed to be registered on the basis of certified copies of their certificates.[1]

These new rules were questioned in Parliament and Mrs Bedford Fenwick was given eloquent support by a Labour Member. Mr Richardson said that the majority of the General Nursing Council 'drove off one committee a woman who has had more experience than any other woman on that council . . . thus taking away the only friend on that committee which the working nurses had'.[2] The Minister gave a lengthy defence of the actions taken by the Council and ended by threatening to repeal the Nurses' Registration Act if they were not approved.

Mrs Bedford Fenwick's opposition to the new rules was not confined to forming strange alliances with Members of Parliament. She held the view that the Council's business was being 'ruthlessly monopolized by the medical, lay, and College nominees',[3] and fought her battle in the General Nursing Council by every weapon she could muster. After the Council had passed, on 21 April, a number of applications by the new procedure, she went and checked them up afterwards and claimed to find errors in four cases out of the twenty she examined. When this was brought up at the next Council meeting it was said that she herself had 'scrutinized' the applications before they had come before the Council. This she hotly denied. The attack on her was 'too scandalous for words. . . . She was not going to be made the scapegoat for the registrar's inefficiency in connection with the matter. She knew that she would have most of the Council against her, but she maintained that they had neglected their duty. If they continued to do so they would live to regret it.'[4]

This was not the first time that the proceedings of the General Nursing Council had ended in an undignified squabble. The *Nursing Times* described it as 'a debate of the type which we

---

[1] And in cases where copies of a nurse's certificates were held by a nursing organization, the registrar was authorized to admit to the Register on inspection of the copy at the office of the organization concerned.

[2] *H of C Deb.*, 22 March 1922, col. 628.

[3] *BJN*, 16 December 1922, p. 385. [4] *NT*, 27 May 1922, p. 517.

regret to say is all too common at the Council meetings'. It continued, 'we are more concerned with what the public would think if it becomes generally known that a body of professional men and women had spent the best part of an hour in heated argument. . . . It is humiliating and undignified; the last thing one could expect to happen in a council of nurses.'[1]

The new rules continued to operate, though no doubt the Registrar and her staff were exercising extreme care with every case they handled. By the time the first elections were held there were only about 12,000 nurses eligible to vote.[2] It was alleged after the election that the General Nursing Council had given undue precedence to College of Nursing members to ensure a majority for those who favoured its point of view. In reply it was said that of the first 6,616 nurses to be registered, only 400 were College members. It is possible that Mrs Fenwick's searching inquiries had held up an excessive proportion of College of Nursing applicants.

The election was hotly contested.[3] The College of Nursing, the Hospital Matrons' Association and the Poor Law Matrons' Association held a joint meeting and selected their candidates, most of whom were matrons. Mrs Bedford Fenwick and her allies stood as independent candidates. 'The policy of the independent candidates', Mrs Fenwick said, 'would be self-government for the nursing profession and power of self-expression.' They stood for 'liberty and self-government'.[4] Only six independents were elected. Mrs Fenwick lost her seat. A question asked on her behalf in the House of Commons failed to reverse this decision.[5]

The election was conducted on a complicated plan. Under the Act the first General Nursing Council had been given power to draw up a 'prescribed scheme' for the sixteen registered nurses to be elected.[6] Such a scheme had been adopted by the Council

---

[1] *NT*, 27 May 1922, p. 509.   [2] *Ibid.*, 10 February 1923, p. 133.

[3] The administrative arrangements for the election were badly conducted. Ballot papers were sent out bearing serial numbers. The first set had to be withdrawn and a new set substituted. Mrs Bedford Fenwick made great play with this 'attempt to violate the secret ballot'. See *BJN*, 9 December, p. 369; 16 December, p. 397; 23 December, p. 413, 1922.

[4] *NT*, 11 November 1922, p. 1098.

[5] *H of C Deb.*, 21 February 1923, cols. 1082-3.

[6] *Nurses Registration Act, 1919*, 9 & 10 Geo 5, Chapter 94, Schedule Section 1 (4).

in February 1921 on a motion of Mrs Bedford Fenwick's.[1] The electorate was divided into compartments in accordance with the different parts of the Register. Eleven seats were reserved for nurses on the general part of the Register, and five for those on the supplementary parts. The eleven seats were sub-divided into further compartments to secure, among other objectives, that six out of the eleven representatives were matrons. According to the chairman of the General Nursing Council, Sir Wilmot Herringham, this was needed to protect the public.[2] This restriction in the electoral system was questioned in Parliament in March 1923[3] and became one of the subjects which the Select Committee on the General Nursing Council were instructed to investigate in 1925. Both the College of Nursing[4] and Mrs Bedford Fenwick favoured the abolition of the restriction and the Committee supported their views.[5] The Government acted on the Committee's recommendation.[6]

At last nurses were being registered in large numbers. The date for closing the Register to existing nurses was 14 July 1923. At this late hour attention in the nursing world began to concentrate on the definition of an 'existing nurse' laid down by the Council. In the middle of 1922 the *Nursing Times* had questioned the right of the General Nursing Council to make one year's training a condition of admission as an existing nurse. '*Bona fide*' nurses had a right by law to registration irrespective of any training.[7] It was a Miss Herbert who championed the cause of the '*bona fide*' nurse.

Letters of protest began to appear in the nursing press. The rule set out by the General Nursing Council was obviously unfair. It required that the year of training should have been done in a hospital approved by the Council. Nurses trained in general nursing homes objected to this restriction and could point out that the matrons of such nursing homes were often fully qualified to train nurses.[8] Existing dentists had been much more generously treated: anyone who had practised dentistry was entitled

[1] *NT*, 25 February 1921, p. 179.

[2] *Select Committee on the General Nursing Council 1925*, p. 17.

[3] *H of C Deb.*, 14 March 1923, cols. 1710–11.

[4] *Select Committee on the General Nursing Council 1925*, p. 34.

[5] *Ibid.*, see pp. 26 and x.

[6] *BJN*, 25 October 1927, p. 231.

[7] *NT*, 24 June 1922, p. 605.

[8] *Ibid.*, 9 December 1922, pp. 1198–9.

to be registered.[1] Worst of all the rule might let in VADs who were 'trained' in military hospitals. The Register was not to be flooded with such women.[2]

The College of Nursing considered this question and advocated the acceptance of existing nurses on their credentials.[3] In March 1923 the Ministry intervened with a tactful letter to the General Nursing Council. First it drew the Council's attention to the strong representations that had been made that VADs might be allowed on the Register through the existing rule, though 'the Minister understands that in fact no such intention has ever been entertained by the Council'. The letter continued:

> The Minister is not unmindful that the intention of Parliament was undoubtedly that existing nurses should be admitted on the most generous terms compatible with the due protection of the public; and he entirely shares what he takes to be the feeling of the Council that the application of the existing rules may result in injustice to individuals whose right to registration would be generally admitted by the nursing profession.[4]

The Council had been warned.

In March 1923 (four months before the Register was due to close) it decided to extend its definition of an existing nurse to include nurses who were '*bona fide*' engaged in practice both at 1 November 1919 and prior to 1 January 1900, subject to 'such special evidence of knowledge and experience as may be accepted by the Council in each individual case'.[5] In other words, nurses engaged in practice in the nineteenth century were to be admitted on their merits. VADs were kept out by a wide margin 'concerning the possible admission of whom there was apparently considerable apprehension'.[6]

The critics were not satisfied. The London centre of the College of Nursing pointed out 'that it is rather unfair to admit a woman with one year's training in a tiny hospital and two years' practice and to refuse a woman with a shorter training and 19 years' practice'.[7] No provision was made for the nurse with three years' training at a good special hospital and experience at

---

[1] *NT*, 16 December 1922, p. 1226.

[2] *Ibid.*, 23 December 1922, p. 1249.

[3] *Ibid.*, 10 March 1923, p. 220.   [4] *Ibid.*, 24 March 1923, p. 274.

[5] *Ibid.*, p. 274.

[6] *Ibid.*, p. 274.   [7] *Ibid.*, 31 March 1923, p. 289.

a general hospital.[1] A correspondent wrote to the *Nursing Times* : 'I am only one of hundreds too young to have been nursing before 1900, and too old to have trained since 1919.'[2] Miss Herbert wrote to say that state registration was becoming 'little more than a dead letter'. There would be 'a large body of practising unregistered nurses, a serious drag on progress in the profession, both educationally and economically'.[3]

When the new rule reached the House of Commons, two amendments were proposed to it. One put down by Lt-Col. Fremantle proposed to change the date of *bona fide* service from 1 June 1900 to 1 January 1910—a more exact method of keeping out VADs. The other amendment proposed by Dr Chapple was more far-reaching.

The Council may accept for registration upon the first register of nurses any applicant who presents—

(*a*) a certificate of good character;

(*b*) a certificate signed by a matron of a general hospital, or an infirmary, or by two medical men setting out that the applicant has been in attendance upon the sick in the capacity of a nurse for a period of not less than three years prior to November 1st 1919; and

(*c*) a certificate signed by a registered nurse and two medical men, one of whom shall be on the staff of a general hospital, setting out that the applicant has adequate knowledge and experience of medical and surgical nursing and is competent to attend upon the sick in the capacity of a nurse.

Provided that the Council may require the applicant as a condition precedent to registration to present herself for special inquiry before a medical officer or officers appointed by the Council.[4]

It should be noted that this amendment was only to apply to female general nurses—not to men or applicants for the supplementary parts of the Register.

In May 1923 the Parliamentary Medical Committee received deputations from the General Nursing Council and the College of

---

[1] On this last question it was the view of the General Nursing Council that 'nurses who, since 1900, had entered private nursing homes for training had deliberately refused to accept the standard that had been universally accepted by the profession'. (*Ibid.*, p. 313.)

[2] *Ibid.*, 21 April 1923, p. 407.   [3] *Ibid.*, p. 407.

[4] General Nursing Council for England and Wales: *Rules and Schedules to the Rules* (1950), p. 14.

Nursing, and heard also the views of Miss Herbert. In the *British Journal of Nursing*, Mrs Bedford Fenwick sounded what she called 'the trumpet call to arms'.[1] She warned registered nurses of the danger which threatened 'not only their professional status but their economic conditions . . . the Register of Nurses might be flooded with VADs, Village Nurses, and Cottage Nurses . . . women who could and should have trained and who shirked doing so during the past 23 years and who have in private homes and otherwise victimised the sick by their ignorance'.[2] 'Are the Registered nurses going to submit to this outrage like dumb, driven cattle, or are they going to appeal to the King in Council and seek redress?'[3]

A debate took place in the House of Commons on 13 June 1923. In support of his motion, Dr Chapple quoted several cases of nurses at present holding senior appointments who were not by the present definition eligible for registration. Other nurses were finding themselves unable to apply for various nursing appointments because they were not on the Register. 'That condition of affairs is going to be increased. In five or six years' time in all probability a nurse who is not on the Register will find it practically impossible to gain a livelihood.'[4] The Minister of Health's defence of the General Nursing Council was not very strong.[5] 'Many of these nurses do not consider that the certificate of a medical man is the best certificate of the competence of a nurse.' Nurses already on the Register would have imposed on them 'a large number whom they do not consider as being of the right stamp'.[6]

By a free vote of the House, Dr Chapple's amendment was adopted. Parliament had taken the questionable step of handing over to a body, composed largely of interested parties, the right to confer a status which might well bring with it economic advantages. By attempting to be restrictive with the granting of this status, the General Nursing Council was deliberately demoting many practising nurses. Parliament did not at this time hesitate to overrule the decisions of the creature it had so recently created, and rose to protect the liberties of the under-

---

[1] *BJN*, 5 May 1923, pp. 275–6.
[2] *Ibid.*, 12 May 1923, p. 299.   [3] *Ibid.*, 2 June 1923, p. 342.
[4] Dr Salter: *H of C Deb.*, 13 June 1923, col. 632.
[5] Mr Neville Chamberlain was at this time Minister of Health.
[6] *H of C Deb.*, 13 June 1923, col. 635.

privileged. It was one of those rare tributes to the working of the British parliamentary system.

The General Council met two days later 'in a state of some bewilderment. . . . Members were indignant that their decision should have been over-ridden.'[1] Parliament had intervened to assert the intentions of the Act. As the *Nursing Times* remarked, this was 'a grave blow to the prestige of the General Nursing Council. . . . To speak plainly [it] has been told that it has failed to appreciate the duty delegated to it.'[2]

In an interview with the *Nursing Times*, Dr Chapple gave his reasons for acting as he did.

I want to say frankly that if the Nursing Council had made a reasonable rule that met the case, if they had interpreted the Act properly, we should not have touched the matter at all. We did not want to interfere. But the Act has not been properly interpreted. The Council and the College misled the nurses; to act as they did, to be narrow and to refuse to play fair is the thing that degrades the profession, and not the admission of *bona fide* workers. To refuse a good nurse because she trained in a nursing home or a special hospital, never dreaming she would be under a disability, was cruel and inconsistent and is not the view and intention of the great body of nurses, who have been put in a false position. Twenty years' practice was an absurd demand, and the other rule demanding one year's training in a general hospital was ridiculous and in fact calculated to lower the standard. What nurse had one year's training? If she left after one year it was probably because she was delicate or unsuitable or because she had spent so much of that year in doing ward maid's work that she didn't care to go on. Till recently nearly the whole of the first year was spent in scrubbing and polishing—is that a nursing qualification?[3]

The rules had been amended only one month before the Register for existing nurses was due to close. In this last month applications for registration almost overwhelmed the General Nursing Council. In the last six weeks 12,000 applications were received of which 4,345 came in the last week and 1,170 on the last day. In total 40,451 applications were received.[4] This was substantially less than the 70,000 or 80,000 expected to register when the bill was debated in Parliament.

While the House of Commons had decided that existing nurses

[1] *NT*, 23 June 1923, p. 599.   [2] *Ibid.*, 14 July 1923, p. 665.
[3] *Ibid.*, 28 July 1923, p. 716.   [4] *Ibid.*, p. 710.

were to be admitted to the Register even though they had not been trained, the Nursing Council laid it down that all other nurses would only be admitted to the Register if they had been trained in an approved training school. This raised the question of defining such a school. At first the Council decided to refuse approval to any hospital or infirmary which had not got a resident medical officer. This was intended as a rough-and-ready test of whether there were enough acute cases for nurses to gain experience.[1] When the rule was sent to the Minister of Health, the Council was told that 'it was not competent to them to make any rule limiting their discretion in dealing with individual applications'.[2] The Council had to consider each application on its merits. The actual decisions taken by the Council led to complaints that they were increasing the difficulties of smaller hospitals in obtaining probationers and generally adding to their financial problems.[3]

The arrangements for the actual training to be undertaken in the approved schools also led to some difference of view between the General Nursing Council and the Minister of Health. The Council proposed to publish not only a syllabus showing in detail the subject-matter on which new entrants to the profession would be examined, but also a syllabus of lectures and demonstrations for education and training. The syllabus of training was to be compulsory for all training schools. Three times the Council sent this forward to the Minister requesting him to make it a statutory rule. But the Council was met with what Mrs Bedford Fenwick called 'absolutely determined and persistent opposition'.[4] The state examination was deferred from 1923 to 1924 and then again from 1924 to 1925.[5]

Eventually the Council decided to make the syllabus of training advisory only. It was drawn up 'in the hope that it may aid the training schools in arriving at a general standard of nursing education'.[6] This controversy was one of the questions considered by the Select Committee on the General Nursing Council (1925) and the Committee upheld the views of the Minister

---

[1] *NT*, 16 September 1922, p. 1881.
[2] *H of C Deb.*, 10 May 1923, cols. 2605-6.
[3] *Ibid.*, 20 June 1923, col. 1423.
[4] *Select Committee on the General Nursing Council 1925*, p. 24.
[5] *H of C Deb.*, 25 April 1923, cols. 463-4.
[6] See *Select Committee on the General Nursing Council 1925*, p. vi.

of Health. The syllabus should not be made compulsory. The Committee feared that the difficulties of small hospitals 'in supplying an adequate training in competition with the larger and better equipped hospitals would be increased, and consequently their supply of nurses, already short, might tend to become still further reduced'.[1]

In 1925 the first state examination was held, and the first 4,005 nurses were admitted to the Register by examination. The inaugural work of the General Nursing Council was complete. The Council had been controlled by nurses from the voluntary hospitals who had sought to restrict entry to the Register. Their behaviour had a parallel in the history of the teachers. Control over the registration of teachers had been vested in a Council, the majority of whose members came from secondary and private schools.[2] Though the secondary school teachers had been unable to exclude elementary teachers they had devised for them an unauthorized second column in the Register, a distinction which Parliament intervened to remove.[3]

Nearly every major decision in implementing the Nurses Registration Act was taken not by the General Nursing Council but by the Minister of Health or the House of Commons. Parliament intervened to preserve the rights of unqualified nurses. The Minister refused to enforce the recommended syllabus of training. Though the profession had been prevented from setting its standards as high as it had wished, the critical problem for at least thirty years ahead was still the shortage of trained nurses.

[1] *Ibid.*, p. vi.
[2] Baron: 'The Teachers' Registration Movement': *British Journal of Educational Studies*, May 1954, p. 136.   [3] *Ibid.*, p. 141.

CHAPTER VIII

Registration and the Shortage of Nurses

A REGISTER of nurses had been established, and regulations had been made to decide who should be admitted to it. A body elected by nurses had been set up to govern the affairs of the profession. After thirty years of agitation the profession had got what it wanted.

The profession had preserved the 'one portal' system of entry as the term was understood in nursing circles. This did not, however, mean that there was only one nursing qualification. There were in fact six separate parts of the Register each with their own training programme. In addition to the general part of the Register, which was only open to females, there was a male part, and parts for children's nursing, fever nursing, mental nursing, and mental deficiency nursing. This meant in practice that there were major restrictions on the mobility of nurses from one field to another. For example, if a registered children's nurse wanted to take up general nursing she had to take two further years of training. If a general nurse wanted to take up mental nursing, she also had to take two more years of training. And there were no means available for a man to be admitted to the general Register which had the highest status. When the women obtained power, they used it to discriminate against men. It was, for example, impossible for a man to become a member of the leading association of his profession—the College of Nursing.

Those who had advocated registration so fervently during the 'thirty years' war' had made extensive claims about the effect it would have on the supply of probationers and on the general standard of nursing—particularly for the higher income groups. If a sharp line were drawn between the qualified and the unqualified, it was hoped that responsible nursing work—if not all nursing work—would increasingly be done by trained women.

IX. Miss Thorold
Matron of the Middlesex
Hospital

X. Miss Burt
Matron of Guy's Hospital

XII. Mrs Bedford Fenwick
—attired for a suffragette procession

XI. (*left*) Miss Ethel Gordon Manson

XIII. Conversazione of the British Nurses' Association at the
Grosvenor Gallery, Bond Street

This in turn would raise the status of the profession and attract more 'superior' women to take the training.[1]

Among those who had opposed registration were the representatives of the small hospitals. They had feared a 'drying up of the sources whence they derive their probationers'.[2] This would involve financial difficulties as the work would have to be done by qualified nurses or unqualified nurses at similar rates of pay. This would be much more expensive. In addition it had been asserted that 'the only nurses who can hope directly to derive substantial benefit from the measure are the "birds of doubtful plumage" . . . those who cannot show the hallmarks of a first-class training. It may happen that the letters R N after their names will make them eligible for public appointments from which they have hitherto been debarred.'[3]

Very soon after Parliament had passed the Registration Act, the central problem facing the hospitals and the public was the shortage of nurses. The Registration Act, as mentioned earlier, was considered by Parliament at the only fleeting moment in the century when there appeared to be not only enough nurses but even a possible surplus. At the beginning of the century there had been a shortage of trained nurses, and in the small voluntary hospitals and poor law institutions there had been a shortage of suitable probationers. This situation, or at least a similar one, reasserted itself soon after the war.

By the summer of 1920, there were editorials, letters, and special articles in the nursing press regretting the shortage of nurses and suggesting reasons for it. The small voluntary hospitals were employing girls who were impatient to start nursing work and were not prepared to wait until they were old enough to enter a proper training school. They also took 'the rejects' from the training schools and a number of older women who wanted a short if unrecognized general training. The small hospitals also found it difficult to get staff nurses, and even some of the larger hospitals with proper training schools could not get as many as they would have liked. Similarly, even poor law

---

[1] According to their critics, the registrationists had claimed too much. 'For every ill', a correspondent wrote to the *Hospital*, 'their panacea is a register of nurses at Westminster. I sometimes wonder if they ever thought of sending their prescription to Messrs Lenin and Trotsky.' (21 June 1919, p. 292.) [2] *Ibid.*, 1 February 1919, p. 384.
[3] *Ibid.*, 6 December 1919, p. 214.

unions with separate infirmaries could not get trained nurses; they advertised for assistant nurses and partially trained women offering much the same salary as a trained nurse would require.[1] There was also a shortage of district nurses in the rural areas. The demobilized VADs had not gone to train for country work.[2]

Complaints about the shortage of nurses continued throughout the twenties and thirties. In 1921, a speaker at the Central Conference of Poor Law Guardians complained of the shortage and regretted 'that it had not been possible to get into touch with the VAD members before disbandment'.[3] In 1922, we find women's organizations pressing for the appointment of a Select Committee.[4] In the next year it was even being suggested that assistant nurses and probationers unable to complete their training should be employed in the infirmaries under the direction of trained nurses,[5] though such a proposal was as yet quite unacceptable to the professional associations. In 1925, the Minister of Health was questioned about the nursing shortage in the House of Commons.[6] And in the same year the Select Committee on the General Nursing Council heard complaints about the shortage from the matrons of smaller provincial hospitals.[7]

The shortage of nurses was the subject of two major inquiries in the inter-war period—one official and one unofficial. In December 1930, the *Lancet* appointed a commission 'to inquire into the reasons for the shortage of candidates, trained and untrained, for nursing the sick in general and special hospitals throughout the country, and to offer suggestions for making the service more attractive to women suitable for this necessary work'.[8] And in 1937, the Government appointed the Athlone Committee with wider terms of reference.[9] The information collected by these inquiries will be drawn on in this chapter and Chapters VIII and IX.

The shortage of nurses in the twenties must be seen against the background of a continuous and substantial increase in the number of persons who stated they were nurses at the decennial

---

[1] *NT*, 29 May 1920, p. 1322.   [2] *Ibid.*, 13 November 1920, p. 620.
[3] *Ibid.*, 25 February 1921, p. 178.   [4] *BJN*, 29 July 1922, p. 68.
[5] *NT*, 13 January 1923, p. 25.   [6] *H of C Deb.*, 19 July 1925, col. 963.
[7] *Report from the Select Committee on the General Nursing Council* (167), 6 August 1925, pp. 42, 45, 49. Mrs Bedford Fenwick attributed the shortage to indifference upon the part of young womanhood to this humanitarian work', p. 26.   [8] *Lancet Commission on Nursing*, p. 7: London, 1932.
[9] See pp. 145–6.

censuses of population. Including mental nurses, there were in 1901 about 63,500 female nurses; by 1921 there were 111,501 female nurses, and by 1931 the number had risen to 138,670.[1] In thirty years the total of female nurses had more than doubled. The expansion was fairly even for each decade. Between 1901 and 1911, the number of women in the profession increased by 20,000 and twenty years later a further 54,000 nurses were reported in the census. Registration did not seem to have led to an unprecedented expansion in the number of nurses at work, though the growth of the profession continued to be substantial.

The number of male nurses also increased. The census of population of 1901 reported that there were about 6,000 male nurses: by 1921 there were over 11,000 and by 1931 over 15,000.[2] The field for their employment was still almost exclusively in the mental hospitals and as mental nurses in domiciliary practice. Their only firm niche in the general hospitals was to look after male patients with venereal diseases. The prejudice against men arose from feminism and snobbery, and probably also from deeper sexual taboos.[3] Even in 1937, there were less than 100 male nurses at work in the voluntary hospitals. The local authorities showed less bias: some of them were deliberately opening up training facilities for men, but in 1937 all the authorities in England and Wales only employed a total of about 1,500 male nurses, most of whom were unqualified.[4] There were however about twice the number of male nurses being trained in non-mental hospitals in 1937 as in 1933; but even in this latter year, the total was not much more than a hundred.[5]

The training of the average nurse had greatly improved. At the beginning of the century, Burdett estimated that only about 25,000 nurses had had some sort of training, though probably only 10,000 of them would have satisfied Miss Nightingale.[6] When the Register for existing nurses was closed in 1925, there were presumably some 120,000 women who considered themselves to be nurses. Of these about 28,000 had satisfied the fairly stiff requirements of the General Nursing Council before the

---

[1] See Appendix I, p. 257.   [2] See Appendix I.

[3] It may have been feared that male nurses would prove harder to order around, or that they would upset the chastity thought appropriate for the females who had been 'called' to nursing, or worse still that some might prove to be homosexual.   [4] See Appendix II, Table 3.

[5] See Appendix II, Table 3.   [6] See p. 57 above.

Chapple amendment made it easier for existing nurses to be enrolled. The Register included a number of retired nurses: Mrs Bedford Fenwick herself was registered though she had retired from nursing many years earlier. On the other hand there were many nurses who valued registration so little that they did not even apply. Others had been advised by their matrons not to register on the grounds that nothing could add to the reputation of the certificate issued by the hospital which was known throughout the world. Many unregistered nurses were highly qualified.[1] It seems likely that at the very least a third of the 120,000 nurses in 1925 had had one year's training in a hospital of which the General Nursing Council would have approved. Certainly the majority had had some sort of training in the sense in which Burdett had used the term.[2]

The members of the profession were gradually conforming to the stereotype created by the introduction of training and the insistence on 'living in'. The proportion of elderly widows and married women among those who told the Census enumerators that they were nurses or midwives declined sharply. In 1901 the Census figures showed that only 55 per cent of female nurses and midwives were single.[3] In 1921 single women had risen to 84 per cent of the total, and in 1931 to 88 per cent. Thus by 1931 only 5 per cent of nurses were married and 7 per cent were widowed or divorced. The average nurse was getting younger. While the total number of nurses had increased, about the same number of women aged 55–64 said they were nurses at both the 1901 and the 1931 censuses (about 11,000). The number of nurses aged 65 and over actually fell between 1901 and 1931 from about 6,000 to about 3,500.[4]

All this indicated the decline of the old type of nurse. Nursing had been an occupation which provided a home and an income for the bereaved. And many married women in the villages used to 'watch the sick' and assist at confinements for a very small

[1] *Nursing Homes, Select Committee Report, 1926* (103) vii, pp. 123 and 124.

[2] In 1927 it was suggested by the *Nursing Times* that there were 100,000 trained nurses 'in this country'. Even allowing for those working outside England and Wales, this figure seems rather high. See *NT*, 12 February 1927, p. 166.

[3] This figure is not strictly comparable with those given for later years. See Appendix I, pp. 258–9.

[4] The figures used for 1901 in these comparisons probably understate the true position. See Appendix I.

fee. It was now less common for nursing to be a casual source of income for the middle-aged and elderly. The average age of patients in hospital was probably increasing. The average age of the nurses responsible for their care declined.

The introduction of training had made it extremely hard for a widow to enter the profession. She could not subsist on the low pay received during training if she had family responsibilities, nor could she live on the hospital premises. The living-in system also tended to keep out women whose husbands were still alive. In addition, there was an unspoken prejudice against married women. Nursing was thought of as a calling which must come before husband and family and which demanded the renunciation of bodily temptations. There may also have been some matrons who would have felt insecure in their relationships with married women.

The expansion of the nursing profession should be seen against the demographic background of the first thirty years of the century. The population was increasing. The number of women aged 15–64 increased from 10·7 million in 1901 to 14·4 million in 1931—an increase of 35 per cent, while the number of nurses increased by 116 per cent.[1] Marriage took much the same proportion of women in the younger age-groups and a somewhat higher proportion of women in the older age-groups. Thus the number of single women aged 15–64 increased between 1901 and 1931 somewhat less than the total of women, from 4·5 million to 5·4 million—an increase of 20 per cent. On the other hand the proportion of single women with jobs was on the increase. Taking the age-group 25–64[2] the number of occupied single women increased from about 1·1 million to about 1·7 million—an increase of 54 per cent. The proportion of occupied women who were engaged in nursing increased substantially.

Although there had been a rapid expansion in the number of nurses and a higher proportion of women were engaged in the work, the demand increased still more. The demand for nurses is partly a product of standards of living and partly a product of the system of medical care, and both had changed considerably since the beginning of the century. There had been substantial developments in the potentialities of medicine, particularly in surgery. Hospitals were no longer the last resort of the sick poor;

[1] The figures given in this paragraph are taken from Appendix I.
[2] Comparable figures for the age-group 15–24 are not available.

the prospects of discharge had improved. And the new panel doctors were sending patients to hospitals to undergo definitive courses of treatment. Dread of admission to hospital remained among the older sections of the population and in the rural areas, but the younger generation was beginning to accept and even demand in-patient care for a variety of conditions.

As more acute sickness was treated in hospital, a higher proportion of the nursing profession was required for hospital work. The increase in turnover, the development of more complicated treatments, the need to teach these procedures to probationers on and off the wards, and the growth of specialized out-patient departments, all added to the demand for hospital nurses. In addition there was pressure to reduce the number of hours on duty to take account of the physical strain of nursing work. If this demand were wholly resisted, nurses might become 'trade union minded'.[1] On the other hand, any concession in this direction made it necessary to employ yet more nurses.

At the beginning of the century there must have been about 11,000 nurses working for the voluntary hospitals.[2] By 1937 there were over 33,000.[3] The nursing staff had been multiplied by about three, while the number of beds provided had increased about half as much.[4] The number of nurses actually engaged on hospital work increased even more than these figures indicate. In 1900, quite a number of hospital nurses were sent out to do domiciliary work, and although this system was still to be found in 1937, the proportion of hospital nurses engaged in it was much smaller. Moreover, by the late thirties it had become quite common for hospitals faced with a shortage of nurses to engage nurses from the co-operatives to work in the wards.[5]

The expansion in the nursing departments of voluntary hospitals was completely overshadowed by the much greater expansion that occurred in the poor law hospitals. More nurses had to be employed if treatment was to be provided which could be compared with that of the hospitals in which the doctors and many of the matrons had been trained. Not only had the number

[1] See Chapter VIII.

[2] See pp. 51–52 above. 16,000 less roughly 5,000 working in poor law institutions.   [3] Appendix II, Table 3, p. 271.

[4] There were 39,184 occupied beds reported in the census of 1901 and about 62,000 in 1937 manned by the nursing staff of over 33,000.

[5] Such nurses received higher pay which naturally caused friction with the regular staffs.

of staff to be increased but in addition the remaining pauper helpers had to be replaced with trained staff. In 1901 there were about 3,200 paid nurses and about 2,000 probationers in all the poor law institutions in England and Wales.[1] In addition there must have been several thousand pauper helpers. By 1937 the local authority hospitals (as many had become) and poor law institutions had about 27,000 female nurses and 13,000 probationers—a total of about 40,000 nurses.[2] In thirty-seven years the paid nursing staffs multiplied nearly eightfold. Better accommodation, shorter hours and higher pay all helped to recruit the larger number of nurses. While the voluntary hospitals were in continuous financial difficulties throughout the inter-war period, the local authorities were able to attract nurses by measures which cost money.

At the beginning of the century, nurses had received much the same pay in both the local authority and voluntary hospital sectors. At the end of the war, voluntary hospitals tended to give slightly better pay than the poor law hospitals.[3] But during the twenties, the pay given to nurses in the poor law service became higher than that paid in the voluntary hospitals. This can be shown in rough average figures for the different types of hospital. In 1930 the pay of probationers in voluntary hospitals was on average about £20 in the first year, £25 in the second year, and £30 in the third year; while the municipal hospitals paid £29, £33, and £40 respectively.[4] In 1937 the pay in the voluntary hospitals was much the same as in 1930, but the local authorities paid a still higher rate to probationers: £33, £38, and £41 in the first three years of training.[5] In 1930 staff nurses in complete training schools started on £52–£55 in voluntary hospitals and £61 in municipal hospitals. By 1937 both groups of hospitals had improved the rates of pay of staff nurses but the local authorities still offered £5 more than the voluntary hospitals. All these rates of pay represent what nurses received in cash. In addition, they were provided with free board and lodging.

[1] P. 51.   [2] Appendix II, Table 3.
[3] See College of Nursing: *Report of the Salaries Committee*, pp. 19–25: London 1919.
[4] *Lancet Commission Report 1932*, p. 235. These figures have been estimated from calculations made on the basis of information given by the Commission.
[5] Appendix II, p. 276.

Both in 1930 and 1937, nurses employed in local authority hospitals worked shorter hours than in voluntary hospitals. There are figures for 1930 for complete training schools. In the voluntary hospitals nurses worked about 117 hours a fortnight in London and 119 hours a fortnight in the provinces, but in municipal hospitals the hours were only 113 per fortnight.[1] A similar advantage for all local authority hospitals existed in 1937.[2]

The drive to improve the medical care provided in local authority institutions received particular impetus from the Local Government Act (1929) which transferred the control of the poor law hospitals from the Boards of Guardians to the Counties and County Boroughs. The plan which Miss Nightingale had outlined for London sixty-five years earlier was implemented all over the country, though some of the bodies which had become responsible for the poor law hospitals were not large enough to be able to provide proper services. Great improvements were made in some of the institutions which were taken over, but progress varied greatly with the will and wealth of different authorities. The scope of the services was extended, more accommodation was provided, and the standards of staffing were improved. Indeed it seems that the nursing staffs of hospitals and institutions outside London increased by over 50 per cent in ten years.[3] The developments in London were spectacular and are described in some detail in the official history of the London County Council.

In October 1935, the Council introduced a revised standard of staffing in twelve out of the twenty-seven acute general hospitals, and brought the remaining fifteen hospitals into line in April 1936. This necessitated an increase of 100 sisters and 500 staff nurses and student

---

[1] These figures are based on information in the *Lancet Commission Report 1932*, p. 248.   [2] Appendix II, p. 277.

[3] The Society of Medical Officers of Health sent out a questionnaire to 53 County Boroughs, 23 Administrative Counties and the Welsh Memorial Association. 'This showed that there had been an increase in the establishments of trained nurses and probationers in general, fever and tuberculosis hospitals from an approximate figure of 9,150 in 1928–29 (before the operation of the Local Government Act) to one of 13,900 in 1938. Similarly in the case of the Surrey County Council hospitals, excluding the mental hospitals, the number of nursing staff had increased from 369 in 1930 to over 700 in 1938.' See Ministry of Health, Board of Education, *Interdepartmental Committee on Nursing Services, Interim Report* (Committee Chairman: the Rt Hon. the Earl of Athlone), p. 16: HMSO, 1939.

nurses. The hours of duty for all nurses were fixed at 54 per week, inclusive of a two hours' study period for student nurses. . . . The Council also introduced a uniform three weeks' preliminary training course for new entrants into general training; later this was increased to one month. . . . In 1938 the special hospitals and those for the chronic sick had their staff increased and the principle of a 96-hours' fortnight was introduced into all hospitals.[1]

One method used by the hospitals—particularly the voluntary hospitals—to recruit more probationers was to lower the age at which they were admitted for training. There was always a fear that a high age of admission would lose suitable candidates to other occupations which could be entered at an earlier age.[2] As Mrs Bedford Fenwick put it, 'we wanted the pick of the basket, not the leavings'.[3] Even as early as 1922 some hospitals were accepting girls at the age of 18, though 20 or 21 was probably the usual age at this time. By 1931 the most usual minimum age of admission was 19 in complete training schools and 18 elsewhere. About a tenth of the hospitals admitted probationers under 18.[4] By 1937 even more hospitals were admitting probationers to ward duty before this age.[5]

The effect of the earlier age of admission to nursing work can also be seen from the census figures. Between 1921 and 1931 the number of single women engaged in nursing (including mental nursing) increased from about 94,000 to 122,000—an increase of 30 per cent. Between the same years the number of single female nurses under 25 increased from nearly 26,000 to about 45,000— an increase of 65 per cent.[6] The physical and psychological needs of mature men and women were being dealt with in hospital by young unmarried girls. And at an early age, girls were being faced with the emotional strains of suffering and death.

The effect of the registration of nurses upon the hospitals was to continue and accelerate developments which had been in progress since the nursing revolution in the middle of the nineteenth century. The trained nurse was given precedence over the un-trained nurse, and now training could be judged by whether or not a nurse was registered. Thus, given the ever-expanding

---

[1] London County Council: *The LCC Hospitals, A Retrospect*, pp. 84–85: London, 1949.   [2] *Lancet Commission Report 1932*, p. 141.
[3] *NT*, 2 October 1920, p. 1155.
[4] *Lancet Commission Report 1932*, p. 221.   [5] See Appendix II, p. 274.
[6] See Appendix I, p. 264.

demand, the shortage of nurses was partly the result of higher standards being demanded of women appointed to do the more responsible work in the hospitals. The shortage of probationers was of a similar character. Before registration, hospitals could adjust the standards demanded of their probationers to the standard of those applying for training. The hospitals with firm reputations could be highly selective while the small voluntary hospitals in the provinces and the poor law institutions had to take what they could get. After registration, the very small hospitals which the General Nursing Council did not approve for training purposes could not take in any *bona fide* probationers at all. Those hospitals which were approved, on the other hand, should have only admitted applicants who stood a reasonable prospect of passing the national examination. Some of the approved hospitals admitted probationers who had little prospect of ever passing the examination even if the training had been well conducted. About 40 per cent of the candidates failed in the final examination.[1]

The General Nursing Council was anxious to raise standards of nurse training, and to stop girls being taken on as probationers by hospitals which used them as 'pairs of hands' and could not or would not provide proper training. The formal powers vested in the Council enabled it to conduct the national examination, and to approve hospitals for training purposes, though any aggrieved hospital had a right of appeal to the Minister of Health. The national examination started in 1925 and was carefully controlled, but the power to deny approval to training schools proved rather ineffective.

Inevitably the withdrawal of approval as a training school was resented by both the management and the matron of the hospital concerned. For the matron it involved a loss of status and acute difficulties over staffing. For the management it involved heavy cost as the work which probationers had formerly done would have to be undertaken by nurses and domestics on higher rates of pay. Thus when in 1927 the General Nursing Council tried to withdraw approval from the Hastings Borough Sanatorium, which had only fifteen occupied beds, the Hastings Town Council appealed to the Minister who overruled the Council's decision.[2] The General Nursing Council was incensed at the time but

---

[1] *Lancet Commission Report 1932*, pp. 34–35.
[2] *NT*, 26 November 1927, p. 1401.

became more cautious in the future. The Council did not wish to be humiliated again.

The powers given to the Council were not used as skilfully as they could have been. Much could have been achieved in the improvement of nurse training by advice and persuasion and by threats of withdrawing approval. For these means to be used effectively, the Council needed an efficient paid staff of inspectors. Such a staff was not created until after the second world war. In the inter-war period, the task of inspection was left in the hands of the members of the Council, many of whom were very busy people and not all of whom had the personal qualities required for this sort of manipulation. The number of candidates who failed in their examinations continued to be large. The Council's rather clumsy answer to this problem was to introduce in 1937 an educational test for probationers starting training.

The expansion in the demand for trained nurses did not only come from the hospitals. More nurses were needed for work in clinics and in the home. Although the state had introduced the voluntary registration of nurses, it was not the policy of the Ministry of Health in the twenties to put any pressure on local authorities to employ only registered nurses or restrict their grants to bodies that employed trained nurses. Indeed, this would have meant pressing 'the claims of the registered nurse as against the nurses who, for one reason or another, had not thought proper to register'.[1] The Ministry took the view that the public had the 'opportunity, if they cared to exercise it, of securing the services of people who had received a certain minimum training'.[2] Nevertheless local authorities increasingly tried to engage registered nurses. And in 1925 the Ministry of Health did lay down that from April 1928 no health visitor should be appointed who was not fully trained.

Early in the century, the typical training of a district nurse was said to be 'some six months in midwifery and for another six months in district work among the poor'.[3] Many of those who had taken up district nursing would have been unable to take an examination of the standard laid down by the General Nursing Council. On the other hand the Queen's Institute, which had been founded with the money subscribed to Queen

[1] *Select Committee on Nursing Homes 1926*, p. 7.
[2] *Ibid.*, p. 7.   [3] *Hospital*, 30 August 1919, p. 545.

Victoria's Jubilee, only supported trained nurses and the role of 'Queen's Nurses' was increasing rapidly. Gradually the lesser-trained village nurses and midwives came under the supervision of a Queen's nurse.[1] The growing proportion of registered nurses used on district work increased the general shortage of trained nurses.

These trends were increased by pressure from the nursing organizations. While the Ministry of Health was hesitant to press the claims of registered nurses, the leaders of the professional organizations were not. Indeed, they made it their business to try and secure that registered nurses were given precedence over those who had not registered. In every field the registered nurse must be employed in preference to the unregistered. The unqualified nurse should, if possible, be kept out of all nursing appointments. This was an admirable objective. But, given the requirements for state registration, it was sadly unrealistic.

In hospitals and in domiciliary work there was pressure to give the registered nurse every advantage. Thus, in 1927, we find the College of Nursing urging upon the Government the principle 'that the person in charge of nursing in the home be a qualified nurse'.[2] Nowhere did the intention to deny the unqualified nurse any role at all appear so nakedly as in the case of nursing homes. The registrar of the College of Nursing stated that nurses in nursing homes should all be trained nurses 'every one of them'.[3] Only grudgingly was a time limit conceded while the untrained left the field. The policy of the College was not only for the person in charge of a nursing home to be registered but eventually for no unregistered nurses to be employed.[4] The Select Committee on Nursing Homes accepted the recommendation that the person in charge should normally have to be a qualified nurse.[5]

After registration, therefore, the hospitals, the local authorities and the district nursing associations all clamoured to employ nurses who had been admitted to the Register. As a result, the shortage of well-trained nurses, which had always existed, became a subject of widespread comment. There were not enough

[1] G. B. Carter: *A New Deal for Nurses*, pp. 69–70: London, 1939.
[2] *NT*, 1 October 1927, p. 1135.
[3] *Select Committee on Nursing Homes 1926*, p. 196.
[4] *Ibid.*, pp. 39–40.   [5] *Ibid.*, p. xv.

registered nurses to go round. Those who were most successful in obtaining them were those who offered the status, pay, or type of work which were most attractive. Thus the trained nurses congregated in the larger hospitals and in district work, leaving unqualified nurses to fill up the gaps. These worked in the small voluntary hospitals, in the institutions for the chronic sick, in the smaller and less 'acute' nursing homes, and in private domiciliary practice.

The most militant group of registrationists had argued that registration would be of major benefit to the richer groups in the community. Instead of being attended, as was often the case, by unqualified private nurses, they would enjoy the attention of registered nurses. How far did this prophecy prove correct?

At least it is clear that the Registration Act failed to correct the abuses of domiciliary nursing. There were still in 1938, as there had been at the beginning of the century, agencies providing untrained nurses (some agencies provided both trained and untrained) and there were members of the public and doctors who did not always inquire about the qualifications of the women they were employing. Some doctors were said to be 'associated with unregistered nurses in private practice'.[1] It was still frequently the case that both trained and untrained received the same pay, and in general the level of remuneration was still higher than that provided in the hospitals.[2] There were still agencies which took high commissions on the earnings of the nurses they employed.[3]

Thus those who employed private nurses frequently got unsatisfactory service. The demand for them was, however, decreasing. By 1931 there was even talk of unemployment among them.[4] From 1900 onwards, and particularly after the first world war, the system of medical care for the richer section of the community had been undergoing a substantial change.

[1] *BJN*, March 1933, p. 57.

[2] A trained nurse in a high-class establishment such as Mrs Coward's Nursing Co-operation earned £140–£150 per year even after allowing for unemployment. Mrs Coward, who had 500 nurses in her agency, told the Athlone Committee that 'a good soldier can easily make £200 or so'. The General and Mental Nurses' Association which had nearly 300 nurses guaranteed £100 per year to female nurses. (Unpublished evidence to the Athlone Committee.)

[3] The General and Mental Nurses' Association took between 15 per cent and 20 per cent.   [4] *NT*, 22 October 1932, p. 1073.

The better-off patients had begun to buy institutional care in acute sickness, though private nurses were still employed for convalescence and chronic sickness. There were many reasons why in acute illness the 'sick-room' gave way to medical care away from home. The medical profession found it more convenient and more efficient to treat their patients in specialized institutions. For example, complex surgery could not conveniently be undertaken in a private house, and specialist departments were developing in the hospitals which could assist in the diagnosis and treatment of the patient. The provision of hospitals for wounded officers during the war accustomed many of the higher social classes to enter hospital.

The development of in-patient facilities for the higher social classes was among the most noticeable developments in the hospital system between the wars. It took two forms—the mushroom growth of nursing homes[1] and the admission of paying patients to voluntary hospitals. In the latter, the best medical care that was available could be provided and the payments made helped to ease the financial difficulties of these charitable institutions.[2] A substantial proportion of charitable funds was channelled into the building of new private wings for the benefit of the middle and upper classes.[3]

Between the censuses of 1921 and 1931, the number of patients in nursing homes and convalescent homes increased from 25,981 to 54,920.[4] Very few of them provided a standard of care which could be compared to that available in the pay-beds of the voluntary hospitals. The converted and specially built premises near the consulting rooms of the leaders of the medical profession were generally, though not always, well conducted. But the large houses adapted, or simply occupied for the purpose, by retired nurses in the fashionable areas of Britain, varied from the satisfactory to the scandalous. Some were run more in the spirit of Midas than Hippocrates. And one of the least satisfactory

[1] *Select Committee on Nursing Homes 1926*, p. 38.

[2] By 1927, 171 provincial hospitals were providing pay beds. See *NT*, 12 February 1927, p. 161.

[3] 'On May 12th at a festival dinner to celebrate the 75th anniversary of the West London Hospital, a vigorous appeal will be launched, the principal feature of which is a scheme for the relief of Hammersmith's middle classes in time of sickness.' (*Ibid.*, 31 January 1931, p. 111.)

[4] *Census of England and Wales 1921. General Tables*, p. 121: HMSO, 1925, and *Census of England and Wales 1931. General Tables*, p. 118: HMSO, 1935.

aspects of the nursing homes was the standard of the nursing staff. The worst of them provided neither the standard of work nor conditions of work which would attract trained nurses.[1] As the Select Committee on Nursing Homes put it, 'patients are frequently quite unaware that the uniformed individuals in charge of them are, in many cases, quite unqualified girls with no real training in their profession'.[2] And what enraged the professional associations, as it had twenty years earlier, was the fact that these unqualified women were paid much the same as qualified nurses were getting—£60 a year all found.[3] 'VADs and such people are paid the same amount as trained nurses' one witness told the Committee.[4]

The poorer sections of the community and also those wealthy persons who were wise enough to insist on the services of trained staff benefited from the registration of nurses. Those who gained least were the middle income groups who could only afford cheap nursing homes and did not enter the large hospitals either as paying patients or as members of the general public. Much depended on the type of case: the care of the acutely sick was undoubtedly improved, while the fate of the chronic sick may have been made worse. In general, the work of the General Nursing Council contributed to the gradual improvement of nurse training all over the country. But one major effect of registration was to bring out into the open and express in terms of unfilled vacancies or improperly filled posts what had always been true—that the number of trained women engaged in nursing work was less than was required.

---

[1] The accommodation was often very unsatisfactory. In one nursing home five nurses slept in one room. In another, a day nurse and a night nurse shared one bed. 'They are not even sure they have their own sheets; in fact you will find that the highest praise a nurse can give a Nursing Home is "I get my own sheets".' See *Select Committee on Nursing Homes 1926*, pp. 128 and 199.

[2] *Ibid.*, p. xiii.   [3] *Ibid.*, pp. 39 and 198.   [4] *Ibid.*, p. 197.

CHAPTER IX

Profession or Trade?

A S time went on the proceedings of the General Nursing
Council became less stormy. After 1925, when the major
policy decisions had been taken, it settled down to the routine of
conducting examinations and approving training schools.

As the time approached for the 1927 election to the General
Nursing Council, the coalition of powerful nursing associations
once again selected their candidates. The College of Nursing,
aided by a subsidy from Lady Cowdray, sent out circulars to
55,000 nurses, canvassing for their votes in support of the agreed
list. There were also 'independent' candidates, but Mrs Bedford
Fenwick herself decided not to stand for election. She stated
sadly that 'the majority of nurses in this kingdom are too ignorant
of the true conditions of nursing politics, and too subject to
economic control, and to financial patronage, to give a free
vote for candidates'.[1]

This did not mean that Mrs Fenwick had retired from nursing
affairs. On the contrary, although nearly 70, she continued to
devote her great energy to the organizations with which she was
connected—the Royal British Nurses' Association and the International Council of Nurses. In May 1926, an endowment of
£100,000 from an anonymous donor[2] led to the foundation of a
new organization, the British College of Nurses, with Dr Fenwick
as treasurer and Mrs Fenwick as president.[3] Both appointments
were for life and carried honoraria. Premises were purchased, a
pension fund was started, and members and fellows were elected
from every part of the British Empire.

The new college was intended as a rival to the College of
Nursing. This was realized by the matron of St Thomas's
Hospital (Miss Lloyd Still). When Mrs Bedford Fenwick wrote
asking for an opportunity to tell the nurses of St Thomas's about

[1] *BJN*, November 1927, p. 258.   [2] A grateful patient of Dr Fenwick's.
[3] *BJN*, September 1927, p. 222.

the new college, Miss Lloyd Still replied that such an opportunity would have to wait until the new body 'had proved its need and worth' and suggested that the new organization should combine with the College of Nursing which was 'devoted to similar aims'.[1] Mrs Fenwick rejected this proposal. The British College of Nurses was an organization controlled by nurses while the College of Nursing had lay and medical persons on its council. She had conveniently forgotten the heavy representation of doctors in the Council of the Royal British Nurses' Association. The old feud was still alive. Only two months before the Royal British Nurses' Association and its allies had actually petitioned the Privy Council not to grant the College of Nursing a Royal Charter.[2]

The British College of Nurses became Mrs Fenwick's main fighting force in the late twenties and it attracted many vocal supporters. Though the College of Nursing was always the predominant body, it regarded the British College as its main rival. But in the light of later history, it can be said that the most dangerous challenge to the power of the College came from another direction. There was talk throughout the twenties and thirties of the general nurses being formed into trade unions which would engage in collective bargaining, and even threaten strike action to improve pay and conditions of service. From time to time it looked superficially as if the older nursing organizations might ally with those who were trying to create nursing trade unions. Mrs Fenwick, although a very blue Tory, was prepared to form alliances with the Labour Party, but this was very different from trade union activity. Although she claimed to be the voice of the working nurses protesting against the tyranny of hospital managements, it was very much a vocational and professional voice. In the last analysis Mrs Fenwick regarded collective action in the full trade union sense as quite unworthy of a body of professional women.

The organization of nurses into trade unions started in the mental field. The National Asylum Workers' Union had been formed before the first world war. The first strike did not, however, occur until September 1918 when 200 employees went on strike at the Prestwich Asylum and 429 employees went on strike at the Wittingham Asylum. In the next month there was a five

[1] *Ibid.*, March 1927, p. 56.
[2] *Ibid.*, January 1927, p. 10. The case was heard on 29 February 1928.

days' strike of the female employees at the Bodmin Asylum.[1]
And in 1919 a strike was threatened in all the London asylums
unless a 48-hour week was granted.[2] The publicity given to
these events stimulated the formation of unions to include general
nurses.

The trade unions found it difficult to recruit general nurses.
Contrary to common belief, the fact that the vast majority of
general nurses were women was not in itself necessarily an
impossible obstacle. Women had been as willing as men to
join some clerical unions.[3] There were, however, a number of
special difficulties in organizing nurses in the hospital service:
the tradition of selfless devotion to the sick, the rapid turnover
of staff, the strong and close personal influence of the matron
who was the immediate representative of management. In
addition there was the opposition to strike action because it
would harm the patient and the evident fact that nearly all
hospitals were non-profit-making. But these were not the only
reasons. Membership of a trade union involves some measure of
sympathy and identification with the working-class movement.
Many nurses were ladies and many others had become nurses in
the hope that they would be regarded as such. Association with
working-class activities would have been in conflict with the
social aspirations of many members of the profession.

Trade union activity started and made more progress in the
local authority hospitals than in the voluntary hospitals. The
former were larger institutions, their nurses came from a lower
social background, and there was some evident source where the
money could come from to pay higher salaries. On 7 December
1918, the Poor Law Workers' Trade Union[4] was established in
an underground room in Holborn for all ranks in the poor law
service including nurses and doctors.[5] Under its constitution a

---

[1] *A History of the Mental and Institutional Workers' Union 1910–31*, pp. 22–24:
National Executive Council Publication, Manchester, 1931.

[2] *NT*, 5 April 1919, p. 305. The *Nursing Times* refused 'to believe that the
women nurses in our splendid asylums will strike and leave the patients
unattended'. It seemed to lack similar confidence in male nurses.

[3] D. Lockwood: *The Blackcoated Worker*, pp. 151–2: London, 1958.

[4] The Union changed its name soon afterwards to the Poor Law Officers'
Trade Union, and again in 1930 to the National Union of County Officers,
and at the end of the war to the Hospital and Welfare Services' Union, and
finally in 1946 became part of the Confederation of Health Service Employees.

[5] Information kindly supplied by Miss D. Westmacott (COHSE).

ballot was required to be held before a strike could take place. It was laid down that 'a sufficient number of officers shall be allowed to remain at their posts to attend to all urgent and necessitous cases subject to the consent of the Central Executive Committee'. Nevertheless it was a trade union. Within nine months it claimed 10,000 members of whom a quarter were said to be nurses.[1] Early in the next year, the Professional Union of Trained Nurses was founded, but a clause in its constitution laid down that no strike could be called.[2] By this time, also, the Poor Law Officers' Association had formed a nursing section. It was reported that 'the nurses had been joining very well'.[3]

An incident at the Brentford Institution in May 1921 indicates the beginnings of militant trade union activity among general nurses. A second-year student was summarily dismissed without notice for an alleged breach of discipline. A petition signed by 75 per cent of the nurses requesting her reinstatement led to further dismissals of the same character. The provincial secretary (Reg Crook[4]) of the Poor Law Officers' Trade Union addressed a mass meeting of representatives of 172 trade union branches in the area. A delegation was sent to the Board of Guardians only to be evicted by the police. The Board of Guardians were voted out in the next elections and a Union nominee became the new chairman of the Guardians. In 1923, the previous Guardians were held by the King's Bench Division to have been guilty of breach of contract when they dismissed the student without notice.

The Labour Party were not slow to try and associate the new trade unions, or at least nurses who were 'trade union minded', with the wider Labour movement. At the end of 1926 it issued a draft policy statement on the nursing profession. In many respects the policy proposed was close to the policy actually implemented under the National Health Service many years later. It advocated a 48-hour week, the separation of nurse training schools from hospitals, and student status for probationers with proper time for study.[5] But one paragraph read 'the only way in which nurses can deal effectively with their conditions, and exercise any sort of equality in bargaining power, is

[1] NT, 18 October 1919, p. 1081.   [2] Ibid., 1 May 1920, p. 521.
[3] The Poor Law Officers' Journal, 25 January 1918, p. 68.
[4] Created Lord Crook in 1947.
[5] NT, 5 February 1927, p. 140.

for the profession to be organized on Trade Union lines'.[1] This was anathema to the professional organizations.

The *Nursing Times*, by this time the official organ of the College of Nursing, attacked the Labour Party's report. It criticized 'the recommendation of an absurdly high salary for the nurse in training', and 'the insistence on authority being in the hands of committees rather than in those of responsible officers'[2] (such as matrons). Above all else it opposed the use of trade union methods by the nursing profession. It argued that the power of trade unions rested upon the threat of, or operation of, a strike (though existing trade unions for nurses had virtually ruled out such a possibility). In the case of nurses it said that a strike would be 'a betrayal of trust' . . . 'putting their own professional advantage before the needs of the people they served'. 'The need for organization had already been met by the establishment of the College of Nursing.'[3]

The Labour Party held a conference for nursing and other kindred organizations to consider the draft report. Mrs Bedford Fenwick and other nursing representatives attended. Ramsay MacDonald made a smooth opening speech. 'I am a tremendous believer in status', he said with more tact than Socialism.[4] When the conference got down to business, it became clear that the issue of trade unionism was the major barrier which would prevent the nursing representatives from supporting the report. Mrs Sidney Webb, who took the chair, sensed the feeling of the meeting and proposed that the words 'purely vocational' should be substituted for 'trade union' in the offending paragraph. According to Mrs Fenwick this was 'a touch of genius'.[5]

Thus the real challenge to the position of the College of Nursing in the twenties came from the growth of trade unionism among the nurses and the possible association of organizations opposed to the College with the wider Labour movement. The more militant spirit among the working nurses arose out of widespread dissatisfaction with pay and conditions of work. The College of Nursing had to concern itself with such matters if it was to claim to speak for the profession. Indeed neglect of such issues might result in the loss of its position as the supreme nursing organization. It was extremely difficult to see what

[1] *BJN*, February 1927, p. 27.   [2] *NT*, 11 December 1926, p. 1136.
[3] *Ibid.*, 18 December 1926, pp. 1165–6.
[4] *BJN*, February 1927, p. 43.   [5] *Ibid.*, p. 27.

could be done. Any large improvement in pay or reduction of hours would cost money, and it was quite clear that few of the voluntary hospitals could afford it while maintaining their existing services, let alone the extended services which new donations on capital account made possible.

All the College of Nursing felt it could do was to bring moderate and responsible pressure to bear on the hospital authorities—particularly on those who paid less than average rates or worked their nurses more than average hours. To do more than this would amount to a challenge to the whole basis of the voluntary hospital movement. For if substantially larger sums were to be found they could only come from public monies; and the voluntary hospitals would have been most unwilling to accept grants which were not in return for services rendered to public authorities. It was partly from this reasoning that the College also opposed any intervention by Parliament concerning the conditions of service of the nursing profession.

In the case of salaries, the College published recommended scales in the hope that hospitals would adopt them. While higher salaries were sought for trained staff, there was no demand for an increase in salaries for probationers. It was thought quite appropriate that the nurse in training should receive low pay. Thus in 1930 the College was recommending a scale starting at £20 and rising to £30 for the three years of training. On average this was the scale actually paid in voluntary hospitals during the thirties; on the other hand, as we have seen, the municipal hospitals were paying probationers substantially more.[1]

In 1937 the College made a clear statement to the Athlone Committee about why it did not recommend higher salaries for nurses in training.

The payment of high salaries to student nurses[2] is not recommended, as it is believed that this does not tend to attract the most suitable type of candidate. The College prefers to regard the nurse in training as a student preparing for a career, receiving professional training practically free of cost and being provided with her maintenance when in hospital together with a small salary. The value of board, lodging, tuition, and medical attention given to student nurses is not

---

[1] See p. 121 above.
[2] The practice of calling probationers 'student nurses' had by this time been adopted by the College and by many of the hospitals.

always realised by parents and guardians, who are apt to have regard only to the monetary return obtainable for services.[1]

This view of the appropriate salary for a probationer had been accepted seven years earlier by the Lancet Commission. 'The standards of the profession could not be maintained merely by an economic appeal.'[2] Evidence for the view that high salaries would attract unsuitable applicants was drawn from the experience of mental hospitals.

There is sometimes such a shortage of suitable candidates that the hospital authorities can exercise little selection, and the hospitals suffer from the presence of a number of women who do not undertake the work because they are interested in it, but because it offers an initial salary and emoluments better than any other open to them. Their presence may make it impossible to allow privileges which would be used and not abused by the good nurse. Their demeanour and their attitude to the work are likely to discourage a girl of good type from joining a service where they would be among her colleagues.[3]

Thus pressure for higher salaries was concentrated on the trained grades. In 1930 the minimum recommended for staff nurses was £62, and for ward sisters £80.[4] At that time the London voluntary hospitals on average paid staff nurses £52 and sisters £75, while the municipal hospitals did pay on average about the recommended starting salary.[5] This was probably more than a coincidence. If the College had recommended still higher salaries it would have widened the gap between what was paid in the two types of hospital. By 1937 the voluntary hospitals had raised the salaries of staff nurses and sisters to the level which the Royal College of Nursing had recommended in 1930.[6] But by this time, the College was pressing for still higher salaries. Its

---

[1] College of Nursing: *Memorandum relating to Conditions in the Nursing Profession for Submission to the Inter-Departmental Committee on the Nursing Services*, January 1938, p. 6. Mrs Bedford Fenwick had made the same point earlier in more colourful language. 'The commercialisation of nursing will not encourage the vocational woman to nurse the sick, and it is this humane type who "reacheth out her hand to the needy" who alone can realize the joys in it, and sun the sweet flower of our work into beneficence.' See *BJN*, March 1931, p. 57.   [2] *Lancet Commission Report 1932*, p. 166.

[3] *Ibid.*, 155–6.   [4] £85 in hospitals with over 100 beds.

[5] See the *Lancet Commission Report 1932*, p. 236, for the source of these estimates.   [6] See Appendix II, p. 276.

representatives told the Athlone Committee that 'every grade is in need of revision, especially those of staff nurse and ward sister'.[1]

The College also pressed hospital managements to introduce compulsory superannuation for nursing staff. By 1930, as the result of strong pressure from the trade unions, 95 per cent of the mental hospitals that trained nurses had compulsory superannuation schemes. Among the complete training schools for the General Register, 81 per cent of London voluntary hospitals and 68 per cent of municipal hospitals insisted on superannuation.[2] The position outside the training schools was less satisfactory. By 1937 about 63 per cent of *all* voluntary hospitals and 84 per cent of *all* municipal hospitals had compulsory superannuation schemes.[3]

The second major cause of complaint was the hours of work. There had been some improvement in this respect since the beginning of the century. At that time the 60-hour week of the Nightingale School was less than had been worked in many other hospitals: 70 hours were worked in the workhouses and at St Bartholomew's Hospital there was said to be an 84-hour week.[4] In 1919 an inquiry conducted by the College of Nursing suggested that hours varied between $52\frac{1}{2}$ and 71 hours per week for day duty, and between $59\frac{1}{4}$ and 84 hours per week for night duty.[5]

A move to reduce nursing hours to 48 per week started at the end of the war. By 1920 the London County Council had adopted, under trade union pressure, a 48-hour week for mental nurses and the Metropolitan Asylum Board had done the same for nurses other than mental.[6] Several Boards of Guardians had also adopted a 48-hour week. In 1919, the College of Nursing recommended 'an average week of 48 hours . . . as a maximum for all Nurses'.[7] Nevertheless as late as 1930 hours worked, as an average of all hospitals, were about 57 per week.[8]

---

[1] *College of Nursing Memorandum to Athlone Committee*, p. 7.

[2] *Lancet Commission Report 1932*, p. 238.   [3] See Appendix II.

[4] These figures are not really comparable with those available for the 1930's. It is not clear whether time spent in meals and otherwise not on active duty have been subtracted as in later figures.

[5] College of Nursing: *Report of the Salaries Committee*, p. 5.

[6] Its mental nurses worked a 50-hour week but had four weeks' holiday— two weeks more than the other nurses. See *NT*, 10 January 1920, p. 29.

[7] College of Nursing: *Report of the Salaries Committee*, p.6.

[8] *Lancet Commission Report 1932*, p. 248. (This estimate is derived from calculations made by the Commission.)

In a number of occupations hours were regulated by Acts of Parliament. It is therefore not surprising that there was talk of introducing legislation of this kind to apply to the nursing profession. In 1920, when there was talk of a bill to limit hours generally to 48 per week, the National Asylum Workers' Union was anxious that this limit should apply to the hours of asylum workers, and in October of the same year the Council resolved to ask the Minister of Health to introduce a special bill to limit the hours of nurses to 48 per week.[1] No action was taken. The next initiative came from a Labour member of Parliament; statutory regulation was to apply not only to hours but also to wages. In December 1930 Mr Fenner Brockway presented his bill to Parliament 'to lay down minimum wages and maximum working hours for the nursing profession'. It was proposed to impose a maximum working week of 44 hours on 'all nurses whether in institutions and hospitals or district nurses'; after every four hours of work there was to be a half-hour break for a meal. The minimum rates of pay mentioned in the bill were substantially higher than those recommended by the College of Nursing—particularly for probationers. It was proposed that probationers should be paid salaries ranging from £40 to £60 in the three years of training. Trained nurses should start at £75 and sisters at £85.[2]

Mr Fenner Brockway introduced his bill without any prior discussions with the nursing organizations. This militated against a good reception in the nursing world. The *Nursing Times* opposed it on principle. 'As long as we take pride in being a "profession" we must go to work by the voluntary method.'[3] 'Can the ideals of nursing grow and flourish under such hard-and-fast regulations? Would doctors, artists, professors or university students call in the law to regulate their hours of study and service? Would they not rather evolve a code for themselves, and from within, as all professions have done before them?'[4]

Mrs Bedford Fenwick in the *British Journal of Nursing* concentrated on the details. How could a nurse working in a private house keep to the statutory hours without harm to her patient? If the bill applied only to registered nurses it would put them

---

[1] *NT*, 18 December 1920, p. 1477.
[2] *H of C Deb.*, 10 December 1930, cols. 416–18.
[3] See 5 December 1931, p. 1298.   [4] *NT*, 28 February 1931, p. 219.

at a disadvantage compared to unregistered nurses as the latter would be able to work whatever hours were needed. Thus the effect of the bill would be to hand over the bulk of private work to unqualified nurses.[1] She thought the bill was most undignified. 'It is the first time, we should imagine, that by legislation a professional person shall be compelled to chew the cud or dip in the trough every four hours, whether she wishes to do so or not.'[2] Mrs Bedford Fenwick's flirtation with 'the left' was at an end. Mr Brockway was prepared to amend his bill, but the damage had been done.[3]

This bill had a bad reception not only from the professional associations but also from the Government. The Prime Minister refused to give it facilities.[4] And when the Labour Government fell, the bill was not presented again as Mr Brockway was not returned to Parliament. Nevertheless the College of Nursing took the opportunity to make an 'earnest appeal' to hospital managements 'to take steps to reduce the hours on duty to a maximum of 56 hours per week'.[5] By 1937 the hours worked had fallen to a rough average of 54. In this year 12 per cent of voluntary hospitals and 21 per cent of local authority hospitals were operating a 96-hour fortnight.

Hours of work and rates of pay were not the only aspects of hospital life which needed to be made more attractive. There had been rapid social changes in other occupations which employed women. Such changes were slow to penetrate the cloistered institutions of medical care. On a number of questions there was a conflict between what was thought appropriate by the leaders of the nursing profession and what was thought appropriate by those outside it.

In 1932 the Lancet Commission summed up the position in the following words:

The nurse's conditions of training and service have fallen into relative disfavour not only with young people in search of a career, but also with their advisers, and with women in other professions. On the other hand, nurses themselves are distressed and even indignant at what they regard as an undeserved prejudice against hospital life. The nursing profession as a whole tends to view the conditions of service and training now available in the light of those

---

[1] *BJN*, March 1931, p. 72.   [2] *Ibid.*, p. 57.
[3] *Ibid.*, p. 153.   [4] *H of C Deb.*, 21 May 1931, col. 2188.
[5] *BJN*, October 1931, p. 283.

offered in the past, even as recently as ten years ago, and finds them immeasurably more favourable; whereas women in other professions, and girls debating their future career are apt to brush aside as irrelevant any description of past conditions, and to survey hospital life as it actually is today, detached from its background of fine tradition.[1]

So, in 1930, we find that the probationer's life consisted of petty restrictions, petty tyrannies, and plenty of heavy domestic work. Attendance at meals was compulsory at 58 per cent of all hospitals.[2] In 84 per cent of the hospitals the nurse was not allowed out after 10 p.m. without a late pass.[3] She often actually had to go to bed by this time.[4] A third of the hospitals did not provide separate bedrooms for the probationers.[5] Only 7 per cent of the hospitals provided senior nurses with a latch key or stated that it was not necessary.[6] Only 10 per cent of the hospitals admitted male guests.[7] The probationer was regarded as 'pushing herself forward' if she sought acquaintance with a nurse outside her own year.[8] All this did not appeal to the secondary school girl whom the hospitals hoped to attract.

Routine domestic work, occupying nine or ten hours a day, was unpopular with probationers. The stalwarts of the profession believed that this work was needed to keep the vocational torch alight.[9] The Lancet Commission recognized that a sense of vocation was essential for a nurse, but did not think willingness to do lengthy domestic chores a necessary test of it.

There was of course strong discipline in the ward and much of this played a part in ensuring that patients got efficient treatment. But there were hospitals where it was laid down that a nurse should never sit in a ward, even if the job she was doing could be done better in that position. And there were hospitals where the night nurse was forbidden to sit by the fire or wear a shawl.

[1] *Lancet Commission Report 1932*, p. 27.

[2] For all meals in 45 per cent of the hospitals, for certain meals in 13 per cent. Leave of absence was granted in some cases. (*Ibid.*, p. 242.)

[3] *Ibid.*, p. 240.   [4] *Ibid.*, p. 170.   [5] *Ibid.*, p. 223.

[6] *Ibid.*, p. 240. When a newly arrived matron of a provincial hospital after the second world war issued latch keys, several of the ward sisters tendered their resignation to express 'their disapproval of this breach of discipline'. See *Working Party on the Recruitment and Training of Nurses. Minority Report*, p. 51: HMSO, 1948.   [7] *Lancet Commission Report 1932*, p. 223.

[8] *Ibid.*, p. 107.   [9] *Ibid.*, pp. 28–29.

In 1920, Dr Comyns Berkeley made a summary of what was offered to the girl who took up nursing.

Three and sometimes four years of strict discipline under the rule of another woman, accompanied by hard physical and mental work, an atmosphere of sickness and suffering, a perpetual sense of unnecessary restrictions, an exile from the world of art and letters and human progress and the narrowing effect of institution life. And all the time there lurks around the spectre of *fear*. For if she thinks for herself and speaks out fearlessly and independently, if she rebels against anything that seems tyrannical or wrong, she will incur the displeasure of the authorities at the present moment, run the risk of losing her certificate, and forfeit the help of her training school when she launches out as a fully trained nurse.[1]

There were many reasons for the restrictive and disciplined life of the nurse. No doubt there were ward sisters whose personality was or had become unsuited for the responsibilities they were carrying. But it would be wrong to attribute everything to the jealousy of the embittered spinster. Nursing skill can determine whether or not the patient recovers, and many an experienced nurse wishes to save the novice from the pain which she may well have herself experienced of knowing that greater effort on her part could have saved a patient's life. Isolated in the hospital community, trying to do the very best without adequate staff to do it, the ward sister may well drive and badger her staff beyond the point where efficiency is increased to the stage where stress and tension lead to negligence and abnegation of responsibility.

All this was bad for recruitment, but there is one other important consequence which should not be forgotten. It would seem unlikely that nurses operating beneath the 'sceptre of fear' were able to give patients the kindly support and comfort they required. How often did junior nurses, themselves the victims of authoritarianism, unconsciously take their revenge on the patients? Was the nurse placed in the appropriate setting to encourage her to 'sun the sweet flower of our work into beneficence'?[2]

Throughout the twenties and thirties there were improvements in the terms and conditions upon which nurses were employed. There were moderate increases in the pay and moderate

[1] *NT*, 30 October 1920, p. 1264.   [2] See p. 136n.

reductions in the hours; there was some relaxation in the restrictions of hospital life and some transfer of domestic work to staff employed for the purpose. Some local authorities in the thirties allowed nurses to be non-resident—an example followed by hardly any voluntary hospitals. On the other hand, developments in medicine were making more intellectual demands on nurses and imposing new disciplines. The improvements did not occur fast enough, or go far enough, to eradicate all talk of trade unionism among nurses.

After the failure of the Wages and Hours Bill, action by the Labour movement switched from the political to the industrial wing. The publication of the report of the Lancet Commission with its 'exposure' of nursing conditions provided the General Council of the Trades Union Congress with an opportunity to extend and co-ordinate its plans to attract nurses to the trade union movement. It stated that

the Mental Hospital and Institutional Workers' Union[1] . . . with the support of large numbers of nurses, male and female, engaged in district nursing and other special branches of the profession, offers its services for the purpose of initiating a professional organization on trade union lines. . . . No steps would be taken which would be detrimental to the dignity of nursing and only such action carried out as the collective wisdom of nurses deemed to be desirable.[2]

In the thirties the National Association of Local Government Officers—an organization which had a 'respectable tone'[3] and was not affiliated to the TUC—made a big drive to recruit nurses to their union. Meetings were held all over the country and there were occasions when all the nurses at a hospital were persuaded to join the union. The senior officials of the local government service tended to be members of NALGO and where the matron had also joined she was able to use her influence to encourage nurses to do likewise. As we have seen earlier, hospital nurses tended to follow their matron's lead in matters of professional organization. On paper, membership was between 5,000 and 10,000: a sufficient number to be a competitor to the College. But the nurses had neither the time nor interest to run local branches. Moreover, there was a rapid turnover of staff

[1] Previously called the National Asylum Workers' Union.
[2] *NT*, 18 June 1932, p. 593.   [3] Lockwood: *op. cit.*, p. 144.

which increased the difficulty of organization. There was no stability in the membership.[1]

At the 1935 Conference of the Trades Union Congress, a resolution proposed by the National Union of County Officers was carried instructing the General Council to use its influence to secure a 48-hour working week for hospital employees. The Minister of Health received a deputation from interested trade unions on 23 July 1936, and NUCO wrote to local authorities asking for the immediate introduction of a 48-hour working week. A bill to secure this objective was presented to Parliament in April 1937. The Royal College sent a circular to members of Parliament opposing the bill.[2]

The TUC launched a direct onslaught on the College of Nursing for its opposition to the bill. It attacked the College for denying membership to male nurses, student nurses, and nurses on the Supplementary Registers, and called it 'an organization of voluntary snobs'—in other words an organization which represented the voluntary hospitals and not the municipal hospitals.[3] The TUC was on firm ground in attacking the unrepresentative character of the College of Nursing. It could not claim to speak for all nurses. And general nurses from municipal hospitals seldom got elected to govern the affairs of the College.[4] The Trades Union Congress was well aware that its potential strength in the field of nursing came from the fact that it had no inhibitions about recruiting male nurses, student nurses, assistant nurses, or even untrained nurses, all of whom were specifically prevented from membership of the College.

The crucial question at issue between the TUC and the College was whether nurses should be organized on an industrial basis or a craft basis. As the *Nursing Times* put it in 1937, should nurses 'throw in their lot with other workers who chance to be employed at the same institutions or by the same employer?' Or had nurses a 'sufficient identity of interest' to combine together as nurses?[5]

[1] The National Union of County Officers, affiliated to the TUC, was also recruiting nurses but no estimate is available of the number of nursing members at this time.

[2] Guild of Nurses: *Hospital and Welfare Services Union*, p. 3: London, 1945.

[3] *NT*, 23 October 1937, pp. 1039–40.

[4] On this last point, however, the Royal College could justly point out that this was not the fault of the College as such but of the registered nurses who elected their representatives.   [5] *NT*, 26 June 1937, p. 617.

In effect, the TUC by attempting to organize nurses was blurring the distinction between a profession and a trade—it was challenging professionalism at its very roots.

Viewed on a strict factual basis, the distinction between a profession and a trade was very slight. And it is for this reason that such meticulous care was taken to preserve and exaggerate such borderline differences as could be found. It was often argued that the possibility of threatening strike action distinguished a profession from a trade. This was untrue. Strike action has been threatened by the medical profession on a number of occasions. But non-payment for overtime was a real difference which was jealously guarded. As the president of the College put it, 'to introduce the principle of overtime work was to strike the industrial rather than the professional note'.[1]

In the year 1937, trade union activity among nurses reached its peak. The Trades Union Congress produced a full charter for nurses including payment for overtime, one month's leave on full pay, thirteen weeks' full pay in sickness, the right to live out, statutory superannuation rights, and a special Whitley Council.[2] And NALGO produced proposals for minimum salary scales: staff nurses were to have a minimum of £75 and sisters a minimum of £95.[3] Criticisms by NALGO of the restrictions imposed on resident nurses were reported in the popular press.[4]

By this time the number of unions that were recruiting nurses had grown. In addition to the National Union of County Officers, the Mental Hospital and Institutional Workers' Union, and the National Association of Local Government Officers, there was the National Union of Public Employees and the Transport and General Workers' Union. In 1937 there was formed an organization called 'The Association of Nurses in support of the TUC Charter for Nurses'.[5] A special section was set up for the most promising field of recruits—nurses who were only partially trained. The Association like many before it hoped to achieve the position in the nursing world which the British Medical

---

[1] *NT*, 26 June 1937, p. 618.

[2] Labour Party: *Notes for Speakers*, 27 August 1937.

[3] NALGO: *Charter for Nurses*, 17 December 1937, pp. 1–3.

[4] Under the headline 'How Many Beauty Aids do You Use?' the *Daily Mirror* reported on 17 December 1937 that nurses at one London hospital were only allowed to display nine objects on their dressing tables. Readers were invited to calculate how many objects they would need.

[5] *NT*, 30 October 1937, p. 1069.

Association had won among doctors. There was thus great duplication of effort among nursing trade unions.

The most militant body at this period was the National Union of County Officers which renamed its nursing section 'The Guild of Nurses'[1] in October 1937 and appointed the first qualified nurse and midwife as full-time organizer (Mrs Iris Brook). The London County Council was showered with leaflets from the visitors' gallery demanding a 96-hour fortnight, and a sandwich board march was organized through London of nurses in white uniforms wearing black masks to avoid recognition (for fear of victimization). In the evening of this historic day a meeting was held in St Pancras Town Hall attended by five hundred nurses. George Lansbury took the chair and the occasion was reported in the popular press.[2] (See frontispiece.)

The growing trade union activity among nurses did not go unnoticed. Even the 'Ministry of Health heard talk of "nurses going Socialist", and joining trade unions which "they were really reluctant to do" .'[3] The Royal College of Nurses became seriously worried. Its policy of bringing pressure to bear on hospital authorities was yielding insufficient results. Voluntary action was failing to solve the problem. The Limitation of Hours Bill was still before Parliament and if passed would involve major state regulation of the profession. This the College wanted at all costs to avoid, but some action was by now essential. Many members of Parliament were agitating for something to be done to improve the lot of the nurse. Eventually the Minister of Health decided, with the support of the College of Nursing, to institute an inquiry into nursing conditions.[4]

In November 1937 the Government appointed a committee, under the chairmanship of the Earl of Athlone,

to inquire into the arrangements at present in operation with regard to the recruitment, training and registration and terms and conditions of service of persons engaged in nursing the sick and to report whether

---

[1] No doubt it was believed that the word 'guild' would seem less frightening to nurses than the word 'union'.

[2] See for example the *Daily Express*, 27 November 1937. I am indebted to Miss Westmacott ((COHSE) for the information in this paragraph.

[3] S. A. Ferguson and H. Fitzgerald: 'Studies in the Social Services': *History of the Second World War*, p. 292: London, 1954.

[4] The College had asked the Ministry of Health to institute an inquiry in 1935.

any changes in those arrangements or any other measures are expedient for the purpose of maintaining an adequate service both for institutional and domiciliary nursing.[1]

In December 1937 the Limitation of Hours Bill was rejected by eleven votes in the House of Commons. It was said to be 'premature' in view of the appointment of the committee.

In its evidence to the Athlone Committee, the College of Nursing came to the conclusion that the time had come for more positive action to improve conditions of service in the nursing profession. 'Previous methods, such as approach to individual authorities, should be replaced by the setting up of national machinery with power and authority to deal with conditions of service for nurses.'[2] It recommended that

National and regional councils should be set up for the purpose of negotiation, giving direct representation to organized nurses in order to grade different types of employment, to agree to uniform scales of salary having regard to regional cost of living for the whole country (or national minimum scales) and to agree on hours of work and holidays.[3]

In its interim report published early in 1939 (no final report was ever issued owing to the outbreak of war) the Athlone Committee made far-reaching recommendations. Trained nurses should have higher pay and a Nurses Salaries' Committee should be established to regulate nurses' salaries. Nurses should work a 96-hour fortnight and have four weeks' leave each year. In a number of hospitals accommodation and catering needed to be improved. More domestic staff should be employed to relieve the nurse of 'the daily repetition of routine tasks'. Unreasonable rules and restrictions affecting the nurse's life should be reviewed in the light of modern conditions.

Most of these recommendations could not be implemented unless more money was found for the voluntary hospitals. This question was faced squarely by one section of the committee. It was recommended that grants should be paid from public funds

[1] Ministry of Health, Board of Education: *Inter-Departmental Committee on Nursing Services, Interim Report* (Chairman: The Rt. Hon. The Earl of Athlone), p. 4: HMSO, 1939.

[2] College of Nursing: *Annual Report for 1938*, p. 12.

[3] College of Nursing: *Memorandum Relating to Conditions in the Nursing Profession for Submission to the Inter-Departmental Committee on the Nursing Services*, p. 20: London, 1938.

XIV. The early Victorian nurse, it seems, made too easy a transition from milk to gin

THE MONTHLY NURSE. (A FACT.)

Brown (to Deaf Nurse). "How is Mrs B. going on?"
Deaf Nurse. "Not just now, thank you. I'll have a drop presently."
B. "Is baby all right?"
D. N. "I'd rather have it in a cup of tea, please!"

XV. 'The Nurse'
(anonymous woodcut, *c.* 1850)

XVI. Singing to Patients, London Hospital, 1902

XVII. Talbot Ward, London Hospital, c. 1905

to the voluntary hospitals to meet the cost of the improvements in the hours, salaries, and other measures proposed. In addition, the majority of the Committee recommended 'the establishment of a system of grants from national funds to all recognized training hospitals in respect of the national work done by the training of nurses'.[1]

These recommendations had serious implications for the Government. Could nursing departments of hospitals be grant-aided? Such a step would involve a long-term commitment for the Treasury and change the traditional relationship between the Government and the voluntary hospitals. It could not be taken lightly. Yet deputations from the nursing organizations and the Trades Union Congress were pressing the Government for action. The Ministry of Health feared that if it did not act criticism would grow.

[The Ministry] urged the local authorities to review their arrangements in the light of the Athlone Committee's report and to take such necessary action as was immediately possible without additional expenditure. . . . When the British Hospitals' Association was asked to address a similar circular to the voluntary hospitals, it needed strong persuasion. Some of the suggestions were considered to be 'not very palatable', and it was feared that the hospitals might take offence.[2]

The Government decided not to offer grants to training hospitals. It was considered ' "neither sound nor proper for the Government to make itself responsible for the payment of salaries to members of a particular profession". A war was needed to change the Ministry's mind.'[3]

[1] *Athlone Committee Report*, p. 70.
[2] Ferguson and Fitzgerald: *op. cit.*, p. 293.   [3] *Ibid.*, p. 294.

CHAPTER X

The Search for the Suitable Nurse

THERE had been many issues on which the different professional organizations had disagreed, but on one they had always been united. There must only be one portal for entry to the nursing profession. With the exception of fever nurses, only those who had undergone a three-year training in a hospital should be allowed to bear the title 'nurse'.

In 1905, the Select Committee on Registration had suggested that there might need to be 'a separate Register of nurses whose training is of a lower standard than that laid down for "Registered Nurses".'[1] But the introduction of such a register had been opposed by the representatives of the profession, and this opposition had reached its height in the first world war, when there was a fear that those who had been members of the Voluntary Aid Detachments might take this short cut to becoming recognized nurses.

The principle of the 'one portal' entry was interpreted very rigidly. For example, when the Lancet Commission proposed that girls should be allowed to take part of the Preliminary State Examination (anatomy, physiology, and hygiene) while still at school,[2] this was interpreted by one section of the profession as a breach of the 'one portal' entry. In addition it was said that it would transfer the control of the examination out of professional and into lay hands. The Council of the College of Nursing did, however, support the proposal which it forwarded to the General Nursing Council. The registrar sent the following reply: 'I am instructed to say that the General Nursing Council have no authority to approve schools for girls as part of the conditions of admission for the Register, nor can they allow any other body or persons not appointed by them to conduct their examinations.'[3]

[1] See pp. 79–80 above.
[2] *Lancet Commission Report 1932*, p. 171.
[3] *BJN*, August 1932, p. 225.

Not until 1953 did the Council change its mind and allow exemption from Part I of the Preliminary Examination.[1] Given the principle of a 'one portal' entry to the profession, much depended on the qualification laid down for entering it. This was why the syllabus of training had been a subject of dispute with the Minister of Health.[2] The General Nursing Council had wanted to impose very high standards of training on all entrants; the Minister of Health had been more moderate; but under the system actually introduced a girl needed a relatively high standard of general education to take the theoretical part of the course. It was hard for a girl who left school at the compulsory school-leaving age to become a trained nurse.

The professional organizations had made no secret of their wish to see *all* nursing done by girls who had attended secondary school. Nursing was a job for educated women and only for educated women. And some writers used the word 'educated' as a polite synonym for high social class. Certain domestic tasks could be delegated to domestic staff but nursing was to be done by nurses: and the range of duties that came under the heading of 'nursing' was clearly intended to be wide.

This view about who should be nurses in the future led to a tendency to indulge in fantasies about who had been nurses in the past.[3] Nursing histories concentrated on the few women of noble birth who were supposed to have taken up nursing and ignored the humbler sort of hospital nurse and village nurse. Even the recent past was romanticized. The impression was created that nursing had been done entirely by dedicated upper class women of the Nightingale type and that a queue of such women had waited for a post to fall vacant.[4] The majority of nursing work, however, had always been done by women without the educational background which the profession now regarded as essential. Indeed the education provided

---

[1] *The Nurses' (Amendment No. 2) Rules, Approval Instrument,* 1953 (SI 1837).
[2] See p. 112 above.
[3] This nostalgia can be detected in the report of the Lancet Commission set up in 1930. '*To restore* the popularity of nursing among educated girls has been the chief objective of our inquiries' (my italics). See *Lancet Commission Report 1932,* p. 12.
[4] In 1921 the matron of London Hospital, Miss Monk, complained that nursing used to be regarded as 'the profession of women of education, of good social standing to enter. This is changing but it ought not to be allowed to change.' See *NT,* 8 January 1921, p. 36.

for girls in the nineteenth century was often inferior to that provided in grammar schools in the inter-war period and this was true even for the higher social classes. Florence Nightingale herself was exceptionally well educated but she was by no means typical of the class from which she came. Even in 1900 nurses from this background had been a small minority of those engaged in nursing work. There had indeed been queues to gain the limited places in the smart voluntary hospitals in London but paid nurses in the infirmaries were often 'of the domestic servant class'.[1] Educated women were a minority of paid nurses in the hospitals and an even smaller minority if account is taken of the large amount of nursing work which was done by paupers. Allowing for the large domiciliary sector, the proportion of 'educated' nurses (in any sense) was very small indeed.

The shortage of suitable nurses in the twenties and thirties was very real. Evidence comes from both the Lancet Commission and the Athlone Committee. The Lancet Commission found in 1932 that the majority of hospitals did not get sufficient replies from suitable candidates to their advertisements for staff nurses and probationers, and in general the shortage of staff nurses was the greater. Municipal hospitals were affected more than voluntary hospitals. Only about a fifth of the London voluntary training hospitals were in difficulties about probationers compared with over 60 per cent of municipal training hospitals.

The position seems to have eased slightly in 1931–32. At least this was the view of the College of Nursing.

The recommendations put forward by the Lancet Commission became unnecessary as the position was remedied automatically by the economic world crisis, which had the effect of diverting into the nurse training schools many candidates who, for financial reasons, could not afford the expensive outlay necessary to qualify themselves in any of the other professions.[2]

But the position deteriorated as the economic situation improved. In 1937 the Athlone Committee found that the shortage was still worse for trained nurses than for probationers. Voluntary and municipal hospitals were in the same relative position in their

[1] See p. 47 above.
[2] Royal College of Nursing: *Memorandum Relating to Conditions in the Nursing Profession for Submission to the Inter-Departmental Committee on the Nursing Services*, January 1938, p. 3.

search for trained personnel: about three-quarters of the hospitals reported increasing difficulty in recruiting trained staff; 71 per cent of the municipal hospitals and 67 per cent of the voluntary hospitals reported increasing difficulty in obtaining probationers. This was true despite the substantially larger pay provided by the municipal hospitals.

These shortages were not caused by any decline in the supply of recruits; both absolutely and relatively nursing was becoming more popular. What was happening was that the demand for suitable nurses was increasing faster than the supply, and the educational standard required of a nurse was being raised.

Some information is available showing the educational standard of probationers during the inter-war period. The local authority and voluntary hospitals were still recruiting girls with different educational and social backgrounds. In 1930 the Lancet Commission found that 61 per cent of voluntary hospitals were able to insist that their probationers had secondary education as compared to only 6 per cent of municipal hospitals. In 1937, the Athlone Committee found that 75 per cent of probationers entering the wards of voluntary hospitals had received secondary education. The corresponding figure in the local authority hospitals was 29 per cent.

If matrons were being forced to accept a higher proportion of unsuitable probationers than in the past, one would expect to find a higher proportion of probationers leaving before they had completed their three years of training. But this was not the case. The Lancet Commission found in 1930 a 'wastage rate' of 26–28 per cent for complete training schools in both local authority and voluntary hospitals.[1] This may be compared with the position at the beginning of the century when about a third of probationers failed to complete their training in poor law institutions[2] and Mrs Wardroper found a similar proportion of girls failing to complete her course of one year.[3]

As the wastage rate was not going up, it seems unlikely that the standard of candidates admitted was going down.[4] After the Registration Act probationers had to take the General Nursing Council's state examination, while before registration the standard

[1] Calculated from the *Lancet Commission Report 1932*, pp. 227–9.
[2] See p. 47 above.   [3] See p. 32 above.
[4] Difficulty with the theoretical work is of course only one of the many reasons for wastage during training.

required for a certificate could vary greatly from hospital to hospital. In view of this, it would seem likely that the standard of candidates was going up. Indeed it would be surprising if, at the beginning of the century, all hospitals and particularly all poor law infirmaries had demanded a standard as high as that of the state examination.

There is further information which supports the view that the educational standard of recruits in the twenties and thirties was higher than earlier in the century. The 1951 Census of Population collected information about the age at which girls left school. A table was published showing this information by age-group for state registered nurses, midwives, and student nurses taken together. As nurse training is normally taken in early adulthood the age-groups recorded in the 1951 Census broadly represent nurses trained at different periods. Thus, nearly all nurses aged 25–44 in 1951 were trained in the late 1920's, 1930's, or early 1940's. Similarly nearly all nurses aged 45–64 in 1951 were trained before 1930.

The information shows that on average the younger a nurse was in 1951, the longer had been her schooling. Only the figures for nurses who continued their education beyond the age of 20 fail to indicate this trend, but the numbers involved are very small. Thus about 18 per cent of nurses aged 45–64 left school between the ages of 17 and 19 compared to 25½ per cent of nurses aged 25–44. And about 19 per cent of nurses aged 45–64 left school at 16 compared to 24 per cent of nurses aged 25–44.[1] This suggests, though it does not prove conclusively, that entrants to the nursing profession had been increasingly better educated during the century. This conclusion could only be avoided if it were the case that an unduly high proportion of the better educated women left the profession prematurely. Were the better educated women more or less likely to marry, take jobs outside the nursing field or retire at an earlier age?

On balance, therefore, the evidence seems to suggest that entrants to nursing were increasingly better educated. Indeed one would expect to find nursing sharing in the higher educational standards of the community. But it might still be the case that while educational standards were going up in nursing they were going up slower than elsewhere—that nursing was gaining a lower proportion of the larger number of girls emerging from

[1] See Appendix I, p. 265.

the secondary schools. This could be read into the statement of the Lancet Commission that 'the nurse's conditions of training and service have fallen into relative disfavour not only with young people in search of a career, but also with their advisers, and with women in other professions'.[1]

Such evidence as there is does not support this conclusion as a long-term trend. Among occupied women with secondary education nursing seemed to have held its place. The information from the 1951 Census of Population shows that the proportion of occupied women leaving school at the age of 16 engaged in nursing was just under 8 per cent of each age-group. But out of the total of women occupied in 1951 who left school between the ages of 17 and 19, nursing had a higher proportion in the younger age-groups than in the older age-groups. Thus about 7 per cent of occupied women with this educational background were nurses in the age-group 45–64 in 1951, and about 12 per cent in the age-group 25–44.[2]

It seems, therefore, that nursing was gaining not only more educated girls but a higher proportion of educated girls. Why, therefore, was the opposite view taken by leaders of the nursing profession in the thirties? A number of explanations could be suggested. Possibly the educated girls were being more fairly distributed among the different training schools. If matrons had themselves been trained in schools with a high proportion of well-educated girls they may have assumed incorrectly that their school was typical of the period and compared it favourably with the school they were in charge of. Alternatively, what was said about education may really have been a polite way of making statements about social class. Possibly nurses were being drawn more from the lower middle classes and less from the upper and upper middle classes. A third explanation could be that matrons accepted uncritically, because it appealed to them, the fantasy of nursing historians.

If it is accepted that nursing was obtaining an increasing proportion of better educated girls, the crucial question for the future of the nursing profession was whether nursing could take a still higher proportion of them. This was what the profession wanted. But given the number of secondary school places, more secondary school nurses could only be gained at the expense of other occupations recruiting such girls. One obvious competitor

[1] *Lancet Commission Report 1932*, p. 27.   [2] Appendix I.

to the nursing profession was the teaching profession, but it would have been a short-sighted policy to try and rob teaching to help the nursing profession.[1] Another major competitor was office work which, like nursing, was gaining an increasing proportion of secondary school girls.[2] Should these girls have become nurses instead? Already in 1951 nearly 12 per cent of occupied women aged 25–44 who had left school between the ages of 17 and 19 were nurses. How many more would have had the personal qualities required for nursing?

The Athlone Committee calculated in 1939 that an annual intake of probationers of about 12,000 was required. 'The whole output of girls from grant-aided Secondary Schools in 1937 of 16 years of age and over (i.e. of those who had completed the period of a normal general school course) was 28,250, while the total number of those who left school at 17 or upwards was 10,600.'[3] Unless there was a large expansion in secondary school education, it was clearly impossible for all nurses to come from secondary schools. Given the standard required for the state examination and the demand for nurses, the limited development of secondary education for girls was the major reason for the shortage of 'suitable' nursing recruits.

Thus, however desirable it may have been in principle for all nurses to be drawn from girls with secondary education, there was a very definite limit to the number of girls educated up to this standard. Irrespective of pay and conditions of employment, the nursing profession was trying to draw its recruits from too narrow a field. Indeed if it had succeeded in its aim, it would have been at the cost to the community of almost monopolizing the output of girls' secondary schools. Given the number of secondary school places the policy of the nursing profession was not realistic.[4]

The effects of the shortage may be seen by studying the distribution of registered nurses at the end of the inter-war period. In 1937, the General Nursing Council issued a questionnaire to

[1] See Appendix I, pp. 267–8. While nursing seemed to have been taking an increasing proportion of girls leaving school at ages 17–19, teaching was taking a declining number of such girls.

[2] *Ibid.*   [3] *Athlone Committee Report*, p. 23.

[4] As late as 1931 we find the Council of the Royal British Nurses' Association expressing the view that if probationers received small or no remuneration at all, the type of women entering the profession would soon begin to show signs of improvement. See *BJN*, February 1931, p. 42.

ascertain the work being done by registered nurses.[1] Out of 78,345 forms, 14,264 were returned stating that the nurse was not in active work and about 6,500 were not returned or not filled in. Out of the 57,606 who reported that they were in active work, 26,091 (45 per cent) held hospital appointments, over 15,199 (26 per cent) were in private work, and 10,368 (18 per cent) were in public health or district nursing. The remainder (about 6,000) were overseas, in the armed forces or in a variety of administrative and para-medical jobs.

With only about 26,000 registered nurses and a shortage of *bona fide* probationers, the hospitals had to employ untrained women on nursing duties. The registered nurses that were at work in the hospitals clustered, like the qualified paid nurses fifty years earlier, in the large hospitals rather than the small, in the hospitals treating acute illness rather than in the institutions that catered for the chronic sick. The prospects of promotion, the attractions of town life, the opportunity to use advanced skills and the desire for status in the profession, were all factors creating this distribution of qualified nurses. Thus numbers had to be made up with unregistered nurses in the small voluntary hospitals and in the large institutions for the chronic sick.

Partly as a response to the shortage of nurses and probationers and partly out of the desire to lighten the load on probationers and enable them to study more, an increasing use was made of orderlies to do the sweeping, dusting and other domestic work in the wards.[2] Orderlies were made use of particularly by the local authorities. In 1933, over 1,400 were employed: by 1937, the total exceeded 2,300.[3] This was welcomed by the nursing profession.

There is a very definite niche [wrote the *Nursing Times*] to be filled by the type of girl who is not the high school type at all. She is often employed in cottage hospitals; she is terrified of examinations and could not pass them if she would; but she does excellent and devoted work under supervision. She is frightened away from the profession by what she hears of the syllabus, yet with a status of her own she

---

[1] General Nursing Council for England and Wales: *Memorandum on Matters concerning the Education, Examination and Registration of Nurses for Submission to the Inter-Departmental Committee on the Nursing Services*, February 1938.
[2] For example under the Middlesex County Council. See *NT*, 18 June 1932, p. 652. [3] See Appendix II, Table 3.

would make an excellent nursing orderly. (The word 'nurse' could be avoided, however, as two grades of 'nurses' are bound to confuse the public.)[1]

The employment of orderlies eased the life of the probationers and made it easier to staff the large, acute and semi-acute hospitals. It could not, however, solve the problems of the large institutions for the chronic sick. Orderlies could be employed to do the scrubbing, sweeping, and dusting, but who was there to do the 'basic nursing'—the work done by probationers in acute hospitals? Registered nurses were not available, so in practice the work was done by the stock of experienced but untrained women who had not registered and by probationers who had failed to complete their training and drifted into this work.[2] In 1933, over 15,000 unqualified nurses were at work in the hospitals: by 1937, the total exceeded 21,000.[3]

In time the local authorities took the bull by the horns and recruited women specifically for the simpler nursing work: formal training courses were introduced. In 1935, Essex County Council planned a course for assistant nurses for nursing the chronic sick.[4] Kent and other local authorities soon followed the Essex example.[5] It was decided after consultation with the College of Nursing that the course should last for two years and this became the standard pattern.

The first reaction of the College of Nursing to these developments had not been favourable. The Council of the College stated in 1935 that the Essex scheme

if developed throughout the country, might prove a menace to the economic conditions of the nursing profession. They also realized that it would be impossible for the General Nursing Council to recognise any standard of training lower than the basic standard prescribed for admission to the Register. They suggested, therefore, that the ideal method of caring for the patients would be to employ non-resident trained nurses.[6]

If this was impossible and untrained women had to be employed they should be called 'attendants on the chronic sick' and given

---

[1] *NT*, 28 November 1931, p. 1271.   [2] See p. 127 above.
[3] See Appendix II, Table 3.
[4] Carter: *op. cit.*, pp. 283–4.
[5] *Ibid.*, pp. 285–6.
[6] College of Nursing: *Annual Report for 1935*, pp. 5–6.

permanent pensionable posts 'to prevent them from competing with trained nurses working amongst the sick of the community'.[1] A year later the College came to the conclusion that there was a need for 'a special grade of nurse' but that it was not desirable to have a supplementary register. Nevertheless the General Nursing Council should be responsible for deciding on the standard of training required and for the maintenance of a roll for such persons. They should still be called 'attendants on the chronic sick'.[2]

In 1937 the British Medical Association stated its views on the subject. The assistant nurse 'is often a valued officer in a public institution. As there is no likelihood of replacing such persons by a fully trained staff, it is highly desirable that their position should be defined and regularised, and a clear demarcation made, so that the public could readily distinguish between the trained nurse and the unqualified assistant.'[3] As the Association pointed out, the existence of the unrecognized nurse could not be ignored; such nurses were going to exist for a long time to come. However much the profession might wish to preserve the 'one portal' entry, failure to regularize the position of the assistant nurse would react against the interests of the profession, as the assistant nurse could easily leave the chronic infirmary and pose to the public as a fully trained nurse. The Association advocated the recognition and training of a second grade of nurse. The nursing profession had to think again.

In the same year as the British Medical Association announced its views on the assistant nurse, the Athlone Committee was appointed and heard evidence on this question. The Committee recognized, as we have seen, that the current output of secondary school girls would not permit all nurses to have this educational background. 'It will not be possible', they wrote, 'for at least some years to come, or perhaps ever, to carry on the nursing services of the country without the aid of assistant nurses.'[4] Many of these women were 'doing excellent work in hospitals and institutions, especially in caring for the chronic sick'. As long as they worked in hospitals and other institutions under trained supervision their employment would be of great help to the community.

The Committee was under strong pressure from a section of

[1] *Ibid.*, p. 6.   [2] College of Nursing: *Annual Report for 1936*, p. 7.
[3] *NT*, 3 July 1937, p. 641.   [4] *Athlone Committee Report*, p. 64.

the nursing profession not to recognize the assistant nurse as this 'would react adversely on the status of the State Registered Nurse'.[1] Nevertheless the Committee decided unanimously that a roll should be established (the use of the word 'roll' as distinct from 'register' should be noted) and a scheme of training should be constructed 'suitable for girls with a practical bent for nursing but without the intellectual equipment necessary to pass all the examinations for State Registration'.[2] The course was to last two years.

The establishment of a roll for assistant nurses raised the problem of the admission of existing nurses in the same way as it had in the case of registered nurses twenty years earlier. The Athlone Committee recommended that 'existing nurses should be admitted to the Roll on a certificate of competence from their employers or from the agency or co-operation through which they were engaged and on evidence that they have practised the nursing of the sick for at least two years and are of good character'.[3]

So far the Committee was united. The Committee could not, however, agree upon the appropriate title for these women. It was argued that the designation should not include the word 'nurse' on the ground that 'these women do not hold the qualifications or do the work of State Registered nurses to whom the word "nurse" should alone be applied in order to avoid confusion and maintain the status of the nursing profession'.[4] Nevertheless the lay members of the Committee wanted to use the term 'assistant nurse' which was already in use. The four state registered nurses on the Committee, however, persisted in their desire to avoid the word 'nurse'. They would not even compromise on 'nursing aid' although at least one member of the Committee would have accepted it as a compromise,[5] but they advocated a more distinctive official description, namely, 'Registered Invalid Attendants'. They seemed to accept that this lengthy mode of address was unlikely to gain popular currency, particularly in emergencies. For they conceded that the new title 'need not prevent the use of the word "nurse" as the normal form of personal address for sick attendants'.[6]

---

[1] *Athlone Committee Report*, p. 65.   [2] *Ibid.*, p. 66.   [3] *Ibid.*, p. 76.
[4] *Ibid.*, p. 59.
[5] Col. Fremantle: *H of C Deb.*, 7 April 1943, col. 645.
[6] *Athlone Committee Report*, p. 81.

The Athlone Committee was only willing to suggest that this recognition should be given to the assistant nurse providing one further step was taken. It seems probable that the nurse members of the Committee would only support the proposal on this condition. The Committee recommended that

it should be made an offence for any agency or cooperation acting in connection with the employment of nurses to supply for gain the services of persons for the purpose of nursing the sick whose names are not entered on the Register or the Roll, or to fail to inform the applicant for the nurse's services to which of these categories the nurse supplied belongs.

To make this effective 'local authorities should be empowered to licence, register, and inspect all such agencies and co-operations'.[1]

The greatest opposition to the recognition of assistant nurses came from the private nurses and this was intended as a measure to give them some protection.[2] The Committee was not prepared to go further towards 'closing the nursing profession' in its interim report. The opinion was expressed that 'excepting nurses in training no persons other than State Registered Nurses, or assistant nurses entered on the Roll should, habitually and for gain, engage in nursing the sick'. But the question of what other legislative steps were to be taken was left for further discussion.[3]

By the time the report of the Athlone Committee was published, the College of Nursing had already accepted the necessity for a second grade of nurse, and by May 1939 we find the General Nursing Council agreeing to start a roll for such nurses on the conditions laid down in the Committee's report. However, the Council 'agreed with the reservations of the nurse members of the Committee about the official title of persons entered on the roll'.[4]

The reaction from Mrs Bedford Fenwick and her supporters was every bit as violent as might be expected. The small but venerable professional organizations that opposed the College (the Royal British Nurses' Association, the British College of Nurses and the Scottish Nurses' Association) marshalled the old arguments. Women were to be placed on a special roll, the majority of whom exploited the suffering public for gain. This would be the death knell of high standards of nursing. Highly

[1] *Ibid.*, p. 68. [2] Carter: *op. cit.*, p. 70.
[3] *Athlone Committee Report*, p. 68. [4] *BJN*, May 1939, p. 158.

educated women would not enter a profession to be undersold in the open market by an inferior grade of worker.[1]

A 'Nursing Standards Defence Fund' was opened and a public meeting of protest was held in the Caxton Hall by the Royal British Nurses' Association which was attended, it was claimed, by 500 people.[2] Readers of the *British Journal of Nursing*, by now a slim, monthly publication, were told that 'clear-eyed, indomitable, courageous State Registered Nurse Number One will once more lead them to victory'.[3] But there were now few nurses willing to follow Mrs Bedford Fenwick's lead.

Thus, twenty years after the Registration Act, it was recognized by a section of the profession, that all nursing work could not be done by persons on the Register. A second portal would have to be opened: but in return for this concession private practice would be regulated. This could be a first step towards the exclusion of unrecognized persons from nursing work. Such was the position at the outbreak of the second world war.

---

[1] *BJN*, February 1939, p. 29.   [2] *Ibid.*, April 1939, p. 96.

[3] *Ibid.*, March 1939, p. 63. According to the popular press Mrs Bedford Fenwick was 'a fiery old lady of 82'. See *ibid.*, April 1939, p. 98.

CHAPTER XI

The Second Portal

THE outbreak of war in September 1939 occurred at a critical time for the nursing profession. Many of the problems of the profession had come to a head and the Athlone Committee had recommended action.

The crucial problem was the shortage of nurses. Both pay and conditions of work were unattractive to prospective recruits and improvements could only be made by giving Exchequer assistance to the voluntary hospitals. But even this unprecedented action would not solve the problem of recruitment, as any large increase in the number of secondary school girls entering nurse training would rob other occupations which needed to recruit from the same field. No one was prepared to suggest that the standards demanded by the General Nursing Council for admission to the General Register should be lowered. The only solution, therefore, was to introduce a new grade of nurse. This would require legislation, which would be violently opposed by a vocal section of the nursing profession.

While a peacetime government could, within limits, disclaim responsibility for the nursing shortage which faced the voluntary hospitals and local authorities, and reacted unfavourably on the civilian sick, the outbreak of war made the problems of nursing more of a national responsibility. Adequate provision had to be made for the medical care of wounded members of the armed services: in addition provision had to be made for air-raid casualties.

Early in 1939, the Ministry of Health worked out the number of nurses that would be needed if war broke out. The armed forces had asked for 5,000 trained nurses, and it was estimated that between 34,000 and 67,000 trained nurses would be needed to man the first-aid posts and emergency hospitals[1] which were planned to care for the vast number of air-raid casualties that

---

[1] Ferguson and Fitzgerald: *op. cit.*, p. 296: London, 1954.

were expected.[1] At this time there were only about 60,000 trained nurses at work in Britain.[2]

If only part of these demands were to be met, drastic steps would have to be taken. The Nursing Sub-Committee of the Committee of Imperial Defence was prepared to cut by half the trained staffs of the ordinary civilian hospitals and fill the gaps with untrained staff. Nevertheless, new recruits were obviously needed. A Civil Nursing Reserve was formed from women of all grades of training and experience which recruited 7,000 trained nurses and 3,000 assistant nurses. In addition to this total of 10,000 experienced nurses, untrained volunteers were recruited who were described as 'nursing auxiliaries'. When war was declared, over 20,000 nurses were ready for action, though not all were able and willing to be sent far away from their homes.

The recruits to the Civil Nursing Reserve, though subject to their own terms and conditions of employment, worked in the Service hospitals, in the civilian hospitals, and in the air-raid posts as required. The VADs had been a cause of friction in the first world war; the new Reserve created similar difficulties in the second. It was no easy task to fit the untrained recruits at one and the same time into the Service world with its discipline, its ranks, its privileges, and the civilian hospital world with its own special traditions of hierarchy and status. In addition, the recruitment of nursing auxiliaries represented no small challenge to the professional nurses. And just as the recruitment of VADs in the first war had led to an almost united demand for state registration, so, in the second war, the Civil Nursing Reserve led to a stronger demand for the recognition of a second grade of nurse.

The armed forces had to decide on the status of nursing personnel who were not state registered. Nurses of the Queen Alexandra's Imperial Military Nursing Service had always enjoyed 'officer' status. Should this be extended to VAD nurses? It was decided in 1940 that 'the nursing member, Grade I, should be given pay corresponding to that of a RAMC nursing orderly, Class I, but should receive certain "officer" privileges, viz. first-class travel in uniform, board and lodging allowance and accommodation such as for the QAIMNS and rank "next and

---

[1] R. M. Titmuss: 'Problems of Social Policy': *History of the Second World War*, pp. 3–11: London, 1950.

[2] See Chapter IX, p. 155.

after the QAIMNS" '.[1] This position was soon recognized to be anomalous. VAD nursing members enjoyed officer privileges while fulfilling 'other rank' functions. There were many non-nursing members of the Voluntary Aid Detachments who held recognized diplomas and qualifications but who had no 'officer' privileges. It was decided to withdraw 'officer' privileges from VAD nurses in 1943. In particular, this meant that they were unwillingly excluded from officers' clubs.

There was, however, a further status anomaly which did not receive attention. A newly qualified female nurse could enter the QAIMNS and attain immediate officer status. A male qualified nurse, however, remained an 'other rank' (Nursing Orderly Class I in the Royal Army Medical Corps or Leading Sick Berth Attendant in the Navy). Thus a female registered nurse could have working under her a male registered nurse who was senior in both age and experience. Civilian discrimination had become codified in the hierarchy of the armed services.

Nursing auxiliaries were given fifty hours' training in hospitals before they were set to work. In the early days their duties were the ordinary domestic work of the wards. This led to complaints being made by the VAD Council, and a large volume of individual correspondence and criticism.[2] A War Office committee, which considered their complaints, stated that 'many VAD members were people of high intelligence and capacity and it was felt that their gifts fitted them for something considerably better than mere routine ward work'.[3] As a result an instruction was issued in 1940[4] which defined their range of duties, relieving them of all heavy domestic work. Thus, in the Service setting, VAD members did not fully take the place of RAMC orderlies, as the latter performed not only nursing duties but also more unskilled tasks from which the VADs were exempt. Male nursing orderlies had to be retained to do this work. Nor were VADs able to undertake all the duties of qualified nurses.

This definition of the duties of VADs created difficulties when it was applied in the civilian hospitals. It meant that when nursing auxiliaries replaced student nurses, more domestic staff had to be employed. This was not only more costly for the

[1] Voluntary Aid Detachments: *War Office Committee Report; 1942–43,* Cmd. 6442 vi, p. 9. Army Council Instruction 1300, 1940.
[2] *Ibid.*, p. 8.   [3] *Ibid.*, p. 10.
[4] Army Council Instruction 249, 1940.

hospitals but was unpopular with the regular nurses. The latter did not believe that fifty hours of training fitted the auxiliaries for the duties which they had been given. Indeed, the early promotion to routine nursing duties represented an affront to the status of regular nurses who had only graduated to such responsibilities after a lengthy and menial apprenticeship. Moreover, full-time members of the Reserve were paid more than student nurses even though they had less experience of nursing work. This the probationers resented.[1] Trained nurses complained that the public seldom appreciated the difference between a VAD uniform and that of a registered nurse,[2] while one auxiliary complained that 'the regular nurse seems to avoid giving the auxiliary too much information for fear that she will become too smart'.[3]

By June 1940, about 6,200 full-time members of the Civil Nursing Reserve were at work in the hospitals; many part-timers were also employed. But in spite of this progress, it was calculated in the summer of 1940 that 100,000 more nurses were needed if all the emergency beds were to be staffed at adequate standards. In the event this estimate proved excessive. While there were not enough nurses to staff all the hospital *beds*, the total number of nurses was sufficient for the total number of hospital *patients* as a high proportion of the emergency beds were unoccupied. 'On the outbreak of war about 140,000 hospital beds had been emptied of patients'[4] to keep them clear for emergencies. Indeed for the total of patients actually in hospital, never before had the total of nursing staff been so generous. In many hospitals, particularly the voluntary hospitals, under-employed nurses awaited the wounded and the shoal of air-raid casualties that never came in the numbers anticipated.

Thus, while there was actually no total shortage of nurses in the hospitals at currently accepted standards, the Ministry of Health believed there would be such a shortage when the war—particularly the air war—began in earnest. It was this belief that determined policy. No longer was it thought possible to brush aside the long-standing problems of the nursing profession.

[1] See correspondence in the *NM*, 19 April 1941, p. 33.

[2] 'How often do we see photographs printed in the national press, showing men of the Forces, and casualties in civilian life, being attended in bed by a young girl with a cross in her cap and on her bosom—and the uninformed public is too often left to assume that this cross is an essential part of the nurse's uniform.' *Ibid.*, 23 January 1943, p. 261.

[3] *Ibid.*, 26 April 1941, p. 42.   [4] Titmuss: *op. cit.*, p. 183.

In January 1941, *The Times* demanded better pay and better status for the profession.[1] The Athlone Committee Report was studied again in official circles and the Ministry of Health decided to implement its major recommendations, both on the salaries of nurses and on the official recognition of the assistant nurse.

The first step concerned salaries. In April 1941, the Ministry guaranteed a cash salary of £40 to students for the first year of training with increases of £5 for each subsequent year. This initial salary of £40 may be compared with the average figures of £21 in the voluntary hospitals and £33 in local authority hospitals which were paid to first-year probationers before the war. By 1941, retail prices were about 30 per cent higher than in 1937.[2] In real terms, therefore, the guaranteed salary was lower than that offered in the average local authority hospital before the war but about a third higher than the pre-war average for voluntary hospitals. Nevertheless the Royal College of Nursing[3] 'found that the new Government rates were too high and did not sufficiently take into account the cost of the expensive professional training'.[4] A starting salary of £30 was held to be sufficient.[5]

For the experienced grades, the Ministry of Health urged hospitals to pay £95 for trained nurses and £60 for assistant nurses.[6] Some financial assistance through the emergency medical service was promised. When allowance is made for the higher price level, these salaries gave trained nurses a slightly higher standard of living than they had received in voluntary hospitals before the war, but no higher than that which had been

---

[1] 'The time has come when all Government Departments must adopt the same attitude to the nursing profession—that it is a profession, a high calling, the members of which are deserving of all the consideration shown to doctors and of such standards of remuneration as will, once for all, mark them out as persons possessed of special and valuable knowledge and skill. An underpaid nurse cannot command the recognition which is her due. Her rank is also a matter of importance. Every nurse ought to enjoy a status comparable to that of a commissioned officer; a lower status is detrimental to her service and therefore a handicap upon her patients.' See *The Times*, 29 January 1941, leader page.

[2] London and Cambridge Economic Service (*The Times Review of Industry*, March 1955, p. xiv).

[3] The College was granted the title 'Royal' in 1939.

[4] Ferguson and Fitzgerald: *op. cit.*, p. 340n. [5] *NM*, 24 May 1941, p. 92.

[6] In addition the nurse received board and lodging in kind.

given in the average local authority hospital. The rates were lower in real terms than the pre-war average for assistant nurses in both types of hospital. A month after the Ministry had sent out this circular, the Royal College of Nursing recommended a salary scale of £100–£150 for trained staff nurses and £150–£200 for ward sisters.[1]

This initiative by the Ministry of Health was intended to do no more than deal with the immediate problem. In the long run, the Ministry would not wish to determine unilaterally the salaries of nurses. It was clearly desirable to follow the Athlone Committee's recommendation and set up a nurses' salaries committee with representatives of employers and employees on the lines of the Burnham committee for teachers. But this proposal was unwelcome to large sections of both employers and employees.

The Royal College of Nursing had decided to press for some sort of negotiating machinery for nurses at the beginning of 1938 but was anxious that 'nurses shall be dealt with as a distinct professional body and not solely as a part of a group including other workers who might greatly outnumber the nurses and who would not have the knowledge of the special problems connected with the care of the sick'.[2] The College was also anxious that any committee which was set up should be on Whitley Council lines. It did not favour the Burnham type of committee which the Ministry had in mind, 'in view of the fact that the Council [of the Royal College] considered that hours and conditions of work demanded as much reform as salaries'.[3] With this in mind the Royal College had co-operated in the setting up of a special committee known as the Local Authorities Nursing Services' Joint Committee to deal with conditions in the nursing services of county councils, county and non-county boroughs, urban and rural district councils and joint boards.[4]

The employers wanted to prevent any negotiating machinery being established. First, they were worried about the cost of paying the higher salaries which might be granted. The Athlone Committee had recommended that the Exchequer should give grants to the voluntary hospitals to enable them to increase nurses' pay, but they feared that such dependence on the Exchequer might become permanent—the thin end of the wedge

[1] *NM*, 24 May 1941, p. 92.
[2] Royal College of Nursing: *Annual Report for 1939*, p. 8.
[3] *Ibid., 1941*, p. 6.   [4] *Ibid., 1940*, p. 5.

of Government control. Secondly, the British Hospitals' Association feared that the existence of a salaries committee might encourage trade union organization among nurses and, therefore, be bad for hospital practice. For these reasons, discussions on a salaries committee made no progress.

In October 1941, the Ministry of Health decided to delay no longer: a salaries committee was constituted for England and Wales under the chairmanship of Lord Rushcliffe.[1] The employers' panel consisted of six representatives of the voluntary hospitals, one representative of the Queen's Institute of District Nursing and thirteen representatives of the local authorities. The employees' panel had nine representatives from the Royal College of Nursing, one from the Association of Hospital Matrons, one each from the British College of Nurses and the Royal British Nurses' Association, three from the National Association of Local Government Officers, and five from the Trades Union Congress. Thus professional organizations had a majority of the seats: the Royal College and the Association of Hospital Matrons had half the seats between them.[2] However, the Royal College asked for still greater representation on the grounds that it represented 8,000 student nurses.[3] The trade unions also thought that they were under-represented. The Guild of Nurses held that there were only five representatives of working nurses 'with many years' experience in the very skilful art of negotiation on Salaries and Service Conditions'.[4]

The original task of the Committee was to draw up 'agreed scales of salaries and emoluments for the state registered nurses employed in England and Wales in hospitals and Public Health Services, including the service of district nursing, and for student nurses in hospitals approved as training schools by the General Nursing Council for England and Wales'.[5] These terms of reference were, however, widened later on—as the result of pressure from both staff and employers' panels—to include conditions of work, such as holidays and sick pay, and also to cover additional groups of nurses such as assistant nurses and nurses training for or on the special registers.

[1] A similar committee was set up for Scotland under the chairmanship of Professor T. M. Taylor.   [2] *H of C Deb.*, 16 October 1941, col. 1494.
[3] *NM*, 25 October 1941, p. 43.
[4] Guild of Nurses: *Hospitals and Welfare Services Union*, p. 7.
[5] *H of C Deb.*, 16 October 1941, col. 1494.

In its first report, published in 1943, the Committee stated that it was anxious to attract more suitable student nurses to enter the hospitals. This did not mean, however, that pay should be high during training.

> In this connection [wrote the Committee] we have had to bear in mind the fact that the student nurse should be regarded primarily as a student, who is receiving a valuable training, with tuition from medical staff as well as nursing staff, although at the same time she is helping to staff her hospital. In other professions it is customary for a student to pay fees for training; the student nurse not only receives hers free, but in addition is paid a salary and provided with emoluments. What is in our view chiefly required as a stimulus to recruitment is that the prospects of the nurse after training, in senior as well as junior posts, should be equitable and attractive.[1]

From this reasoning the Committee concluded that it was to the trained grades that higher pay should be granted.

Thus no more was recommended for student nurses than the Ministry of Health had offered in 1941, but staff nurses received £5 above the 1941 minimum. The major change was to increase the maximum pay for staff nurses and sisters. The salary scales for trained and experienced nurses were placed firmly on an incremental basis. The cash salary for a resident ward sister began at £130 but could rise to £200 after ten years' service. Even a resident assistant nurse whose starting cash salary was £55 could reach a maximum of £95. In 1943, prices were over 40 per cent higher than in 1937,[2] so in real terms the minimum cash salaries for qualified grades were not very different from the average of those paid in 1937; the maximum salaries were substantially higher. In general, the Committee's report was welcomed in the nursing world. According to the *Nursing Mirror*, the profession had been regularized 'on a basis which compares reasonably well with that of other professions for educated women'.[3]

The Committee recommended that the hours of work should be 96 per fortnight 'as soon as conditions permit'. Night duty should be limited to six months for sisters and staff nurses, and three months for student nurses. There should be one complete

---

[1] Ministry of Health: *First Report of Nurses Salaries Committee*, Cmd 6424, p. 7: HMSO, 1943.   [2] London and Cambridge Economic Service Index.   [3] 20 February 1943, p. 325.

day off duty a week and 28 days' leave with pay. Sick pay should vary from one month's to three months' full pay according to length of service with an additional period on half pay.

It was estimated that the cost to local authorities and voluntary hospitals of implementing these proposals would be between £1½ million and £2 million per annum. The Government commended the report to the bodies concerned and agreed to pay 50 per cent of any increased expenditure which was caused by introducing them.[1] The recommendations were not, however, made compulsory, although the Minister of Health was pressed to do so by a Labour member of Parliament (Dr Edith Summerskill); the Minister pointed out that he had no power to direct hospitals.[2] Thus, in the middle of the war, action was taken on the Athlone Committee's recommendations.

While these steps were being taken to improve nurses' pay, there was also some progress during the early years of the war towards the recognition of the assistant nurse. The Civil Nursing Reserve had recruited 'assistant nurses' right from the start. This in itself implied some official recognition. At first, assistant nurses were described as 'those who were only partially trained but who were or had been earning their living by nursing'. In April 1941 they were formally defined as persons who 'had had two years' experience when they entered the Reserve'.[3] New applicants for enrolment as assistant nurses needed a period of not less than two years' training in hospital, though not necessarily in a hospital recognized by the General Nursing Council as a training school.[4] The publication in 1943 by the Rushcliffe Committee of a salary scale for the assistant nurse was a further step towards recognition.

During the war years, both hospital managements and trained nurses were becoming more willing to accept the new grade. The employers favoured recognition because of the activities of the nursing co-operatives. These employment agencies were experienced in securing high pay for those on their registers. As a result assistant nurses were often better paid than state registered nurses, and hospital authorities objected to paying high rates for nurses who were not always efficient. Moreover

---

[1] *H of C Deb.*, 11 February 1943, cols. 1422–3.
[2] *Ibid.*, 18 February 1943, col. 1930.
[3] Ministry of Health Circular 2540, 11 April 1941, Appendix II.
[4] *NM*, 19 April 1941, p. 26.

some women were leaving the Civil Nursing Reserve to be re-engaged at higher rates through the nursing co-operatives. The employers naturally wanted some minimum standard of competence to be laid down for someone calling herself an assistant nurse.

The profession itself was also more in favour of limiting and defining the activities of assistant nurses. It was quite clear by now that such women would continue to work in the hospitals for many years to come. It was felt that their position should be regularized if only through fear that the nursing auxiliaries, introduced by the Civil Nursing Reserve, might pose as assistant nurses after the war and take jobs from persons more fitted to do them. Already there was 'leakage of candidates from the intensive training available under the Civil Nursing Reserve to the undiscriminating and ever-open doors of the nurse supply agencies'.[1] In 1940, the Royal College sent a deputation to see the Minister of Health which 'stressed the dangers to the profession of competition with unqualified persons and the need for legislation to control the assistant nurse in order to meet the situation likely to arise at the end of the war'.[2]

In November 1941 the Royal College of Nursing set up a Nurses' Reconstruction Committee under the chairmanship of Lord Horder to consider ways and means of implementing the recommendations of the Athlone Committee's Report. The first report of the Committee, dealing with the assistant nurse, was published in August 1942.[3] It stated that

The Assistant Nurse of the future should become one of the most stable elements in our national nursing service—an integral part of the profession, and a person whose status offers the key to the improved training and employment of her senior partner, the State Registered Nurse. Moreover it is only when the services of the Assistant Nurse have been defined and regulated that matters affecting the State Registered Nurse can be brought into line—her student

[1] Royal College of Nursing: *Nurses' Reconstruction Committee*, Section I 'The Assistant Nurse', 1942, p. 8 (Committee Chairman: Lord Horder).

[2] Royal College of Nursing: *Annual Report for 1940*, p. 7.

[3] The Committee produced four reports. The last one was not published until 1949. Half the Committee was appointed by the Royal College and a half was appointed by kindred organizations which were invited to send representatives. The latter included the British Hospitals' Association, the British Medical Association, and the Society of Registered Male Nurses.

status assured when in training and her skill used to the best advantage when she is trained.[1]

The Royal College's desire to see recognition given to the assistant nurse arose out of the desire to protect the status of registered nurses. There was a shortage which was likely to continue. The shortage disturbed the training for state registration in two main ways. First, it meant that the nurse in training could not be treated entirely as a student. There were jobs in the hospital which had to be done and only the students were there to do them. They had to undertake work which was not essential for their training.

Secondly, student nurses were tempted after their second year of training to abandon their course and join a co-operation or an agency as an assistant nurse. 'She can return to her training school in that capacity at a far higher rate of remuneration than her colleagues, though no better qualified than they. The prospect of quick returns at no cost to themselves is a strong temptation to the other student nurses to follow suit.'[2] It had been found in Scotland that over 80 per cent of assistant nurses enrolled with the Scottish Reserve had at one time been students in training for one or other of the State Registers.

If the assistant nurse was recognized, there would be more nurses to do the work of the hospitals and the training of students could be improved. There was, of course, another solution to the nursing shortage—to lower the theoretical standard for the State Examinations so that the type of girl who became an assistant nurse could take them. The type of girl who was now becoming state registered could continue her training by post certificate courses. It was, however, argued that a curriculum suitable to the assistant nurse type of girl would waste the more promising student's time. Such a 'drastic reduction of standards' was less desirable than instituting elementary tests for the assistant nurse.[3]

Given that there were to be assistant nurses, the next question to be settled was where they should work. The criterion suggested by the Horder Report was the quality of service required, but the fields named happened also to coincide with the areas of current shortage. Not only should the assistant nurse look after

---

[1] *Horder Committee Report*, Section I, 1942, p. 5.
[2] *Ibid.*, p. 8.   [3] *Ibid.*, p. 5.

the chronic sick; there was a place for her, under proper safe-guards, 'in factories, in certain health clinics, in nursing homes, and in many small institutions at present trying to solve their staffing problems largely by means of student labour'.[1]

The assistant nurse should no longer 'be regarded as an inferior type "second grade" or "helper"; instructed in such essentials as will enable her to carry out the work which trained nurses find uninteresting and therefore will not do'.[2] She was to be the junior partner. However, student nurses and assistant nurses were not to be taught together.[3] Every possible step was suggested to distinguish the senior and junior partners—there were to be separate uniforms and separate badges. While student nurses were 'trained' in 'preliminary training schools', attended 'lectures' and satisfied 'examiners' for admission to the 'Register', assistant nurses were to be 'instructed' in 'classes' at 'preliminary training centres' and were to satisfy 'assessors' for admission to the 'Roll'. Such was the proposed partnership.

The Horder Committee suggested stricter tests for the admission of existing assistant nurses to the 'Roll' than those recommended by the Athlone Committee. For nurses over the age of 30 a certificate of competence and evidence of five years' experience were to be required. For nurses under 30 evidence of two years' service in a hospital under supervision was suggested. The Athlone Committee had been content with a certificate of competence and evidence of two years' practice from all applicants.

Similarly the Horder Committee wanted to go further towards 'closing the profession' than the Athlone Committee. Co-operations and agencies were not only to be inspected, they were to have a state registered nurse as professional supervisor.

---

[1] *Horder Committee Report*, Section I, 1942, p. 7.   [2] *Ibid.*, p. 8.

[3] The *Nursing Times* elaborated the reason for this recommendation as follows: 'Were the two types of nurse to train in the same wards, the more simple duties and the less interesting work would fall to the assistant nurse in training which would probably lead to a feeling of inferiority in the lower grade. If the two grades are kept separate, each group will have the whole interest of the care of the patients in her ward, though in the case of the assistant nurse, the State registered ward sister will do the major nursing treatments herself. In this way nursing snobbery will surely be avoided, and the two groups of nurses will both learn that the nursing care each patient receives depends not on his purse, but on his nursing needs.' (27 March 1943, p. 198.)

Assistant nurses were only to work in private practice under supervision. With the exception of student nurses in training and assistant nurses under instruction, the practice of nursing was to be limited by law to state registered nurses and state enrolled assistant nurses. 'Nursing' was to be defined as 'tending for reward a sick person or persons under the charge of a registered medical practitioner'.

The Committee recognized that it would not be fair to 'close the profession' without making some arrangement for nurses who could have registered but failed to do so. It was not, however, prepared to see the Register itself reopened, which the trade unions had been demanding for several years. Instead, it suggested that a special temporary roll should be set up for 'practising nurses'. The conditions for admission to this roll, however, were to be stricter than those which had actually operated for existing nurses in 1925. In addition to what had been laid down in 1925, the practising nurse would be required to have either a certificate of three years' general training or a total of ten years' practice. The General Nursing Council was to have discretion to refuse enrolment in any case.

Early in 1943, the Minister of Health introduced his Nurses Bill. It followed fairly closely the proposals of the Horder Committee which had been set up by the Royal College of Nursing. Co-operatives and supply agencies were to be licensed and the selection of the nurse to attend each case was to be made by a state registered nurse or a doctor. But the profession was not to be 'closed' in the way in which the Horder Committee had recommended. It was held to be impracticable to define 'tending a sick person for gain'. A compromise had been reached whereby the title 'nurse' was, with a number of exceptions, to be restricted by law to state registered nurses and enrolled assistant nurses.

The General Nursing Council was made responsible for forming and keeping the Roll of assistant nurses. As in the Registration Act, the Council was to admit existing nurses who 'for a prescribed period' had been '*bona fide* engaged in practice as nurses under conditions which appear to the Council to be satisfactory for the purposes of this provision and have such knowledge and experience as to justify their enrolment'.[1] The Council was to frame the exact rules. For the list of practising

[1] *Nurses Act 1943*, 6 & 7 Geo. 6, Section 2 (2) (c).

nurses the Act was made more specific. Persons were to be admitted who held satisfactory certificates from an institution showing that they had completed before July 1925 'a course of training in nursing in the institution, and who satisfy the Council that they are of good character and have adequate knowledge and experience of nursing'.[1] Admission to the list was to depend upon training. The Horder Committee had been prepared to allow a nurse to qualify for admission on ten years' practice and no training.

During the debate in the House of Commons, fears were expressed that the General Nursing Council might be too restrictive in exercising the powers entrusted to it.

Frankly I am afraid that if these matters are left entirely in the hands of the General Nursing Council that body may adopt the somewhat restrictive methods which now operate. There is at the present time an acute shortage of nurses, both state registered and assistant, but notwithstanding, many hospitals with training schools have very long waiting lists and many months have to elapse before an applicant for training is admitted. In addition, many of the training schools have very high entrance fees. I am very apprehensive that the General Nursing Council may apply these somewhat restrictive methods to assistant nurses.[2]

The list for practising nurses was also criticized. Some members, briefed by the trade unions concerned, asked for the Register to be re-opened and nurses 'on the list' to be allowed to have the same rank as state registered nurses. The Minister of Health was asked to stand up to 'that formidable body the General Nursing Council [which] is opposed to the re-opening of the Register'.[3] Mr Cocks, another speaker in the debate, championed the cause of 'experienced nurses with the highest qualifications who omitted to register in 1919'. 'They feel now that they have been penalized under the Bill and graded below nurses who have no higher qualifications and less experience than they.'[4] The Minister's reply was not convincing: 'If they want admission to the general register, surely they must conform to the standards which have been applicable since the period of grace expired'.[5] The new bill, however, was making admission

---

[1] *Nurses Act 1943*, Section 1 (2).
[2] Mr Burden: *H of C Deb.*, 7 April 1943, cols. 660–1.
[3] Mr Messer: *ibid.*, col. 681.
[4] *Ibid.*, 7 April 1943, col. 682.   [5] *Ibid.*, col. 685.

to the general register much more valuable than it was when nurses, often on the advice of their matrons, had failed to take advantage of the period of grace under the 1919 Act.

Mrs Bedford Fenwick was opposed to the whole bill. She returned to her post in the central lobby of the House of Commons, accompanied by Miss Isabel Macdonald and the two weighty red volumes of the Register of nurses which were her constant companions. Her favourite phrase 'one portal' was explained vigorously to any member of Parliament whose attention she could attract. Once again she attempted to form an alliance with the trade unions. She summoned their representatives to meet her in the lobby without explaining that she was opposed to the enrolment of assistant nurses. The trade unions were vigorous supporters of the bill, and no arguments of hers could persuade them to support her. She was left to fight her losing battle with what had now become almost a stage army.[1]

Thus nearly forty years later the recommendation of the 1905 Select Committee on the Registration of Nurses was implemented. There were two grades of nurse. This had some historical parallels. Early in the nineteenth century there had been, though not so rigidly, two grades which had been separately recruited: the nurses and the sisters. Later there had been probationers and lady-pupils. Now the higher class had a minimum of three years' training, and the lower class was to have a minimum of two years' training. There seemed reason to hope that the shortage of nurses would at last be eased.

---

[1] In an editorial entitled 'The Rise and Decline of the Profession of Nursing in England and Wales' Mrs Bedford Fenwick registered her protest. According to her the Act provided 'for the enrolment [registration] of semi-trained nurses, known as Assistant Nurses, and the recognition of thousands of women with nebulous, untested qualifications, who, during the past twenty years, have failed to qualify themselves by examination for State Registration. . . . Future generations of nurses will suffer from the disastrous legislation thus inaugurated.' *BJN*, April 1943, p. 37.

CHAPTER XII

The Shortage Continues

BY the end of 1943 the major recommendations of the
Athlone Committee had been implemented. A national
negotiating body had been set up, and Exchequer money was
used to underwrite the rates of pay it had recommended. In
addition a new grade of nurse had been recognized. These
measures did not, however, put an end to the shortage of nurses.

The Civil Nursing Reserve had estimated in 1942 that 12,200
more nurses were needed,[1] and new attempts were made to
recruit them. In April 1943, anyone aged between 17 and 60
who had had nursing experience in the preceding ten years was
compelled to register with the Ministry of Labour. This was a
vast administrative operation—a list of over 400,000 names was
compiled—but it found few additional nurses.

More successful was a large-scale publicity campaign to
attract recruits: volunteers came forward both to become
students and to become nursing auxiliaries. The success of this
campaign was largely due to the fact that women were being
conscripted for war work. Faced with the alternatives of factory
work or the women's Services, many girls, particularly those of
middle class background, chose nursing as their form of war work.

Between 1941 and 1944 when hospital nursing staff reached
its war-time peak, the total of hospital nurses in England and
Wales increased from about 89,000 to 98,000—an increase of
about 9,000.[2] During this period the number of auxiliaries
increased by only about 2,000; the number of trained nurses
actually *fell* by about 1,500 and there was also a fall in the
number of assistant nurses. The major change was in the number
of student nurses. There were about 9,000 more students in the

[1] *Horder Committee Report*, Section II, 'Education and Training', 1943,
p. 59.
[2] The figures cover all hospitals except mental and maternity hospitals.
See Ferguson and Fitzgerald: *op. cit.*, p. 335.

hospitals in the middle of 1944 than in the middle of 1941. The change in the intake of new students was dramatic. In 1938 it was estimated that a total of 11,200 students entered general training in both voluntary and municipal hospitals in Great Britain. In the peak year (1943) 15,400 students entered training.[1] Thus in the war emergency, the increase in the number of probationers which had been continuously sought between the wars was achieved.

In spite of all the controls imposed in wartime, no attempt was ever made to compel nurses to remain in training. It was thought unwise to use conscripts to nurse the sick. In spite of the high level of recruitment, the wastage rate for general training was actually a little lower during the war than it had been before it. In 1937, 37 per cent of students in voluntary hospitals and 52 per cent of students in municipal hospitals left before completing their three years of training. Among students admitted between 1938 and 1942, the wastage rate in voluntary hospitals varied between 33 per cent and 35 per cent in each year except one.[2] In municipal hospitals the wastage rate varied between 41 per cent and 47 per cent.

The shortage of nurses during the war was not spread evenly throughout all the different fields of nursing practice. There never was a shortage of nurses to look after the casualties from the armed forces. Indeed it became recognized, by the middle of the war, as it had been in 1917, that there was a danger of the armed forces absorbing too many nurses. Work with wounded servicemen was more popular with nurses than work with the civilian sick—particularly the chronic sick, the mentally sick and the tuberculous cases. Moreover the Service Departments were in a powerful position when they made demands for resources to fight the war. Their establishments had to be limited.

The shortage was felt by the maternity hospitals, the tuberculosis hospitals, the hospitals for the chronic sick and the mental hospitals. These had always been the less popular fields of nursing practice. Moreover, as the increase in nursing staff largely took the form of an increase in students taking general

[1] Ministry of Health, Department of Health for Scotland, and Ministry of Labour and National Service: *Report of the Working Party on the Recruitment and Training of Nurses*, p. 88: HMSO, 1947 (Chairman: Sir Robert Wood, KBE).

[2] It was 40 per cent of the 1939 intake. See *Wood Committee Report*, p 89.

training, the general hospitals were relatively well-staffed. During the war, the number of patients in tuberculosis and chronic hospitals was increasing rapidly for a number of reasons, but the required nursing staff was not available. The mental hospitals were particularly badly hit because they used such a high proportion of male staff. Many men had left to join the Forces and the recruitment of male students was negligible for obvious reasons. The recruitment of females was also low: the intake of students in Great Britain fell steadily from 9,700 in 1938 to 3,700 in 1943.[1] Moreover wastage during training, which had always been heavy, became alarming. The pre-war figure of 62 per cent rose to between 67 per cent and 80 per cent for women and even touched 100 per cent for men.[2] Steps had to be taken to redistribute the available nurses, so that more would care for the ordinary civilian sick.

In September 1943, the Control of Engagements Order which covered women from 18 to 40 years of age was applied to nurses and midwives. Nurses had to obtain appointments, and employers had to obtain nurses only through an Appointments Office of the Ministry of Labour. It was laid down that a nurse who left her post had to choose her new one from the fields where there was a shortage of staff; nurses could, however, leave to take up further training. This measure proved inadequate.

In April 1944 the Ministry of Labour decided to direct newly qualified nurses away from their training schools. Thus, for the first time, nursing staff could be compulsorily transferred from one post to another. Even this measure proved less effective than had been hoped, as about half the newly qualified nurses chose to take further training rather than take a post in one of the understaffed fields. There was a sharp increase in the numbers taking midwifery training. While this greatly assisted the maternity services, the problem in tuberculosis, mental, and chronic hospitals remained acute. Only 9 per cent of the newly qualified nurses chose to work in these fields.

All these efforts managed to increase the number of nurses working in tuberculosis hospitals and hospitals for the chronic sick between the middle of 1942 and the middle of 1944 by only about 2,000.[3] But the number of patients also increased rapidly, with the result that the ratio of nurses to patients changed very

---

[1] *Wood Committee Report*, p. 90.   [2] *Ibid.*, p. 90.
[3] Ferguson and Fitzgerald: *op. cit.*, p. 337.

little. As the war came to an end, the position deteriorated again; by November 1946 it was worse than it had been in the middle of 1942.

The total nursing staff of all hospitals was declining. From the peak of 98,000 in England and Wales in the middle of 1944, the total fell to about 94,000 in the middle of 1945 and by November 1946 had fallen to about 80,000.[1] The number of trained nurses and assistant nurses fell only slightly. The number of student nurses also held up well. Indeed in 1945, 14,000 entered training in Great Britain compared to 11,200 in 1938.[2] The municipal hospitals had about the same number of students as before the war while the voluntary hospitals were in a better position. The overwhelming reason for the fall of the hospital nursing staff at the end of the war was the departure of the nursing auxiliaries. In the middle of 1943 there had been a peak of 12,800 at work in England and Wales; by November 1946 there were only 1,700, though by October 1945 between 3,500 and 4,000 nursing auxiliaries had become student nurses.[3]

One step taken by the Minister of Health to deal with the immediate situation was to start in April 1946 short courses of a year for candidates who held certain nursing ranks in the Services. After this training the candidate was admitted to the Register. The General Nursing Council approved this step as a wartime emergency measure, but in July 1949 the Council asked the Minister how long these courses were expected to continue as 'they could not be considered to be entirely satis-factory'.[4] The Minister replied that he did not think the time had yet come to dispense with them and asked the Council what concession the Council would give to candidates who could have taken them when they were discontinued. 'The Council informed the Minister that such candidates would be allowed to complete their training for admission to the Register in a period of two and a half years.'[5] The one-year courses continued until October 1953.

Neither the implementation of the Athlone recommendations nor these emergency measures solved the nursing shortage.

---

[1] These figures cover all hospitals except mental and maternity hospitals. See Ferguson and Fitzgerald: *op. cit.*, p. 335.   [2] *Wood Committee Report*, p. 88.

[3] These figures cover all hospitals except mental and maternity hospitals. Ferguson and Fitzgerald: *op. cit.*, p. 335.

[4] *General Nursing Council Annual Report 1949–51*, p. 4.   [5] *Ibid.*, p. 4.

Indeed the national negotiating machinery had reinforced the effects of the war by making the distribution of nurses worse rather than better. Before the war, local authorities had been able to compensate for the lower status of their hospitals by paying higher salaries than the voluntary hospitals for all grades, including students. The effect of the Rushcliffe Committee's report had been to reduce these differentials. The standard scales for students were 'looked on with extreme disfavour by the less well known hospitals, which maintained that their only hope of attracting candidates was to offer financial inducements from the start'.[1]

The legislation on the assistant nurse had given a legal status to existing practising nurses, but training schools for assistant nurses were slow in getting under way. 'Those in charge of Public Assistance institutions were unwilling to provide the training until their additional responsibilities had been recognized by an adjustment in their salary scale.'[2] Nor was the assistant nurse training popular with those starting work in the hospitals. It was felt to be an inferior grade recruited to do the unpopular work among the chronic sick and the word 'assistant' in the title deterred prospective trainees. Most important of all was the fact that more could be earned as an orderly than as an assistant nurse. Those who *were* willing to take some form of training tended to get accepted as student nurses. In the year 1947–48, only 678 pupil assistant nurses entered training.[3] According to one observer (Dr Cohen) the scheme was 'dying a natural death'.[4]

The price which had been paid by the Ministry for the recognition of the assistant nurse was to grant the profession legal restrictions in the use of the title 'nurse'. The profession had asked for unrecognized persons to be forbidden 'to nurse the sick for gain'. The restriction of the use of the title 'nurse' had been a compromise which the profession had accepted. It proved very difficult if not impossible to administer. Thus, a woman trained as a nurse abroad might be asked her occupation at the port of entry and find that she had broken the law with the first word

[1] *Horder Committee Report*, Section IV, 'The Social and Economic Conditions of Nurses', 1949, p. 31.   [2] *Ibid.*, p. 23.   [3] *Ibid.*, p. 23.
[4] Ministry of Health, Department of Health for Scotland and Ministry of Labour and National Service: *Working Party on the Recruitment and Training of Nurses (Ministry Report)*, p. 46: HMSO, 1948.

ₒhe uttered on British soil. In addition, there were many persons who regarded themselves as 'nurses' whom it would have been somewhat unreasonable to drag before the courts if they persisted in adopting the title. Thus the Minister drafted a special regulation with three pages of exceptions to the prohibition.[1] Under the first regulations, for example, Christian Science nurses were allowed to remain 'nurses', though this concession was withdrawn as the result of indignant representations a year later.[2]

Foreign nurses, however, presented a special problem. As the General Nursing Council had no powers under the 1919 Act to register nurses trained abroad, the Minister of Health had opened a 'list' of foreign trained nurses. Nurses on the list were paid as trained nurses and permitted to call themselves 'nurses' as long as they gave some indication of the country where they were trained. For example, a nurse trained in France could legally call herself a 'French nurse'. Under the 1949 Nurses Act, the General Nursing Council was given powers to admit foreign trained nurses to the Register. The Council accordingly pressed for the list to be closed as those on it paid no fees, were subject to no disciplinary procedure, and in many cases had received training which was below the standard of that required in Britain. But the Council would not allow those nurses whom they were unwilling to admit to the Register or Roll to continue to describe themselves as such (with their country of training). The list therefore remained open until 1957, when the Council granted this not unreasonable concession.

Meanwhile plans were being developed for a National Health Service. This would clearly increase the demand for nurses and the Ministry felt that a comprehensive review of nursing services was required. Accordingly a Working Party was set up in January 1946 under the chairmanship of Sir Robert Wood to examine such questions as 'What is the proper task of a nurse? What training is required to equip her for that task? What annual intake is needed and how can it be obtained? From what groups of the population should recruitment be made? How can wastage during training be minimized?'[3] The Working Party consisted of

[1] Minister of Health: *Nurses England and Wales*, Statutory Rules and Orders 1945 No. 638.
[2] *Ibid.*, 1946 No. 1141.
[3] *Wood Committee Report*, p. iii.

only four persons in addition to the chairman: a doctor, a psychologist, and two nurses. The nursing organizations were not consulted about its composition.[1]

A majority report was published in the next year and a minority report in 1948 by Dr John Cohen (the psychologist).[2] Although Dr Cohen did not sign the majority report his way of thinking strongly influenced it. In the short time it sat, the Committee assembled a range of new empirical evidence which would have done credit to many a leisurely Royal Commission. It did not take formal evidence in the usual way. Instead it concentrated on field work undertaken by trained investigators. It attempted 'to carry out a scientific study of the problems confronting the nursing profession'.[3]

The Wood Committee wanted above all else to increase the number of trained nurses. They planned to achieve this by attracting more students and reducing wastage during training which was 'the key problem of the present training system'.[4] Wastage was attributed to hospital discipline, the attitude of senior staff, food, hours, and pressure of work, in that order.[5] Indeed the report contributed the most outspoken and well-documented condemnation of the attitudes and behaviour of senior nurses in hospitals that has yet been published. It is no wonder that the report was not well received by the Association of Hospital Matrons, and that the nurse members of the Committee were, to put it mildly, not popular with many of their colleagues.

'Nurses in training', the Committee wrote, 'must no longer be regarded as junior employees subject to an outworn system of discipline. They must be accorded full student status so far as the intrinsic requirements of nurse training permit.'[6] The Committee undertook a job-analysis of the work of a small group of

---

[1] *NT*, 13 September 1947, p. 629.

[2] In his lively minority report Dr Cohen pointed out with a wealth of supporting data that insufficient information was available from which estimates could be made of the number of nurses that were needed or decisions taken about the training which they should be given. He recommended that both the training and examination of nurses should be made the responsibility of the Divisions of Nursing at the Health Departments. The question of the future existence and possible role of the General Nursing Council should be examined by a committee of inquiry. He suggested an extensive programme of research.   [3] *Wood Committee Report*, p. 1.

[4] *Ibid.*, p. 78.   [5] *Ibid.*, p. 41.   [6] *Ibid.*, p. 78.

student nurses. It was found that the first-year nurses in the group devoted 33 per cent of their training hours to domestic duties 'which could be properly performed without any nurse training at all'.[1] In the second year 24 per cent of training hours were spent in this way, and in the third year 16 per cent. By relieving the student nurse of domestic work and other nursing duties dictated solely by the staffing needs of the hospitals, the Committee believed that a period of two years would suffice for the general training.

The Committee outlined the changes which were needed to enable nurses in training to be treated as students. First, there must be adequate nursing and domestic staff in training hospitals. Secondly, the course of training must be dictated by the needs of the student and not by the staffing requirements of hospitals. Thirdly, the finance of nurse training should be independent of hospital finance. Fourthly, students should be under the control of the training authority and not of the hospital, except as necessary for teaching and care of patients.[2] This last point involved a major change. Presumably the training authority would be able to refuse requests from the matron of the hospital for students to undertake any duties other than those needed for their training.

The Committee believed that nurse training schools were too small. In England and Wales there were 389 complete, 167 affiliated and 5 associated general training schools. 'It is unlikely', wrote the Committee, 'that so large a number of training schools could all have adequate clinical material, proper training facilities and equipment, well-trained sister tutors, or students in the numbers needed to run a training unit efficiently.'[3] Accordingly, the Committee recommended that composite training units should be formed. Even the large hospitals would need to be associated with hospitals of other types to cover the whole field of nursing.

The work of the various training units would need to be co-ordinated. For this purpose, the Wood Committee recommended that a Regional Nurse Training Board or Committee should be set up for each hospital region. This was to be a powerful body equipped with a permanent staff and Regional Director of Training. The principal duties of these Boards would be the planning and co-ordination of training facilities, the co-ordination

---

[1] *Ibid.*, p. 46.   [2] *Ibid.*, pp. 79–80.   [3] *Ibid.*, p. 43.

of standards of admission and the allocation of students to training units with due regard to the candidate's choice, the approval of supervisors for the year of supervised practice and the formation of advisory centres to stimulate interest in nursing and advise potential students.[1]

If complete training was to be given in two years, then the position of the assistant nurse had clearly to be reconsidered. The Committee was not in favour of perpetuating this grade. It recommended that no more pupil assistant nurses should be recruited. The duties undertaken by assistant nurses should be allocated partly to the trained staff and partly to a new grade of nursing orderly. Statutory recognition and the use of the title 'nurse' was not justified for this grade which would only need three to six months' training. The nursing orderly grade would be concerned with the simpler routine nursing duties.

The Wood Committee's report became known as the 'pink peril' in certain nursing circles, but some of its recommendations were well received by the nursing journals. The *British Journal of Nursing* was delighted at the proposal to close the roll for assistant nurses and expressed its pleasure in its usual style.[2] The *Nursing Times*, on the other hand, questioned the reduction of training from three years to two. Would a two-year trained nurse 'understand the why and wherefore of every skill? Would she be practised in observing all the signs and symptoms of a patient's condition?'[3]

Four years earlier, the second report of the Horder Committee had made the same point. 'The critics of the repetitive tasks inherent in a nurse's training underestimate the variety . . . of almost all routine tasks which fall to the lot of the nurse. . . . No two patients are alike and there is always something to learn from each.'[4] The *Nursing Times* questioned in 1947 the introduction of auxiliary workers into the wards of training schools.

We feel that this may lead to the student nurse gaining too little practice in bedside nursing. . . . Some may feel that it is a pity that even the simple nursing duties should be carried out by other than

---

[1] *Wood Committee Report*, p. 80.

[2] 'At last the gloom and darkness of the night have been pierced by rays and beams of light, and now the Dawn of a new Day is already lighting the distant horizon, and its rosy glow gives promise of a bright day to come.' October 1947, p. 111.   [3] 13 September 1947, p. 630.

[4] *Horder Committee Report*, Section II, 1943, p. 12.

nurses and argue that it would mean a reduction in the amount of actual nursing service that the patients would receive, but we have got to decide what sacrifices will be needed if we wish to obtain the status of student for our nurses in training.[1]

In the middle of 1948, the General Nursing Council published its views on the Wood Committee's report. The Council accepted the concept of the 'student nurse' but considered that

the *reduced* length of training which it is claimed would be sufficient to cover an *increased* content would, if carried out, be a retrograde step . . . such a crammed training would not recruit additional student nurses and would cause serious wastage amongst the trained staff in hospital.[2]

It is essential that the nurse throughout her training should continue to undertake repetitive nursing duties. . . . The elimination of so-called 'repetitive duties' on which the reduced training is based would result in robbing the student nurse not only of the ability to nurse but of satisfaction in nursing.[3]

The Council opposed the suggestion that training schools should be separated from the hospitals:

The Council cannot accept the suggestion that training units should be under the control of independent Directors rather than that of the Matron of the principal hospital in each training unit. The proposed dissociation of responsibility would result in the loss of much that experience has proved of the greatest value in the training of nurses.[4]

It also objected to the idea that either control over training schools or their inspection should be the responsibility of anyone but itself.[5] Tartly, the Council concluded that it 'desires to draw the attention of the Minister to the fact that the Report of the Working Party would appear to have been drawn up with insufficient thought of the needs of the patient which in fact form the basis on which any conclusions relating to nurse training must be built'.[6]

In the case of the assistant nurse, the Council believed that

---

[1] *NT*, 9 August 1947, p. 541.

[2] *Memorandum on the Report of the Working Party on the Recruitment and Training of Nurses* submitted to the Minister of Health by the General Nursing Council for England and Wales, p. 15.

[3] *Ibid.*, p. 3.   [4] *Ibid.*, p. 6.
[5] *Ibid.*, p. 9.   [6] *Ibid.*, p. 14.

the training could not be reduced from two years. The roll of assistant nurses should remain open until there were sufficient trained nurses in the country. Higher salaries would stimulate recruitment for this Roll, and compensate for the limited possibilities for promotion. The Council approved the establishment of ward orderlies but not nursing orderlies and urged the Minister of Health to encourage recruitment for this grade.

Whether use should be made of ward orderlies whose duties were purely domestic, or of nursing orderlies who would be allowed to undertake some basic nursing duties, was a critical problem for the nursing profession. The experience of the war had led a section of the profession to favour the use of nursing orderlies. Experienced nurses working with the armed forces had learnt the value of male nursing orderlies; civilian hospitals had found that nursing auxiliaries had a useful contribution to make and were feeling the effects of the large-scale departure of this grade at the end of the war. The London County Council had even reacted to the post-war shortages by deliberately recruiting between 1,100 and 1,200 women orderlies who performed duties which brought them into closer contact with the patients than hospital domestics. It was reckoned that two orderlies were needed for a ward of thirty beds.[1]

The role envisaged for the hospital orderly was a limited one, and as long as it remained closely confined, there could be no professional objection to employing them. 'The duties of hospital orderlies are domestic,' wrote the *Nursing Times* in 1948, 'but they have a definite status, and increasing numbers are coming forward. . . . Every member who increases the ward team in the hospital service is valuable. . . . Teaching orderlies the dangers of infected tea towels or improperly cleaned feeding cups makes them realize that their work is important, and gives them further interest and that sense of responsibility which every worker should have.'[2] 'Let us welcome all comers,' the *Nursing Times* suggested later in the same year, 'but not labelling all as nurses or nursing staff regardless of their qualifications.'[3]

While there were many matrons who recognized the value of the orderly or auxiliary grade, there was also support for retaining the grade of assistant nurse. Those matrons who had established the training feared that its abolition would make the task

---

[1] *Horder Committee Report*, Section IV, 1949, p. 24.
[2] *NT*, 20 March 1948, pp. 201–2.   [3] *Ibid.*, 20 November 1948, p. 844.

of staffing the chronic hospitals more difficult. There was also some opposition to the use of auxiliary grades by the more traditional section of the nursing profession. Some even held that such usage was a contravention of the spirit of the 1943 Act which had restricted the use of the title 'nurse'. The 1949 Report of the Horder Committee (set up by the Royal College of Nursing) held that such a step could only be taken if there were appropriate safeguards.[1] There was always the danger that members of this unrecognized grade would find their way to nurse supply agencies. Even as late as 1949, it was reported that some supply agencies were seeking to evade the provisions of the 1943 Act. Some even 'stipulated that those of their staff who may not legally use the title "nurse" be addressed as "Sister" '.[2]

The fourth report of the Horder Committee was cagey about the whole issue. It did not commit itself on what type of assistant should work with the trained nurse.

The trained nurse's skill can be still further economized by delegating the simpler *nursing* tasks to staff who are less highly qualified. The question whether the patient would be best served by assistant nurses or by nursing orderlies is a matter of controversy which can only be decided in the light of further experiment.... All that can be said at the moment is that in view of the manpower situation, a large body of subsidiary workers is essential.[3]

The recommendations of the Working Party about training schools went somewhat further than the profession was prepared to go. The Horder Report of 1943 had recommended that there should be a reduction in the number of training schools and that small hospitals without facilities for a complete training should 'be relegated to a more limited though still well-defined role in group schemes'.[4] It had also pressed for the thorough inspection of schools 'analogous to the inspection carried out by the Board of Education in schools, and present methods be supplemented by a paid, full-time inspectorate'.[5] But the Working Party had gone further than this in arguing that training units should be taken out of the hands of hospital matrons and handed over to separate directors or principals. In practice, this would probably mean that the 'apprenticeship system' of nurse training would

---

[1] *Horder Committee Report*, Section IV, 1949, p. 22.
[2] *Ibid.*, p. 22.   [3] *Ibid.*, pp. 24–25.
[4] *Horder Committee Report*, Section II, 1943, p. 9.   [5] *Ibid.*, p. 35.

be superseded. This was not acceptable to the majority of the profession. It did not want nurse training to be completely separated from the work of the hospital. 'Will this produce', asked the *Nursing Times*, 'the type of nurse teacher who is interested in nurse education, but is not interested in the hospitals and the nursing service that they provide?'[1]

The essence of the Wood Committee's proposals was to achieve full student status. The difficult training and working conditions in hospitals were well known to potential recruits. Until these were improved, attempts to increase recruitment by publicity campaigns might tend to defeat their own ends. The fundamental difficulty was that the achievement of full student status would reduce the amount of nursing labour provided in hospitals at a time when there were already insistent demands for more nursing services to be provided. Thus the vicious circle which had existed in nursing for most of the century would need to be broken before the plan could be implemented. A hospital, unlike a factory, cannot close down when faced with a staff shortage. Somehow the needs of the sick must be met. The routine work of the nurse, the long hours, even the discipline under which the nurse works, were in a large measure a response to the nursing shortage.

The Committee reckoned that for the whole of Great Britain 14,000 nursing orderlies would need to be recruited and trained. But in addition an extra 22,000 or 24,000 trained nurses would be needed. It was suggested that a ready welcome should be given to male nurses, married nurses, and part-time nurses.

The use of part-time nurses had been recommended during the war,[2] but they had never made a substantial contribution to the work of the hospitals. Part-time nurses were believed to be unreliable—they were not willing to take their share of the less popular duty times (week-ends, evenings, and night duty) as they were mostly married women and had their own domestic responsibilities to attend to. But after the war, because of the acute shortage, part-time nurses were employed in hospitals for the chronic sick. Gradually the system extended to all types of hospital: matrons became more willing to cope with the administrative problems involved and began to appreciate the contribution they had to make. Between the beginning of 1946 and

[1] 13 September 1947, p. 630.
[2] See, for example, *NM*, 10 April 1943, p. 17.

March 1949 the number of part-time nurses in Great Britain increased from 3,000 to 26,000.[1]

In 1949 we find the fourth Horder Report recognizing that the part-time nurse had a permanent part to play. It summed up in the following words:

If the scheme for the employment of part-time staff is adequately prepared, and administered with sympathy and understanding, if both participants—employers and volunteers—realise its potentialities and limitations, a real sense of loyalty can be built up and difficulties minimised. With the development of loyalty comes willingness to volunteer for the less popular hours.[2]

Many more male nurses were at work in the hospitals after the war than before. The number of students had increased from about 120 in 1937 to about 2,400 in 1949 and the number of registered male nurses had increased from about 300 to about 1,300 in the same period.[3] The prejudice against men, already diminishing in the local authority hospitals before the war, was further reduced by the war itself. Many matrons and trained nurses had seen the skill of male nursing orderlies when working for the armed services and many men who had done nursing work for their war service took advantage of the chance of becoming state registered under the special short courses available after the war. But some prejudice still remained. As the Confederation of Health Service Employees remarked rather infelicitously in 1946, the male nurse was the 'Cinderella' of the profession. It was common for younger nurses 'to regard their male "opposites" as "male attendants" who are useful at times (when convenient) but who have little knowledge of nursing and can hardly be trusted to take a temperature'.[4]

Thus the war and its aftermath had changed some traditional attitudes of matrons. There was more willingness to make use of male nurses, married nurses, and part-time nurses. And untrained orderlies and aides were increasingly used in the wards. The leaders of the nursing profession were not, however, willing

---

[1] See p. 25.　　[2] *Horder Committee Report*, Section IV, 1949, p. 28.

[3] The figures for 1949 cover all hospitals in England and Wales other than mental, mental deficiency and neurosis hospitals. Thus the staff of psychiatric wards in general hospitals are included. The figures for 1937 are taken from Appendix II.

[4] COHSE: *The Hospital Services*, p. 19: London, 1946.

to sanction the performance of basic nursing duties by these grades. They intended that all such work would be reserved for registered nurses, assistant nurses, and those in training for these grades.

There was no support from the leaders of the profession for the more radical proposals of the Wood Committee. In particular they refused to accept a reduction of the training period for state registration from three years to two years. The supply of nurses was increasing, but the demand was increasing even more. There remained, therefore, after the war, as there had been before it, too few recognized nurses to meet all needs.

CHAPTER XIII

The Whitley Council

ON 5 July 1948, the National Health Service was established. The community had accepted full responsibility for the care of the sick, and nearly all the hospitals in England and Wales became publicly owned. No longer could governments play a mediatory role between a loose alliance of local authorities and an even looser alliance of voluntary hospitals. The quality of medical care, the terms and conditions of service of the staff working in the hospitals, and the power and privileges of professional bodies became all on one day matters with which central government was immediately concerned. At last it was possible for dramatic improvements to be made in the training and working conditions of the nursing profession.

The planning of the hospital services was delegated to fourteen Regional Hospital Boards. The large planning unit which Florence Nightingale had recommended eighty years earlier had been set up. The new boards had control over all the hospitals except the teaching hospitals; the latter were given their own Boards of Governors directly responsible to the Minister of Health. The day-to-day management of the non-teaching hospitals was handed over to Hospital Management Committees. The Royal College of Nursing preferred these arrangements made for the hospital services to those which had been suggested in the 1944 White Paper. It had 'expressed apprehension' at the idea of so many nursing services being brought under local government.[1] While the functions of planning and management were delegated, the negotiation of salaries and conditions of work was centralized. As nearly all the money spent on the hospitals was to come from the Exchequer, the salaries of hospital employees was a matter of national importance.

The negotiations for the different grades of staff working in the hospital service obviously needed to be co-ordinated. Any

[1] Royal College of Nursing: *Annual Report for 1946*, p. 4.

settlement for one grade would raise questions of relativities with other grades. As it would be cumbrous for one body to settle the pay of such a large number of different occupations, separate negotiating bodies were set up for different groups of staff—*functional* Whitley Councils.[1] In addition a *general* Whitley Council was appointed to negotiate the conditions of service which affected all grades. In the case of nurses and midwives, the Rushcliffe Committee for England and Wales and Guthries Committee for Scotland were replaced by a Nurses and Midwives Whitley Council for Great Britain.

This Council had 64 members. The staff side had 41 seats and the management side had 23 seats (voting was by sides). Of the 23 seats on the management side, 5 went to the government departments concerned, 8 to local authorities and 10 to the newly created hospital authorities (Regional Hospital Boards, Boards of Governors, and hospital management committees). Representation was not allocated according to the proportion of nurses employed. On this basis, hospital authorities were under-represented and local authorities were over-represented. The bodies that represented the local authorities had been able to press their claims strongly when the Council was set up. At this time the hospital authorities were still very new and weak. Under the arrangement that emerged the central departments and the local authorities had an overall majority if they voted together.

The staff side team was much the same as those of the committees it was replacing, but there were some minor changes. The professional associations were determined at all costs, however large the staff side should become, to hold a majority of the seats. They secured over half of the 41 seats, and neither the British College of Nurses nor the Royal British Nurses' Association was among the associations represented. The seats which had previously been held by the Trades Union Congress were handed over to specific trade unions. The National Union of Public Employees got 4 seats and the National Union of General and Municipal Workers got 3 seats. 4 seats were also given to the Confederation of Health Service Employees which had been

[1] The use of the term 'Whitley Council' to describe a negotiating body stems from the Committee on the Relations between Employers and Employed set up in October 1916 under the chairmanship of Mr J. H. Whitley, later Speaker of the House of Commons.

formed in 1946 by the amalgamation of the Hospital and Welfare Services Union with the Mental Hospital and Institutional Workers' Union.

Membership of the staff side of the Whitley Council did not follow the proportions of active nurses that were attached to the different organizations. For example, the Royal College of Nursing had twelve representatives.[1] In 1950–51 the College claimed a total of 45,720 members of which 26,000 were subscribing members, 2,000 were 'life' members, and 16,000 were 'founder' members. Moreover a nurse remained a 'member' until her subscription was two years in arrears. Thus by no means all the 45,720 were actively engaged in nursing. The Confederation of Health Service Employees, on the other hand, with only four places on the Council claimed a membership of 2,800 general nurses and 23,500 mental nurses in 1958. The Women Public Health Officers' Association had one place for only 3,000 members, not all of whom were nurses.

The traditional practice, accepted by the Rushcliffe Committee, had been to pay hospital nurses net salaries. In other words nurses who lived in received a payment in cash plus free board and lodging and other benefits in kind known as 'emoluments'. The value of these emoluments was counted for superannuation purposes. Thus in 1948 the salary of a first-year student was £70, a second-year student got £80, and a third-year student received £90: in addition there were the emoluments in kind valued at £75 for superannuation purposes. Nurses who lived out received in addition to their basic salary a 'living-out allowance' of £55 (i.e. £75 less £20 to allow for the value of the meals and other services received at the hospital).

The management side of the Whitley Council was anxious to change from the system of net salary plus the value of emoluments or living-out allowance to a gross salary from which payments were made to the hospital for services provided. It was felt that paying a gross salary would help to raise the status of the profession. It was also believed that it might help recruitment if the salary of a nurse was quoted inclusive of the value of services. Prospective entrants tended to forget the value of the services received in kind, when calculating the monetary rewards which the profession offered. However, the change involved one

[1] At this time, Her Majesty Queen Mary was patroness.

important effect which should not be overlooked: the value of emoluments became liable to income tax.[1]

It was because of this point about income tax that many hospital nurses wanted to keep the net salary system. Some sisters to whom the point was of considerable importance felt that 'it was sheer quixotry to incur income tax on the value of emoluments merely for the sake of prestige'.[2] Later, however, the fourth Horder Report welcomed the change, pointing out somewhat unconvincingly that 'the nurse who pays for her room has a right to complain, or to vacate the room altogether if the service is unsatisfactory, or there is undue emphasis on discipline and she feels she can fare better elsewhere'.[3]

The management side had one further objective in mind when the negotiations started: it wanted to increase the spending money of the non-resident nurse in relation to the resident nurse so that more nurses would be able to live away from their hospitals. It was held that this would be good for recruitment. Trade unions that recruited nurses were also very keen to see this happen.[4] But this could only be achieved if the gross salary were substantially increased. Not only would the change in the system of payment involve higher income tax commitments, but also higher deductions for superannuation. Unless the salary of resident nurses were increased, they would actually have less money available for spending.

The first negotiations of the new Whitley Council were complicated by one further factor. At the same time as the National Health Service was introduced, nurses, in common with the rest of the population, had to pay National Insurance contributions at a much higher level. Previously nurses had only had to pay the contributions to National Health Insurance of 1s. 4d. per week. From July 1948, they had to pay 3s. 10d. per week for the wider range of benefits available under the revised National Insurance scheme. For the first-year student nurse earning £70 in cash, an extra deduction of £6 10s. per year for National Insurance was a heavy burden, and the management side feared

---

[1] Emoluments had previously been exempt from tax because it is a general principle of Income Tax law that a benefit in kind received by an employee from his employer is not assessable to tax if it is not capable of being converted by him into cash.

[2] COHSE: *The Hospital Services*, February 1946, p. 16.

[3] *Horder Committee Report*, Section IV, 1949, p. 35.   [4] *Ibid.*, p. 35.

that it would be bad for recruitment. For this reason, among others, students were the first grade to be discussed by the new Council.

The question of the remuneration of student nurses had always been a delicate issue. Before the war, when local authorities had tended to pay students more than the voluntary hospitals, the Royal College of Nursing had condemned the local authorities for paying too much.[1] But while the College had favoured low pay for students, the trade unions had frequently complained of the 'exploitation of students on low salaries'. In 1941, the Government had paid students more in the hope of improving recruitment and the Royal College had objected that the Government had given too much.[2] In 1943, the Rushcliffe Committee had left the pay of students unchanged when increases were laid down for trained grades; it had supported the Royal College on this issue.

The second report (1943) of the Horder Committee set up by the Royal College had drawn an analogy with medical students and recommended that 'when possible, the student should pay for her training, but that no good potential nurse should be debarred from training through lack of money. . . . The Committee views with concern the increasing tendency to entice student nurses into the profession with liberal remuneration during their training.'[3] In 1947 the majority report of the Working Party found the analogy with other students irrelevant as it did not

take into account the type, hours and conditions of work and the future prospects of promotion. . . . The fact is that we are faced with the practical and pressing problem of providing an adequate number of nurses of the type required by the community. . . . The nursing needs of the community will not be met unless the training grant given to a student nurse is adequate to cover reasonable personal expenses (including on vacation).[4]

Thus the pay of the nurse in training was a delicate problem for the staff side of the new Whitley Council. The trade union representatives were prepared to press the case of the students and management was prepared to pay more in the hope of

[1] See p. 135 above.   [2] See p. 165 above.
[3] *Horder Committee Report*, Section II, 1943, p. 14.
[4] *Wood Committee Report*, p. 57.

encouraging recruitment. The departure of the British Hospitals Association from the negotiating machinery had led to a more liberal attitude towards pay for students. Moreover, the trade unions probably hoped that management would be induced to extend any improvement given to this grade right up the whole salary structure. The professional associations led by the Royal College, on the other hand, feared that high pay for students would damage their claim for student status and encourage hospitals to regard nurses in training simply as employees. The whole standing of the profession demanded that entry should be by training analogous to that provided at universities. Moreover the acceptance by management of the idea that the nurse under training was a student was important for the representation of the Royal College on the Whitley Council. Nurses in training could not be members of the College itself, but if they were regarded as students, the College could claim to speak on their behalf. If nurses in training were regarded merely as employees, the only organizations of which they could become members were trade unions. And the trade unions might ask for larger representation on the Whitley Council.

The changes contemplated by the management side of the Whitley Council at the start of the National Health Service led to delay in the first negotiations of the new Council. In addition the question of the student nurse strained the uneasy partnership between the trade unions and professional associations on the staff side of the new Council. Both sides of the Council saw the need for a swift settlement, but owing to the many issues involved the negotiations were not speedily completed.

The student nurses who were already paying the higher National Insurance contributions did not take kindly to the delay. By early in July 1948, the first month of the National Health Service, student nurses in certain London hospitals were threatening to hand in a month's notice on 1 August unless they received an adequate rise in salary.[1] It was argued that nurses had always had free medical care and they could not see why they should suddenly have to start paying for it.[2] The students appealed directly to the Minister of Health, who told them to place their claim before the Whitley Council 'through their representative associations'. This raised the awkward question of what *were* their representative associations. As the *Nursing*

[1] *NM*, 3 July 1948, p. 273.   [2] *Ibid.*, 14 August 1948, p. 316.

Mirror stated in 1950, 'students have no alternative but trade union membership'.[1] Some students protested to the Royal College of Nursing, and others who were members of the Confederation of Health Service Employees demanded that the union should itself organize a public demonstration.

The Confederation of Health Service Employees decided to place itself at the head of the protesting students, partly to see that the demonstration was well conducted and partly to prevent the discontent being manipulated for political purposes which it would have held to be undesirable. Thus it called on its nurse members to join in a public demonstration and demand a minimum wage of £5 a week. A group of nurses, male and female, some in uniform, gathered in Trafalgar Square on the Sunday before the Whitley Council was due to meet and marched to Hyde Park, where leaders of the union and student nurses addressed the crowd from a coal waggon.[2] A resolution was passed demanding a £5 a week minimum and emergency action from the Minister of Health if the Whitley Council failed to act expeditiously. One of the speakers took the opportunity to criticize the number of seats on the Council held by the Royal College of Nursing.[3]

A more dignified meeting was held by the Student Nurses' Association Unit of St Mary's Hospital, Paddington, which resolved that 'student nurses' salaries should be increased by a minimum of £40 per annum. . . . If other student nurses are in agreement with this resolution they should also send their resolutions to the Student Nurses' Association, at the Royal College of Nursing, who are in a position to negotiate our claims with the Whitley Council.'[4] The president of the Student Nurses' Association was at this time Her Royal Highness Princess Elizabeth.

These demonstrations did not go unnoticed in the nursing world, and came as something of a shock to the more traditionally minded. In one hospital where the students had written a letter of protest to their local Member of Parliament, those concerned were severely reprimanded for 'degrading the profession of nursing to the level of manual labour'.[5] The *British Journal of Nursing* was particularly shocked by the whole proceedings:

[1] *Ibid.*, 1 December 1950, p. 72.   [2] *NT*, 21 August 1948, p. 607.
[3] *NM*, 21 August 1948, p. 321.   [4] *Ibid.*, p. 334.
[5] *Medical Press*, 18 August 1948, p. 117.

'Twenty years ago young women of sound principle . . . would [never] have presumed to have assessed their talents in the same category as those of our incomparable Miss Nightingale even in private, much less from a coal cart to a public audience in Hyde Park!' Students had 'an inflated idea of their own usefulness and importance' and were making 'the most extravagant demands upon their fellow countrymen'.[1] The *Nursing Mirror* also had doubts about these extreme measures: 'Florence Nightingale, were she alive today, would have been the first to agitate for good pay . . . but we cannot help feeling that she would have found a subtler and more certain way to get what she wanted than marching with banners into any park in London.'[2]

The measures were effective. At least, the Whitley Council held meetings on 20 August, 24 August, and 3 September. Early on the principle was accepted that nurses in training were students to the extent of calling their pay a 'training allowance'. The staff side asked for £130 for a first-year female student with free board and lodging. The management side offered £180 with a deduction of £100 for board and lodging. The staff side rejected this offer and the management side offered £200 with the same deduction of £100 'as a final gesture, if that would provide a settlement'. The staff side then said it would accept £175 with a deduction of £75 which would have left the student who lived in with the same net sum of £100 which had been offered. No sooner had the spokesman for the management side accepted this than a representative of the trade unions on the staff side said that the trade union members could not be parties to the settlement. It was then pointed out that 'if the staff side were unable to present an agreed viewpoint, it was obvious that there could be no Whitley negotiating machinery for the nursing profession'. After further meetings the staff side accepted the management side's 'final offer' of £200 with a deduction of £100 for residence.

Later in the same year the Royal College's fourth Horder Report was published. It withdrew somewhat ungraciously from the position it had taken up six years earlier.

Today all education, up to and including secondary school standard, can be obtained free of cost, and the general tendency is to extend this principle. Thus the difference in salary between those who may have to contribute towards the cost of their training and

---

[1] *BJN*, September 1948, pp. 101–2.   [2] 25 September 1948, p. 401.

those whose training is automatically free will ultimately tend to disappear. This tendency is accelerated in a public service such as nursing, where the authority responsible for providing the service will go to considerable lengths to overcome any shortage of recruits not only by paying the necessary training costs but by meeting the student's financial needs.[1]

The Horder Committee saw the weakness in the position it had previously taken up. To the older generation of nurses low pay during training was not only hallowed by their own experience of it, but was even regarded as one of the hallmarks of the profession. It was clear, however, that this distinction between the professional and non-professional occupations was breaking down. The professional associations, moreover, had taken up a position which was unrealistic. However desirable it may be for the student nurse to be regarded and treated as an undergraduate, she did in practice contribute to the work of the hospital and did expect to be paid for this work. Secondly, it was perhaps too readily assumed that the girl who took nurse training regarded herself as starting upon a lifelong career. No doubt many of the leaders of the profession had decided right at the start to dedicate their whole lives to nursing and others may have later come to believe they had done so. But was this true of the typical new entrant? Did she picture herself as entering a lifelong career and weigh up the total rewards she would receive from this work? Or did she regard herself as filling in respectably and valuably the years between school and marriage? If this last were the more typical situation, immediate financial rewards compared with other occupations influenced the level of recruitment.[2] Those who argued that high pay during training

[1] *Horder Committee Report*, Section IV, 1949, p. 34.

[2] Analysing opinions expressed in 1949 by about 190 girls aged between 12 and 21 on the possibility of becoming a nurse, Miss Pearl Jephcott emphasised the importance of pay. The girls 'mentioned pay more frequently than any other single reason why they decided against nursing for themselves. . . . They seem to refer to pay in general, not to the student nurse's salary. The latter's £200 p.a. (with £100 deducted for board, etc.) is above what many girls of 18 earn, of course. The trouble is that £100 "keep" has not the same value as a couple of pound notes in your handbag each Friday night. From the latter you can meet the dilemmas of the week.' 'If you are a nurse, the girl argues, you have only £2, not £4 for any crisis, let alone for future, unforeseen, needs like saving to get married. Neither can you step up your income temporarily like a girl on piece work can.' *NM*, 24 September 1949, p. 412.

would attract undesirable recruits lacked confidence in the ability of matrons to select their candidates and observe those they had admitted during their training.

Thus, in the autumn of 1948, students won training allowances which provided a much higher standard of living than ever before. But this was only the start of the first general review of all nurses' salaries undertaken by the new Whitley Council. Claims followed for the other hospital grades. For the staff nurse, the staff side claimed a gross minimum salary of £380 with a board and lodging charge of £120.[1] The board and lodging charge of £120 was accepted by the management side which, as we have seen, wished to increase the relative salary of the nurse who lived out. But instead of the gross minimum salary of £380 claimed by the staff, an agreement was reached for a minimum salary of £315 rising to a maximum of £415.

Soon after this agreement, the Government introduced its wage freeze policy, and management refused for a time to make any decisions about other grades of staff. But in the winter of 1950–51, salaries were fixed for the more senior nurses in the hospital service and all the increases were back-dated to 1 February 1949. 'The rationale of the increases for senior grades seems to have been to give roughly the same *net* increase (after deductions for board and lodging and taxation) to them as to the junior grades.'[2] Thus while the Rushcliffe Committee's decisions had widened differentials proportionately, the first decisions of the new Whitley Council had the opposite effect.

The first ten years of the National Health Service were years of fairly continuous inflation. The increase in the cost of living led to regular claims from the staff side for increases in nurses' salaries. New salaries were negotiated for hospital nurses which came into effect in June 1952, in December 1954, in April 1956, in July 1957, and in March 1959. A brief description of the negotiations will be found in Appendix III. Only one of the increases granted, that which came into effect in July 1957, was on a straight proportionate basis. Each of the other settlements

---

[1] The principle of a gross salary with a charge for board and lodging instead of a net salary with a 'living-out allowance' was accepted by the staff side at an early stage in the negotiations.

[2] H. A. Clegg and T. E. Chester: *Wage Policy and the Health Service*, p. 43: Oxford, 1957.

altered relative differentials. Up to 1956 proportionate differentials were reduced. They were restored in March 1959.

The reduction in differentials in the first eight years of the National Health Service arose from the general climate of opinion. Inflation had come to be regarded by leaders of public opinion as the major problem of the post-war era. It was widely believed that the continuing rise in the price level was due to extravagant public expenditure—particularly on the social services—and the cost of the National Health Service came in for special criticism. In addition post-war governments, like Boards of Guardians many years earlier, were under strong pressure from influential quarters to reduce the level of the taxes they levied. For these two major reasons, governments attempted to avoid expenditure on the health services and economized in those fields which would do no *immediate* harm to the Service. The reaction, therefore, of the Ministry of Health to pressure from the Treasury was to impose absurd limits on capital expenditures and to grant only such salary increases or improvements in terms of service as could not be avoided.

This general approach of the Ministry of Health was reflected in the attitude of the management side of the Nurses and Midwives Whitley Council. Although the health departments had a minority of the seats, the influence of government was much greater than its formal representation suggests. The Whitley Council machinery would deserve several chapters in any textbook written on the art of government manipulation. Both the secretariat and the spokesmen of the management side were drawn from whole-time members of the Department. They were in general more experienced and more knowledgeable than the part-time representatives of hospital authorities. And it must not be forgotten that members of Regional Hospital Boards and Boards of Governors were appointed to these positions of status by the Ministers concerned. Thus, Ministers had manœuvred themselves into the comfortable position of carrying no small weight in the deliberations of the management side of the Whitley Council without formal responsibility for its actions in the House of Commons.

The objective of the staff side of the Nurses and Midwives Council was, of course, to increase the general level of salaries. The greatest pressure was exerted to improve the pay at the lower levels of the salary structure. Two reasons can be suggested for this. First, the considerable number of experienced negotiators from the trade union movement hoped that if substantial increases were granted at the lower level, there would be a movement later on from the management side and the professional associations to restore proportionate differentials. Thus the most effective way of raising the whole level was to start by raising the bottom. Secondly, the majority of those whom the staff side represented were at the rank of staff nurse or below. While the Royal College may have been primarily concerned about the long-term prospects of registered nurses, the trade unions had a special interest in the lower grades.

The first settlement by the Whitley Council had given senior grades flat-rate net increases. The second claim by the staff side was for a flat £100 for all grades from the staff nurse upwards; it eventually accepted a gently graduated increase which narrowed still further proportionate differentials. The third claim made by the staff side in 1954 was a cost of living claim and was therefore on a proportionate basis. The management side's offer was flat rate for the grades of staff nurse and above: it came into force after a decision by the Industrial Court. The fourth claim made by the staff side in 1956 was substantial and the management side responded by offering moderate increases on a proportionate basis which were accepted by the staff side, subject to an amendment which increased the salaries of the lowest levels. Thus each decision up to 1956 narrowed proportionate differentials. The fifth decision made in 1957 was largely a cost of living award and was therefore on a strict percentage basis.

In the early post-war years the salaries and earnings of many professions (excluding superannuation and other fringe benefits) were lower in real terms than before the war. The gap between the pay of wage-earners and professional people had in many cases become narrower. In the fifties, professional people reasserted their claims, and the view became widely held that the differentials which had existed before the war, when government played a much smaller role in financing the education of professional people, should be re-established. The first and most important step in this direction was the Danckwerts' award to general practitioners made in 1952. This intended to provide family doctors with the same standard of living under the National Health Service as had been enjoyed in the less secure days before the war. Gradually what may be termed the upper middle class counter-revolution spread to local government employees, to judges, to university teachers, to civil servants, to school teachers, and finally in 1958 to administrators in the hospital service.

Such was the background to the negotiations conducted in the Nurses and Midwives Whitley Council during the winter of 1958–59. It was probably felt in government circles that senior nurses were falling behind among professional people. Two groups were particularly relevant to the position of hospital nurses. First, the teachers had had substantial increases, and teaching was the major rival to nursing in the recruitment of young women. Secondly, the salaries of hospital administrators were greatly improved and similar increases may have been thought necessary for matrons 'to maintain their status in the hospitals'.

Towards the end of 1958, a substantial claim was submitted for mental nurses by the staff side and it was implied that a similar claim was being prepared for general nurses. While the claim for mental nurses was still unresolved, an interim cost of living claim was presented for all nurses. The management side replied that they proposed themselves to undertake a complete review of salaries. As a result, they made an offer of substantially improved salaries which was eventually accepted with minor amendment. Students' allowances and salaries of assistant nurses were increased by $4\frac{1}{2}$ per cent to 7 per cent. The salaries of staff nurses were increased by about $12\frac{1}{2}$ per cent and of ward sisters by about 20 per cent. By this agreement, the proportionate differential between the staff nurse and the sister was restored to what had been agreed at the start of the National Health Service. The proportionate differential between registered nurses and students was increased above the 1949 level. If the comparison is taken back to 1943, the percentage increase since that date for students, staff nurses, and sisters were fairly similar. Broadly it can be said that the agreement which took effect on March 1959 was a re-enactment of the proportionate differentials established by the Rushcliffe Committee. The increases which had been won for student nurses in 1948, had been extended up the salary structure.

All these calculations have been made in terms of gross salary and are thus relevant to the nurse who lived out. The position of resident nurses depended not only on the gross salary but on the board and lodging charges. The management side of the Whitley Council had intended to increase the effective charges for living-in so that it would be possible for more nurses to live out. In practice it did exactly the opposite. Resident nurses got larger relative increases in spending money than non-resident nurses. Charges for residence increased much less than salaries.

If income tax is ignored, the effective residence charge can be traced back to the first nationally negotiated scales of 1943. Between 1943 and 1959 effective residence charges rose by between 70 per cent and 105 per cent for various grades, gross pay rose by between 120 per cent and 166 per cent, and net pay rose by between 197 per cent and 292 per cent. On average, the effective residence charge rose less than the cost of living. If the effective residence charge was right in 1943, by 1957 the resident nurse was overpaid and the non-resident nurse was underpaid.

The resident was certainly receiving services which cost the hospital more than she paid for them. From March 1959 the residence charge was £128 for students, £165 for enrolled assistant nurses, £180 for staff nurses and £205 for ward sisters. Without any allowance for the rental of rooms the average resident nurse was costing the hospital service about £6 per week.[1] Indeed the residence charge was seldom sufficient to pay for the cost of providing meals alone. With a modest allowance for rent based on current replacement costs (£1 per week) the student was paying about a third of what she was costing the hospital service (excluding all training and teaching expenses).

The whole *economic* incentive was to live in; this faced hospital authorities with pressures to build or adapt staff accommodation. By relatively underpaying non-resident nurses, there was less economic incentive for married nurses and nurses with family responsibilities to take up hospital work. It was therefore less possible to relieve 'the shortage of nurses' by drawing upon the most promising pool of recruits to the fullest extent. In addition it was held to be impracticable to allow resident nurses to pay separately for each of the services they received. For example, would a student really choose to spend £1 a week of her remuneration on domestic services in her residence, or would she look after herself?

[1] An inquiry undertaken by the South West Metropolitan Regional Hospital Board in 1959, covering over 2,000 residents, showed that the cost per week varied between £4 8s. 9d. and £7 6s. 9d. in different hospitals.

How did the net salary of a nurse compare with that of before the war? The minimum for a staff nurse had increased by 340 per cent since 1937, using the average paid in municipal hospitals, and by 372 per cent, using the average paid in voluntary hospitals. The maximum had increased by 445 per cent and 486 per cent using the same respective bases. During the same period retail prices increased by about 180 per cent and the average earnings of female wage earners over the age of 18 rose by 268 per cent. Since before the war, the net salaries of resident nurses had increased more than the earnings of women in industry and very much more than the cost of living.

These bare comparisons of net salary do not give a full picture of the changing position of nurses in the salary and wage hierarchy. First, there were items such as uniforms, which some hospitals before the war had expected the nurse to buy out of her pay and which, under the National Health Service, were provided by the hospitals. Secondly, the nurse received more in kind than before the war, though her cost to the hospital had probably not increased as much as her salary. Thirdly, nearly all nurses were in a generous superannuation scheme, while before the war superannuation was not compulsory in many hospitals.[1] The nurse contributed 6 per cent of her salary and the employer 8 per cent.[2] Pensions were, however, related to earnings in the last three years of employment, which meant that in practice the Exchequer would have to pay much more than 8 per cent.[3] Fourthly, provisions for leave, sick pay, and other terms of service had improved greatly since 1938.

The number of hours worked must also be considered. In 1937 the average nurse worked about 104 hours per fortnight.[4] Less than one-fifth of all hospitals were operating a 96-hour fortnight. In 1943 the Rushcliffe Committee accepted the principle of a 96-hour fortnight, and the practice extended. In 1949 the Minister of Health pressed hospitals to operate it wherever

[1] See Appendix II, Table 10.

[2] See *National Health Service (Superannuation) Regulations*, 1950, Statutory Instrument No. 497.

[3] This arises partly because nurses had their pensions based on their last and normally most senior appointment while contributions were geared to all the appointments they had held, and partly because of the effects of inflation. Contributions were paid on salaries whose general level proved to have been far below the level on which pension was calculated.

[4] See Appendix II, p. 277.

possible.[1] Though these hours were not always observed in practice, differences from the standard week were not large.[2] Before the war, the regulation of hours had been sought by the trade unions and vigorously opposed by the Royal College. Regulation was imposed under the National Health Service with the full support of the staff side of the Whitley Council.

Soon after the National Health Service started, local authority employees were granted a 44-hour week.[3] In 1957 a 44-hour week was introduced for domestic and ancilliary workers in hospitals. It became clear that an 88-hour fortnight could not be long delayed for hospital nurses, and in 1957 the Whitley Council set up a Working Party to consider the reduction in hours of duty. As a result, in 1958 the Whitley Council made recommendations to the Minister, who advised hospital authorities that an 88-hour fortnight should be introduced when circumstances permitted. By the beginning of 1959, the majority of hospitals were working an 88-hour fortnight: progress was slowest in the London teaching hospitals although they had the largest ratio of nurses to beds.

The reduction in hours is of considerable economic importance. A hospital needs to be staffed to some extent throughout the 24-hour period and in general a reduction in hours involves the employment of more nurses. Since the beginning of the century the average cash pay of student nurses had multiplied by about twelve, and of staff nurses by even more. Hours were reduced by over a third, and students were much more often at work in the classroom than fifty years earlier. As a result, the cost in terms of cash salary of providing an hour of nursing services was multiplied by at least twenty, while the general price level multiplied by about four. This has been a major factor accounting for the increasing cost of medical care in this century. At present the cost of nursing staff is almost a quarter of the cost of the whole hospital service.

In general, the formal terms and conditions of service of nurses were considerably improved. They did better than most other grades of hospital employees; they secured higher pay, shorter hours, generous superannuation, and many other advantages.

[1] Regional Hospital Board Circular (49) 99.
[2] See *Overtaxed Nurses*, the report of a committee set up by the *Nursing Mirror* in 1955 and published in February 1957.
[3] Clegg and Chester: *op. cit.*, p. 71.

In addition, female nurses benefited from the decision taken by the Government in 1955 to grant equal pay in the public services. The establishment of the National Health Service in 1948 opened up a new and much more prosperous era for the nursing profession.

Viewed broadly, as a means of settling levels of remuneration and other conditions of service which were generally accepted, the Whitley machinery, with perhaps excessive assistance from the Industrial Court, was not unsuccessful. The Council was, however, criticized on many counts. It was frequently blamed for delay, particularly in its earlier days.[1] On a number of occasions government policies of wage restraint were more successfully imposed on the public sector than the private sector, and such policies led to stalling by the management side. Other delays were caused by the complexity of the negotiations and by no means all such delays could be justly blamed on management.

There was no scientific way of determining the pay of the nursing profession. There remained anomalies in the salary structure of the National Health Service and the staff side were not slow in drawing attention to them. Male orderlies received, and female domestic workers in certain circumstances could receive, more current cash than trained nurses. Nurses' salaries would have needed to be substantially higher if this were to be avoided. The general nurse was on an incremental scale and was not paid for overtime or granted special rates for split duties and other inconveniences. A standard salary with increments was regarded as a mark of professional status; in the lower reaches of that scale a trained nurse could receive less cash than the staff working under her direction.

The introduction of national salary scales had disadvantages. As the *Nursing Mirror* pointed out in 1949, 'the less attractive hospitals found it difficult to attract nurses, since they could not offer higher salaries as compensating inducement where conditions were not so good as elsewhere'.[2] The standardized board and lodging charge led to many complaints, particularly from matrons living in inferior accommodation.[3] Standard charges were levied for unstandardized accommodation.

---

[1] See, for example, *NT*, 5 February 1949, p. 101; and *NM*, 24 September 1949, p. 405; 16 December 1949, p. 226; 12 May 1950, p. 118; 3 June 1955, p. 651.   [2] *Ibid.*, 1 October 1949, p. 1.

[3] See, for example, *NT*, 21 February 1953, p. 189.

Looking back over the past twenty years during which central government increasingly intervened in the nursing world, it may well be asked how this affected the nursing organizations. Before the second world war, the professional organizations were losing ground to the trade unions, and in 1937 nursing knew one of its brief moments of militancy. The central government by its intervention, by its choice of representatives on official committees, by its ratification and financial support of the decisions of those committees, strengthened the position of the professional associations.

The trade unions became recognized partners in the negotiating process but the professional associations, and the Royal College in particular, did not necessarily lose by this arrangement. If anything was gained by the tougher methods of negotiation that characterize the trade unions, the benefits accrued to the professional associations as well as the trade unions. Indeed, as the professional associations held the majority of the seats on the Whitley Council, they may have gained more from the trade unions' toughness than the trade unions themselves. For the loss of support for the existing machinery might well have led to larger recruitment of nurses by trade unions and the reconstitution of the negotiating machinery with the trade unions playing a larger role. To some extent the skill of the trade unions in collective bargaining promoted the status and membership of the Royal College of Nursing.

CHAPTER XIV

Training for the General Register

THE shortage of nurses continued. In the war, emergency assistant nurses had gained recognition and official negotiating machinery had been established. Immediately after the war, the departure of most of the nursing auxiliaries and the prospect of a National Health Service led to new proposals for the training of nurses. By 1949, however, though the shortage of nurses was still large, the drive for radical changes in training had lost much of its impetus. The steps taken by the Government were no longer adventurous.

The hospital management committees that took over the non-teaching hospitals in July 1948 found within their groups hospitals staffed and equipped at very different standards. There were the ex-voluntary hospitals, some rich, some poor; there were hospitals which had been modernized when the major local authorities became responsible for them in the middle of the inter-war period; there were hospitals which had been upgraded under the emergency medical service; and last but not least there were a number of 'hospitals', particularly those that housed the chronic sick, which retained the standards and equipment thought appropriate many decades earlier. Where the number of staff had been kept low by a shortage of charitable funds and by the unwillingness of local authorities to incur expenditure from the rates, these limitations were removed by the nationally-financed health service.

By binding together in largely geographical groupings hospitals and institutions of widely different standards and traditions, the National Health Service presented a challenge to the new hospital managements. The committee members were largely drawn from local government, from the old voluntary hospital committees, and from senior members of the medical profession and the nursing profession.[1] On the whole they were

---

[1] The Royal College had strongly pressed the Minister to appoint nurses to hospital authorities.

more used to the acute type of hospital which had enjoyed the higher standards of equipment and staffing, and they found much that was inadequate in their new heritage. Thus there was pressure to upgrade the more neglected institutions that were taken over. Among other needs, nursing staff was urgently required.

There was one further reason why there was an expressed demand for more nurses at the start of the National Health Service. The 1946 Act had enhanced the status of many matrons. The Nightingale revolution had gradually improved the standing of the matron in the voluntary hospitals.[1] She had come to be recognized as the head of an independent department directly responsible to the committee. Progress had been much slower in the workhouses and infirmaries where the lay administrator and medical superintendent respectively had continued to be the heads of the establishment and thus senior to the matron.[2] Under the National Health Service the principle of tripartite administration, under which the medical, lay, and nursing heads each had access to the committee, became increasingly accepted.[3] Matrons were thus more often but by no means always able to approach their committees directly and ask for an increase in the nursing establishment.

The search for more nurses at the start of the National Health Service has to be seen against a background of major demographic changes. By comparing the census of population of 1931 with that of 1951, it can be shown that the number of young single women, the group from which nurses had traditionally been drawn, declined sharply. Not only were there fewer girls reaching the age of 18 in 1951 than in 1931, but more and earlier marriage was reducing the period for which nurses might be expected to remain in full-time service.

Between 1931 and 1951 the number of women increased. The total in England and Wales between the ages of 15 and 64 rose from about 14·4 million to about 15·1 million, but the number fell in the younger age groups.[4] In 1931 there were about 6·8 million women aged 15–34; in 1951 there were only about 6·1 million. Moreover, a higher proportion of women in all age groups were married or widowed. The change was very large in

---

[1] See pp. 25, 28 above.   [2] See p. 48 above.

[3] There were, of course, notable exceptions to which the Association of Hospital Matrons was not slow in drawing attention.

[4] See Appendix I, p. 260.

the younger age groups as women were marrying earlier. The proportion of single women in the age group 20–24 fell from about 74 per cent in 1931 to about 52 per cent in 1951, and in the age group 25–34 from about 33 per cent to about 18 per cent. As a result, the number of single women aged 15–64 declined from about 5·4 million in 1931 to about 4 million in 1951. The largest change occurred in women between the ages of 20 and 34. The number in this age group fell from about 2·4 million in 1931 to less than 1·4 million in 1951.

These unfavourable developments for the recruitment of unmarried female nurses were somewhat counteracted by the effects of full employment—by an increase in the proportion of single women who were occupied. In 1951 about 87 per cent of single women aged 25–34 were occupied, compared to about 80 per cent in 1931; and about 81 per cent of single women aged 35–44 were occupied in 1951, compared to about 73 per cent twenty years earlier. Nevertheless, the basic problem remained: there had been a very large fall in the absolute number of single women.

In spite of these changes in population which were unfavourable to the recruitment of single female nurses, the number of student nurses was larger during the early years of the National Health Service than it had been before the war. The number of student nurses in Great Britain (including those in mental hospitals) had risen from 43,000 in 1938 to 51,000 at the start of the National Health Service. One reason for this increase was the larger number of girls staying on at school beyond the compulsory school-leaving age. Over half the student nurses were probably drawn from girls leaving school at 16 or over.[1] Although there were fewer teenage girls than before the war a much larger proportion were staying on at school. In 1938 about 30,000 girls left grant-aided schools over the age of 16, compared with about 45,000 in 1948.[2]

Including the students there were about 39,000 more nurses than before the war. But the demand for nurses had risen much more than the supply. Not only were matrons and hospital authorities anxious to improve staffing standards where they were low, but there was a general desire among all concerned to see the 96-hour fortnight introduced in all hospitals. It was

[1] See Appendix I, Table 15, p. 265.
[2] See *H of C Deb.*, 5 February 1959, *Written Answers to Questions*, cols. *121–2*.

officially estimated after the new hospital managements had surveyed the position that 48,000 more nurses were needed in the hospitals.[1] This took no account of the growing demands for nurses to work in industry, in the community health services and elsewhere.

For a decade government had tried to overcome the 'shortage of nurses'. The total position was, however, much better than it had been before the war. The shortage was due to an increase in the demand, not to any reduction in the number of nurses. Indeed, the number of nurses had increased substantially, as may be seen by comparing the figures from the census of population of 1951 with those of 1931. The increase had, however, come largely from part-time nurses, male nurses, and married nurses. Single women played a much smaller part than before.

During this twenty-year period the total number of nurses (male and female) in terms of full-time equivalents rose from about 154,000 to about 225,000—an increase of about 71,000.[2] In 1901, the total number of nurses had been just under 70,000. In this year about 26,000 nurses worked in the hospitals. By 1951 about 130,000 of the 225,000 nurses worked in 'hospitals' and nursing homes. In 1901 less than 40 per cent of nurses had worked in 'hospitals': by 1951 nearly 60 per cent were employed in hospital work.

In absolute terms, the number of nurses increased faster after 1931 than before, though proportionately the increase was somewhat slower. Male nurses played a larger part in 1951 than twenty years earlier. In 1931 there were about 15,000; by 1951 there were about 25,500. There had been virtually no part-time nurses in 1931, but by 1951 out of the total of about 199,000 female nurses in full-time equivalents, part-timers contributed over 8,000 units—there were about 16,500 persons at work. The vast majority of these women were married (84 per cent).

Among the full-time women engaged in nursing in 1951, about 22 per cent were married as compared with about 5 per cent in 1931. The proportion of widowed nurses had continued its secular decline. By 1951 only about 4½ per cent of full-time

---

[1] Lord Shepherd: *H of L Deb.*, 9 November 1948, col. 308. This number was estimated to make it possible to guarantee a 96-hour fortnight and to staff the beds that were closed. It included mental hospitals and applied to Great Britain.

[2] For the source of these figures and those quoted on the next few pages, see Appendix I.

female nurses were widowed or divorced. Thus out of the grand total for both sexes of about 225,000 full-time equivalents, single women contributed about 141,000.

In the ten years between 1921 and 1931 the number of single female nurses increased from about 94,000 to about 122,000—an increase of about 28,000. In the *twenty* years between 1931 and 1951 the number of single female nurses increased from about 122,000 to about 141,000—an increase of about 19,000. Thus the average increase per year in the number of single female nurses in the thirties and forties was a third of that which took place in the twenties. Out of the total increase of about 71,000 in full-time equivalents between 1931 and 1951, about 52,000 were men, part-timers, and married women. It was the recruitment of these groups which made it possible to increase the number of nurses per 1,000 of the population from 3·85 in 1931 to 5·13 in 1951.

Nevertheless the increase in the number of single nurses between 1931 and 1951 of about 19,000 meant that a much higher proportion of occupied single women were attracted to the profession. There was little change in the proportion of the older age groups that went in for nursing. The increase came from the younger women. Between 1931 and 1951 the proportion of occupied women aged 35–44 engaged in nursing went up by 1 per cent from 4¾ per cent to 5¾ per cent. In the age group 25–34 the increase was much greater—from about 4 per cent to 6¼ per cent. Most remarkable of all was the change among the under-20's. As figures do not exist in the appropriate form for 1931, the position in 1951 must be compared with that of 1921. In this last year, only 0·1 per cent of single occupied women aged 16–17 were nurses and 0·8 per cent aged 18–19; by 1951 the percentages had risen to 1·9 per cent and 3·8 per cent respectively. Thus, while there had been about 5,000 nurses under 20 in 1921, by 1951 the total had risen to over 27,000. Virtually the whole of the increase of 19,000 in the total of female single nurses between 1931 and 1951 came from the under-20 age group.

This increase in the number of young nurses occurred in spite of the fact that the school-leaving age was being raised. Moreover the younger nurses in 1951 had had longer schooling than the older nurses. About 35 per cent of nurses aged 20–24 had left school between the ages of 17 and 19, compared with about

18 per cent of nurses aged 45–64. And 25 per cent of nurses aged 20–24 had left school at age 16, compared with 19 per cent aged 45–64. This was not just due to the expansion in secondary education for girls. Nursing had a higher proportion of longer-educated occupied women in the younger age groups than in the older age groups. About 15 per cent of occupied women aged 20–24 who left school between the ages of 17 and 19 were nurses, compared to about 7 per cent of occupied women with this educational background aged 45–64. It would seem likely, therefore, that the general educational standard of nurses was higher than it had been in the past.

Nurses were probably better educated, but it does not follow from this that the social class of their parents was higher than it had been in the inter-war period or before the first world war. The social groups from which nurses had been recruited at the beginning of the century had varied widely. Many daughters of the upper and upper middle classes had taken nurse training and risen to the highest posts in the profession: nursing, teaching, and 'slumming' were virtually the only careers open to women. The nursing profession had also recruited girls of the 'servant class' who had taken their training in the workhouses[1] or had been given special short courses on the district.[2]

An inquiry carried out by the Wood Committee indicated that in 1946 only about 5 per cent of nurses had fathers with professional occupations (Registrar-General's Class I), while the fathers of 34 per cent were in minor professional and business occupations (Class II), and of a further 34 per cent were clerical workers and skilled manual workers (Class III). The fathers of 11 per cent of the nurses were in semi-skilled or unskilled occupations. The remaining 16 per cent were not allocated to any social class.[3] It may be the case, therefore, that nursing had become less attractive to girls of the highest social class. Careers had been opened for women such as medicine, the law, and professional social work which had higher status and usually involved a university education. There was also a wide range of para-medical occupations such as occupational therapist, physiotherapist, and almoner which such girls may have found more attractive. Thus while nursing had risen educationally, it may have fallen in social esteem.

[1] See p. 47 above.   [2] See p. 59 above.
[3] *Wood Committee Report*, p. 13.

Nursing, like teaching, was a means of rising in social class. It was also a means of leaving home. It proved particularly attractive to those who lived in areas where there were few suitable jobs for women. Thus, it was found by the Wood Committee in 1946, that 12 per cent of the total hospital nursing staff was born in Eire.[1] And an inquiry conducted by the Social Survey in 1943 showed that 14 per cent of student nurses were farmers' daughters, while farmers and farm labourers combined represented only 8 per cent of the male working population.[2] It will be recalled that Miss Nightingale had particularly hoped to attract girls from the farm to nursing work.[3]

There were thus many more nurses after the war than before. The total number of single girls had decreased but a larger proportion of them had entered the profession. The increase in the number of nurses had come from girls under 25, from girls from Eire, from married women working both on a part-time and whole-time basis, and from male nurses. The immediate prospect for further recruitment of girls was not very favourable as less girls would be reaching the age of 18 in the fifties. On the other hand, there was a trend for girls to remain longer at school. It was against this background that the Government studied the Wood Committee's report in the autumn of 1948.

The Committee had hoped to solve the nursing shortage by increasing the number of state registered nurses. This was to be achieved by recruiting more students, by reducing the period of training from three years to two years, and by conducting the training in such a way that the recruits would stay to finish the course. It was believed that this could be brought about if the needs of the nurse in training could be made the only determinant of the student's curriculum. Thus training schools should be separated both financially and administratively from the hospital and should operate under the control of powerful regional committees. All this was summed up in the phrase 'full student status'. At first it seemed that the Government was prepared to go quite a long way along these lines. Speaking for the Government in a House of Lords debate in November 1948, Lord Shepherd said 'policy on the question of separation of responsibility for training from the hospitals is being considered by the

[1] *Ibid.*, p. 13.
[2] Kathleen Box: *Recruitment to Nursing*, p. 8: London, 1943.
[3] See pp. 21–22 above.

Government. . . . We believe that for training there should be some other authority than merely the management of the hospitals.'[1] The Government seemed to be bracing itself to stand up to 'that formidable body the General Nursing Council'.

The Government moved cautiously. In April 1949 a new Nurses Bill was introduced in the House of Lords. It proposed to follow the recommendations of the Wood Committee by increasing the number of appointed members on the General Nursing Council. There were to be 34 members, of whom 12 were to be appointed by the Minister of Health (of these 6 were to be nurses), 3 by the Minister of Education and 2 by the Privy Council. The other 17 members were to be elected by nurses— 14 general nurses on a geographical basis to prevent an excess of London matrons.[2] While previously any registered nurse could be elected, under the new bill general-trained candidates for election had to be still engaged in nursing work or work related to nursing. This subtle change, which kept out retired nurses, lowered the average age of the Council and brought its thinking more in line with that of practising nurses.[3]

The new bill also gave the Minister power to set up Standing Nurse Training Committees for each of the regional hospital areas. On these committees would be representatives of the Regional Hospital Boards, Boards of Governors, the General Nursing Council, the Central Midwives Board, local health authorities, local education authorities, and universities. The Wood Committee had recommended such committees and had thought of them as powerful bodies, planning and co-ordinating training facilities, allotting students and approving supervisors.[4] Under the new bill, the duties allotted to the committees were much less forceful. They were 'to promote improvements in nurse training . . . to advise and assist training institutions in preparing and carrying out training schemes, to advise and assist the General Nursing Council on the approval of training institutions'. Though the finance of nurse training was to be

---

[1] *H of L Deb.*, 9 November 1948, col. 310.

[2] The trade unions had pressed strongly for this.

[3] In 1946, the COHSE had described the eleven nurses elected for the General Register as '7 voluntary hospital matrons, 2 voluntary hospital sister tutors, 1 author of text books for nurses and 1 superintendent of health visitors'. See COHSE: *The Hospital Services*, p. 20.

[4] *Wood Committee Report*, pp. 64–65. See pp. 183–4 above.

channelled through these committees, the student remained under the control of the hospital and not under the control of separate training authorities. The system of training remained firmly and wholly in the hands of the General Nursing Council which was empowered but not compelled to carry out experiments.

The bill also provided for the amalgamation of the male part of the Register with the general part when the General Nursing Council had made the requisite rules,[1] and the closing of any other supplementary part of the Register by order of the Minister on the request of the General Nursing Council. In addition the 'list' of nurses under the 1943 Nurses Act was to be opened again to admit those who had been prevented by the war from applying in time.[2]

The bill was strongly supported by the Royal College of Nursing, but it sought amendment and clarification on a number of detailed points. For example, it insisted that nurses should be in the majority on the new training committees; that these committees should be autonomous and in no way under the Regional Hospital Boards; and that the budgets of teaching hospital training schools should not be submitted to the area committees but to the General Nursing Council itself.[3]

When moving the second reading of the bill, Lord Shepherd described it as

a fine balanced document, trying to please as many as possible of the parties interested in nursing. . . . The subject has been discussed at representative meetings . . . the Minister's views have been considerably modified in the light of opinions expressed. Thus, while it cannot be claimed that the provisions of the Bill will satisfy every interested party . . . it is certain that the Bill has been framed with full knowledge of, and with careful regard to, the view of all the responsible authorities and organizations.

---

[1] Mr Messer, briefed by the nursing trade unions, had suggested this to the Minister of Health in 1942 but had been told that 'this is a matter for the General Nursing Council. An amendment of their rules would be required to give effect to the suggestion.' See *H of C Deb.*, 3 December 1942, col. 1322. Accordingly a delegation of male nurses went to see the General Nursing Council in 1943. The Council took the view that legislation would be required. Thus no progress had been made.

[2] In fact only 2,234 names were ever entered on 'the list'.

[3] *NT*, 30 April 1949, pp. 345–6.

After further preliminaries, Lord Shepherd read to the House the following words from his brief:

to exercise especial care in putting the point before your Lordships; . . . The Government accept the Working Party's view that, under the present arrangements, the training of nurses tends to be subordinated to the staffing needs of the hospitals, and their conclusion that, so far as may be practicable, training should be dealt with independently of hospital administration—in particular that the finance of training should be separate from the finance of administration. How far in the circumstances attending the administration of the hospital service the student nurse can be given the full status which the Working Party recognised as the ideal remains to be seen. The Bill, while leaving this question open, creates the conditions in which the answer to it may be evolved by trial and experiment.[1]

It was clear that the bill was not designed to lead to speedy action. Lord Crook, in the course of the debate, criticized the Government's lack of courage:

the powers of experiment given to the council . . . may cause delay in reaching decisions on general principles which would help us in solving the problem of the shortage. . . . The three years' training argument . . . will be shelved for a period which . . . may well be ten years from the date on which the Working Party was set up. . . . This Bill gives the General Nursing Council powers to experiment in January 1951. We cannot hope to start planning an experiment before the middle of that year, and shall not embark upon an experiment until 1952. If the experiment runs the whole period of three years, which one would expect to be the very minimum—the year 1956 becomes very clearly the year for decision on the point whether there shall be certification of any kind at the end of two years, or whether the three-year period is to be maintained . . . I am clear that the Ministry of Health . . . cannot afford to put off for a long period of years a decision on a vital question of that kind.[2]

Another critic of the bill, though from a different viewpoint, was Lord Moran, who feared 'a lowering [of] the standard, because it will be difficult for these regional committees, under the pressure of local opinion, which is naturally agitated by the desire to get nurses, to maintain the standards as they have been in the past'.[3] He also protested against the teaching hospitals

[1] *H of L Deb.*, 3 May 1949, cols. 162–4.   [2] *Ibid.*, cols. 183–4.
[3] *Ibid.*, col. 179.

being 'put into regional machinery for this purpose of training of nurses'.[1]

Lord Moran's views were also held—though much more forcibly—by the *British Journal of Nursing*. The recommendations for the Regional Committees embodied 'the entire disintegration of the One Portal Examination to the State Register. . . . The position of the Nursing Profession will revert to the epoch when training schools were a law unto themselves.'[2] In an editorial for the June number headed 'Thirty Years After' the viewpoint of the journal was forcibly re-stated.

WE HAVE NOT KEPT THE FAITH, AND WE HAVE NOT STOOD FIRM. Slowly but surely, one at a time, and with scarcely a struggle, we have allowed our privileges to be filched from us. . . . Unskilled persons have cast envious and resentful eyes upon the fair rewards of State Registration. The exalted and powerful position of the General Nursing Council aroused smarting jealousy in the breasts of those who would like to wield the power of the Council, but who have no longer hopes of so doing. . . . Powerful opposition was successful in reducing the very necessary training period to two years, for a second grade of 'Nurses'; whilst discipline, so essential where life and death are in conflict, was mocked and derided as archaic and conventional. . . . Regional Hospital Boards are now empowered to set up training committees who will be responsible for the better education of nurses. . . . As student nurses now receive a generous training allowance, they could quite well contribute to their own education and thus relieve the hard-pressed public a little.[3]

Except for this outburst from what remained of the Fenwick faction, the new bill was well received in the nursing world. A meeting was held of the National Council of Nurses and its decisions were forwarded to members of the House of Lords.[4] The representation of nurses on the new regional training committees was considered and it was decided to reject a suggestion made by the Minister of Health that it should be arranged that too many should not be matrons. The Council pressed for a nurse majority on these committees and suggested that they should be renamed

[1] *Ibid.*, col. 180.   [2] May 1949, p. 42.   [3] June 1949, pp. 51–52.
[4] The National Council had been formed in 1904 (see p. 76) and represented the nurses of Great Britain and Northern Ireland at the International Council of Nurses. Mrs Bedford Fenwick was president from 1904 to 1945. Both the Royal College of Nursing and the British College of Nurses were affiliated to it.

Regional Hospital Training Committees.[1] No further important amendments were suggested.[2]

The *Nursing Mirror* in its review of the bill expressed surprise that it did not go further in some respects. It had expected the abolition of the roll of assistant nurses. And it regretted that the bill, in addition to re-opening the 'list' to nurses who could not be entered on it owing to war circumstances, did not also re-open the Register. 'There are still nurses in this country, who for merely technical reasons have not been able to get on the State Register, although they are as well qualified as thousands of their colleagues, whose names have been admitted to the Register.'[3] 'With the re-opening of the Register the List with its insidious distinctions should be swept away.'[4]

This last suggestion was incorporated in the Act.[5] Section 14 directed the General Nursing Council to make rules for the admission to the Register not only of 'persons whose names are included in the list' but also

persons who hold certificates issued by institutions which appear to the Council to be satisfactory for the purpose of the provision stating that they completed before the beginning of July, nineteen hundred and twenty-five, a course of training in nursing in the institution and who satisfy the Council that they are of good character and have adequate knowledge and experience of nursing.

In 1949, the trade unions were granted what the professional associations had successfully obstructed in 1943.

The changes made in the Nurses Act of 1949 did not lead to any dramatic alterations in the basic training for the General Register. Not until 1 June 1951 were the new Area Nurse-Training Committees actually set up. The General Nursing Council was pleased to report that each committee had a majority of registered nurses and described them, perhaps significantly, as 'this new link between the Council and *its* Training Schools' (my italics). 'The Council continue to maintain,' the Council reported in 1951–52, 'and indeed it is essential that they should always do so—their direct contact with the individual

---

[1] In the Act they were eventually named Area Nurse-Training Committees.   [2] *NM*, 4 June 1949, p. 159.   [3] *Ibid.*, 23 April 1949, p. 49.
[4] *Ibid.*, 28 May 1949, p. 129.
[5] *Nurses Act 1949*, 12 & 13 Geo. VI, Chapter 73.

hospitals but . . . the closest liaison is maintained with the relevant Area Nurse-Training Committee.'[1]

By 1955 it had become clear that 'the fullest possible use was not being made of the advice and assistance which the committee could provide, particularly in relation to the formulation of new schemes of nurse training or the recasting of existing schemes'.[2] In a circular issued in May 1955[3] hospitals were reminded 'that the area nurse-training committees . . . were in a position to see any new proposals against the background of the existing schemes and to ensure that the new proposals were suitably related to the general pattern of training in the area'.[4] Without the powers envisaged in the Wood Committee's report, the area committees served a very limited purpose.

Nearly all the experiments in nurse training approved in England and Wales by 1958 reduced the total time needed to qualify for more than one part of the Register. In other words, they made less rigid the firm barriers which had been erected between different fields of nursing under the original Registration Act. None of them made it possible to become a registered nurse in less than three years. By 1957 there were 15 courses combining children's nursing with general nursing, most of which reduced the time taken from five years to four years. There were 71 courses which combined general training with mental nursing and reduced the time taken from five years to four and a half years, or in some cases to four years. Schemes were also introduced combining general nursing with mental deficiency nursing or fever nursing, or mental nursing with mental deficiency nursing or fever nursing with the nursing of sick children. In total, there were 134 experimental schemes in England and Wales, including two providing integrated training as nurse and health visitor.[5] Meanwhile, in September 1956 the first experiment of a two-year course of training for the final examination in general nursing was started at the Royal Infirmary, Glasgow, with the approval of the General Nursing Council for Scotland. After a further year working under supervision, the students were eligible for registration.

The number of student nurses in National Health Service hospitals increased steadily. At the end of 1949 there were about

---

[1] *General Nursing Council Annual Report 1951–52*, p. 2.
[2] *Ministry of Health Annual Report 1955*, p. 110.   [3] *Ibid.*, p. 45.
[4] *Ibid.*, p. 110.   [5] *Ministry of Health Annual Report 1957*, Part I, p. 113.

40,000 in England and Wales—by the end of 1952 there were nearly 45,000, but the rate of increase was slowing down.[1] By the end of 1953, the number had fallen to about 44,000.[2] Commenting on the fall in his annual report for 1953, the Minister of Health said the staffing position was

by no means wholly satisfactory. . . . it is clear that no further great increases in the student nurse intake can be expected, bearing in mind that the total population in the young age groups from which recruits are largely drawn is some 25 per cent less than it was immediately before the war, and competition from other professions for the available women was greatly increased.[3]

The total remained at about 44,000 at the end of 1954, but during 1955 there was an improvement in recruiting which was maintained during the next three years. By September 1958 about 3,500 more students were working in the hospitals than at the end of 1954, and about 7,500 more than at the end of 1949.[4]

There was no reason to be satisfied with this increase in the number of student nurses. When recruitment was related to the number of girls reaching the age of 18 in each year, it seemed that some progress was being made. Much more significant was the comparison with the number of girls leaving school over the age of 16, which was not made either in the reports of the Ministry of Health or the General Nursing Council. Between 1948 and 1957, the number of girls leaving grant-aided schools at the age of 16 increased by 28 per cent (from about 26,000 to about 33,000), at the age of 17 by 14 per cent (from about 10,000 to about 11,400), at the age of 18 by 54 per cent (from about 8,000 to about 12,000). When allowance is made for the high proportion of students drawn from these groups, for the fact that a considerable number of students came from Eire, from the Commonwealth and from the colonial territories, recruitment was less than might have been expected. It may be the case that the suggested trend of the thirties and forties towards a higher

---

[1] These figures and those that follow exclude students in mental and mental deficiency hospitals. They are taken from the annual reports of the Ministry of Health.

[2] Part of the fall may have been due to a new rule restricting entry of students under the age of 18. See General Nursing Council: *Annual Report 1952–53*, p. 3.   [3] pp. 36–37.

[4] *Ministry of Health Annual Report 1957*, Part I, pp. 172–3.

proportion of better educated girls entering nursing was reversed in the fifties.[1]

The trend in the recruitment of male nurses was even less
encouraging than the trend for female nurses. In 1949 there had
been about 2,400 male students in the hospitals. By the end of
1955 the number had fallen to about 1,450 and remained at
about that figure until the end of 1958. The large number of
students in the early years of the National Health Service did
lead to an increase in the number of male trained nurses. At the
end of 1949 there had been about 1,300; by 30 September 1958
there were over 2,700. However, the number of male assistant
nurses fell from about 2,600 at the end of 1949 to under 1,900
at the end of September 1958. And while the number of female
pupil assistant nurses increased greatly during the period, there
was no increase in the number of male pupils. The post-war
boom in male recruitment was over.[2] One reason for the failure
of the hospitals to recruit and retain more male nurses was the
limited prospects for promotion. Very few men had been promoted by their matrons to the rank of charge nurse (the male
equivalent of ward sister). While the 1949 Act had abolished
formal discrimination against men, it had not abolished all
prejudice.

[1] Out of the total of student nurses, trained nurses, and midwives aged
20–25 in the 1951 census of population about 36 per cent left school over the
age of 17, 25 per cent at the age of 16, and 39 per cent under the age of 16.
(See Appendix I, Table 15.) If students admitted to the index for general
training in 1952 had a similar educational background, and if all students
had entered training from grant-aided schools in England and Wales on
reaching the age of 18 (or on leaving school at the age of 19), the nursing
profession recruited in 1952 about 29 per cent of the girls leaving school over
the age of 17, 12½ per cent of girls leaving school at 16, and 3 per cent of girls
leaving school below the age of 16. If these percentages are applied to girls
from grant-aided schools becoming 18 (or leaving school at the age of 19) in
1957, there would have been over 1,000 more student nurses on the Register
in 1957 than actually was the case. Of course, this statistical exercise rests
on a battery of assumptions and does not *prove* the suggestion made in the
text. It does, however, suggest a useful line for further research. (For information on the ages at which girls left grant-aided schools, see *H of C Deb.*,
5 February 1959, *Written Answers to Questions, cols. 121–2.*)

[2] The figures given in this paragraph cover all hospitals in England and
Wales other than mental, mental deficiency, and neurosis hospitals. Thus
the staff of mental and mental deficiency beds in chronic, long-stay, and
general hospitals (there were 9,500) are included. These figures have been
kindly supplied by the Ministry of Health.

'Wastage' during training remained as much of a problem after the Nurses Act of 1949 as it had been before. During each of the first ten years of the National Health Service between 14,000 and 17,000 new names were entered on the General Nursing Council's index of student nurses for the General Register.[1] The number who discontinued training varied between the low figure of 4,993 in 1949 and the high figure of 8,596 in 1956. The number of these withdrawals which were due to marriage increased during the ten years, but it was always less than 2,000; between 1,000 and 2,000 students tended to return to training later on, but the number that left for good remained large: about one-third of those who entered training. 'Wastage' during training was as high as it had been before the war.

Each year the General Nursing Council expressed its dissatisfaction with these figures of 'wastage'. It saw two means of reducing them. The first was to prevent any student nurse being accepted for training below the age of 18. Some students were beginning training at the age of $15\frac{1}{2}$ or younger.[2] The Council regarded early entry to training as 'no less than an exploitation of young people'.[3] With the approval of the Minister schools were forbidden to admit students under the age of 18 after the beginning of August 1952. This step, however, had no noticeable effect on the figures of 'wastage'. Nor did it stop the misuse of young people. In a report published in 1956 the Royal College of Nursing said that young people in hospital cadet schemes were frequently employed on nursing duties in unsuitable circumstances.[4]

The second measure favoured by the Council was the reintroduction of 'a Test Educational Examination, waived in September 1939, in order that those candidates who, through lack of intellectual capacity or educational attainment, are unable to benefit by the course of training shall be eliminated at the outset'.[5] Such a step needed the approval of the Minister of Health, which was not obtained. In 1948 the National Institute of

---

[1] The figures given in this paragraph were kindly supplied by the General Nursing Council for England and Wales.

[2] *General Nursing Council Annual Report 1949–51*, p. 11.

[3] *Ibid., 1951–52*, p. 3.

[4] Royal College of Nursing: *Observations and Objectives*, p. 6: London, 1956.

[5] *General Nursing Council Annual Report 1951–52*, p. 3.

Industrial Psychology had devised a test specifically for the General Nursing Council which had been tried out on some 2,000 candidates entering training in 1948. The Minister studied the report on this experiment for nine months and decided in February 1952 that he could not consider the reinstitution of a test by the Council.[1] In 1953 the National Institute of Industrial Psychology prepared a final report on its experiment which showed that the test 'would not have eliminated all those who ultimately failed to complete their training through reasons related to lack of education or intellectual ability, and indeed would have eliminated a very small proportion of those who had subsequently completed their training successfully'.[2]

The Council still wanted to try out the test on all applicants for training who did not already hold appropriate educational qualifications. The Minister, however, considered 'the test submitted was not suitable for general adoption by hospital authorities. . . . The mode of selection of candidates was best left to the unfettered discretion of the hospital authorities, using such methods as experience had shown to be effective.'[3] Thus the disputed test was used only by those hospitals that wished to do so.

The Wood Committee had said there were too many training schools. At that time there were 389 complete, 167 affiliated, and 5 associated general training schools. At the end of March 1957 there were 401 complete training schools, of which 52 consisted of more than one hospital. In addition 242 other hospitals played some part in training for the General Register, but only 3 of these were affiliated training schools where admission to the General Register took four years.[4] The Wood Committee had wanted to see even the large hospitals associated with hospitals of other types. This had only occurred to a very limited extent.

Gradually the General Nursing Council became conscious of the deficiencies of the small training schools, many of which had been pointed out by the Wood Committee in 1947. A study of the problem, started in November 1956, had shown that the small schools offered inadequate clinical experience, were uneconomic in terms of both staff and equipment, lacked the services of enough outside lecturers and could not retain qualified sister tutors. Moreover, they tended to accept as students, girls

[1] *Ibid.*, p. 3.   [2] *Ibid., 1953–54*, p. 3.   [3] *Ibid.*, p. 3.
[4] *Ibid., 1956–57*, p. 19.

who had little prospect of ever passing their examinations, and when ward staff was short failed to provide proper bedside teaching. After prolonged discussion with all concerned, the Council drafted plans to remedy the situation.

In 1948, before the new hospital authorities had found their feet, it might have been possible for drastic action to be taken without much of an uproar. By 1959, the Council felt it had to move warily in face of the hospital authorities. Thus the operative date for its new proposals was tentatively put at 1 January 1962. By then it was hoped to have reduced the number of student nurse training schools for the General Register until all had three hundred beds with the appropriate departments and specialities. The much disputed test was to be introduced compulsorily for all recruits who could not claim exemption through some other educational qualification. At the same time it was proposed to abolish the preliminary examination and develop a closer link between the theoretical and practical work. It was hoped that hospitals no longer able to train student nurses would seek approval as assistant nurse training schools.[1]

At its annual general meeting in June 1959, the Association of Hospital Management Committees passed the following resolution:

That the Association is deeply concerned as to the possible effect on the staffing of hospitals if the General Nursing Council's proposals for new conditions of approval of hospitals as training schools for student nurses are implemented as suggested by the 1st January, 1962, and urges the Minister of Health to appoint a Working Party to consider all aspects of the proposals before making a decision in this matter.

Despite the high proportion of students who left before completing their training, and despite also the ever-increasing demand for nurses in public health work, the number of trained staff working in the hospitals increased. By the end of 1955, there were 8,500 more whole-time trained nurses and 4,000 more part-time trained nurses than at the end of 1949. By the end of September 1958 the number of whole-time trained nurses had risen by a further 1,000 and about 2,000 more part-timers had entered hospitals. Compared with the end of 1949, there were about 7,500 more students, nearly 9,500 more whole-time trained

[1] *General Nursing Council Annual Report 1957–58*, pp. 18–20.

nurses, and over 6,000 more part-time trained nurses at work in National Health Service hospitals.[1]

The Wood Committee had estimated that between 22,000 and 24,000 more trained nurses were needed in Great Britain. At the start of the National Health Service the Government had stated that the hospitals needed 48,000 more nurses. By September 1957 there were 15,000 more state registered nurses (in terms of whole-time equivalents) at work in the hospitals of Great Britain (including mental hospitals) than at the end of 1949.[2] The staffing problems of the hospitals were not solved by an increase in the number of trained nurses. Not only were many hospitals far below their establishment for nursing staff, but at the end of 1957 over 14,000 beds were closed for lack of staff and over 430,000 patients were on the waiting lists.[3]

The Wood Committee had recommended radical changes in the training of nurses: a course of two years provided in a reduced number of training schools administratively separated from the hospitals and directed by powerful regional committees. The General Nursing Council had opposed these recommendations partly because they would reduce its own authority and partly because it disagreed on principle, and the Government had taken no steps that the Council was not prepared to support. In the twenties, when the Council had just been created, Parliament could overrule its decisions; in the war emergency a new grade of nurse could be imposed; but after the war, Ministers did not risk an open quarrel with the entrenched power of the profession.

The point at issue was a technical one: the system of nurse training. Parliament had intervened in the twenties to protect the liberties of unqualified nurses and in 1943 to establish a new grade of nurse. It was a different matter for a Minister of the Crown to try and convince the House of Commons that he knew better than the profession itself how nurse training ought to be conducted. In such a situation the House might well side with the profession against the bureaucracy. Mr Bevan thought it wiser to attempt to win the day by infiltrating and persuading the General Nursing Council.

[1] Excluding mental and mental deficiency hospitals.

[2] These figures are drawn from information published in the *Annual Reports* of the Ministry of Health and kindly supplied by the Department of Health for Scotland.   [3] *Ministry of Health Annual Report 1957*, pp. 160, 162.

CHAPTER XV

The Third Portal?

NURSES in training had been granted some measure of
'student status', their hours and curriculum had been
improved, and training allowances had been granted which were
worth much more than had been paid before the war, but all
these measures had failed to recruit enough trained nurses to
staff the hospitals of the National Health Service. There were
still shortages. Married nurses and part-time nurses were
increasingly employed but their numbers were insufficient to fill
all the gaps.

Both students and registered nurses were unevenly distributed
between different types of hospital. At the end of March 1958,
the acute hospitals operated by Regional Hospital Boards had
about 20 trained nurses to a hundred beds; the provincial teaching hospitals had about 25 trained nurses to a hundred beds,
while the London undergraduate teaching hospitals had over
29 trained nurses to a hundred beds.[1] The rates for student nurses
varied even more. For every hundred beds, the Regional
Hospital Boards' hospitals had 26½ students, the provincial
teaching hospitals had 50 students and the London undergraduate teaching hospitals had 64½ students. A sub-committee
appointed by the National Consultative Council recognized that
there was some justification for teaching hospitals having a
higher rate of nurses. 'Nevertheless', their report continued, 'we
are satisfied that the disparity is considerably greater than is
justified by the differing needs.'[2]

The position also varied widely between individual hospitals.
Those with fine reputations, with attractive locations, with good
working conditions and marital opportunities, or with matrons
who were popular with nurses, were able to recruit more than

[1] *Report of the Sub-Committee appointed by the National Consultative Council on
the Recruitment of Nurses and Midwives*, Ministry of Health Circular NCC 17,
1959, p. 1.   [2] *Ibid.*, p. 2.

their share of the available trained staff. In such hospitals there was little pressure to economize with skilled manpower. Jobs which had been traditionally undertaken by nurses—the care of the flowers, the serving of meals, the clerical work of the nursing office and the outpatients department and even domestic duties —could continue to be done by students and trained nurses. It could, moreover, be said with some justification, that nurses often did these jobs better than other grades of staff and thus the patient was provided with a better service. By this reasoning those who criticized such arrangements could be comfortably dismissed as laymen who failed to put the patient's interests first. In other hospitals, domestic work continued to be done by nurses because the hospital authority could not or would not recruit enough domestic workers.

In a report published as late as 1958, the Royal College of Nursing developed this familiar theme. 'Far too many nurses in training spend time, particularly at week-ends, on tasks which should be undertaken by ward orderlies or domestics.'[1]

In some hospitals student nurses on night duty are still required to complete a heavy programme of non-nursing tasks, such as cleaning offices and sluices, mending linen, washing and ironing masks and bandages and ruling up books. The employment of domestic orderlies in the hospital at night to do the cleaning, prepare drinks, set break-fast trays, make empty beds and act as runners would release the night nurses for their real nursing duties.[2]

Trained nurses were also wastefully used in some hospitals. They undertook such tasks as 'locking up nurses' homes, calling maids (and sometimes nurses) and manning telephones',[3] and spent 'considerable time on work which should be carried out by clerical staff'.[4]

The traditions of the profession were only one reason why such work continued to be done by nurses; there were also difficulties in recruiting domestic staff, and some Regional Boards which allowed generous establishments for nursing staff were unwilling to allow more domestic workers to be employed. But where these practices arose out of tradition in a generously staffed hospital, the price was paid by the patients in those hospitals which did

---

[1] Royal College of Nursing: *The Problem of Providing Continuous Nursing Service Especially in Relation to Night Duty*, November 1958, p. 13.
[2] *Ibid.*, p. 8. [3] *Ibid.*, p. 5. [4] *Ibid.*, p. 14.

not enjoy these advantages. Moreover, there was little such a hospital could do to improve its own position. Indeed a vicious circle was often set in motion: once it was known that a hospital was understaffed, it became less attractive to potential recruits.

Before the war, it had been possible for an understaffed hospital to pay higher salaries. Nor was this practice unreasonable: work in an understaffed hospital was hard, and compensation for doing less attractive work was not unknown in other occupations. Though this meant that hospitals with the highest reputations often paid the lowest salaries, it was still true that work in a junior position in such a hospital was the most certain road to a senior post elsewhere. Differential salaries were no longer possible for nurses under the National Health Service; the same salary was laid down for every hospital for the physically sick. Almost the only means of competition available to hospitals was in the standards of accommodation and services provided in return for the standardized board and lodging charge. Where hospital managements knew that the major barrier to recruitment was the attitude of senior nursing staff, there was little they could do about it: incompetent administration was not sufficient for dismissing or demoting a senior nursing administrator.

There were hospitals with a high proportion of trained staff and hospitals with a low proportion of trained staff. In general, it seems likely that the hospitals for the 'acutely sick', particularly the training schools, gained most from the increase in the numbers of students and trained nurses during the first ten years of the National Health Service. The improved recruitment did not do much to help the 'chronic sick'. There were many fields of nursing practice both inside and outside the hospital service which had always proved more attractive to trained nurses than work with the chronic sick. Hospital managements wanted to improve the staffing of the chronic sick hospitals they had taken over, but trained nurses did not offer their services in sufficient numbers for this type of work.

The system of training assistant nurses had been developed by local authorities before the war in the hope of relieving the shortage of nurses for the 'chronic sick'. After consultations with the Royal College of Nursing, it had been decided that the training should last for two years. When the Roll had been opened under the 1943 Nurses Act, two years' training had been laid down for future candidates, which was to include not less than one year spent in nursing the chronic sick. The majority of the nurses on the Roll, however, were admitted because they had fairly extensive nursing experience rather than any formal training; by the end of 1946, 27,300 such nurses were on the Roll. In 1947 the Wood Committee, while recognizing that it would be essential to continue 'for some time to come to use . . . the services at least of those Assistant Nurses now recognized and employed' did not 'favour perpetuating a grade such as the present Assistant Nurse with a two-year training'.[1] The Committee had in mind a shorter training of three to six months, which could 'hardly justify statutory recognition and the use of the title "nurse" ',[2] nor regulation by the General Nursing Council.

The Council was responsible for the training of assistant nurses and it wanted to keep this grade of nurse with the two years of training; it had drafted detailed proposals to bring the scheme into effect. According to the Confederation of Health Service Employees, these proposals were 'impractical'.[3] The Confederation saw an acute danger of the Council 'running away with itself and by its decisions, and the development of its "authoritative" powers and its policy of creating an increasingly high standard of qualifications, doing untold harm in the future'.[4]

In November 1949 the General Nursing Council, as the result of pressure from a number of quarters, made considerable revisions to its original scheme. There were three important changes which were introduced from 1950: first, the minimum training period was reduced from two years to one year, followed by a further year of work under supervision to qualify for admission to the Roll; secondly, the pupil no longer had to spend one year nursing the chronic sick;[5] thirdly, any type of hospital was able to apply for approval as an assistant nurse training school.

In November 1951 the written part of the test for pupil assistant nurses was altered. Previously it had been in the nature of a 'quiz' taken on the day before the practical assessment. The new arrangement was for a paper containing simple questions of a practical type which were answered in writing in the ward on

---

[1] *Wood Committee Report*, p. 77.　　　[2] *Ibid.*, p. 78.
[3] COHSE: *The Hospital Services*, p. 4.　　　[4] *Ibid.*, p. 5.
[5] *NT*, 19 November 1949, p. 1008.

the day of the practical assessment.[1] In May 1955 there were further slight changes in the system of assessment. The written work was to be done first under supervision and half an hour was allotted for this purpose. The practical assessment then followed and was not to take more than an hour.[2]

Once again a compromise had been reached. The requirements for the second grade of nurse were slightly eased but the period of training was by no means as short as the Wood Committee had recommended. It had hoped that there would be rapid recruitment to its new proposed grade of 'nursing orderly' and that a place would be found for them in every type of hospital; it was suggested that 14,000 orderlies would be needed for Great Britain 'over the whole hospital field as it now exists'.[3] The decision to keep a longer training for the 'second grade' meant that fewer persons were recruited to it.

The training for the assistant nurse was extremely slow in getting started. Not until March 1949 was the first test conducted by the General Nursing Council, and in the first year only 189 assistant nurses were admitted to the Roll by assessment. The General Nursing Council maintained an index of pupil assistant nurses similar to that for student nurses. In the year 1951–52 only about 2,100 new names were added to the index; in the year 1955–56 the number of new names had risen to only about 2,650. The number of pupils in training, however, increased more than proportionately, from about 3,100 to about 4,800; it frequently took more than a year to pass the 'test'.

The number of hospitals approved to provide the training grew more rapidly. At the end of March 1951, there were 210 hospitals taking part: by March 1956, 426 hospitals were participating. The General Nursing Council felt there was still ample scope for an increase in the number of training schools:

Indeed the Council would welcome applications from training schools which find difficulty in providing a first-class training for student nurses, because of a limited amount of clinical material, to become recognised instead for the training of pupil assistant nurses.... It is difficult to encourage such action, however, when it is realised that such a change in the status of the training school would result in a decrease in the salary of the Matron.[4]

---

[1] *General Nursing Council Annual Report 1951–52*, p. 6.
[2] *Ibid.*, *1955–56*, p. 13.   [3] *Wood Committee Report*, p. 72.
[4] *General Nursing Council Annual Report 1955–56*, p. 13.

The increase in the number of both pupils and schools did not, however, lead to an increase in the number of enrolled assistant nurses at work in the hospitals. The annual number of assistant nurses admitted to the Roll by assessment increased from about 189 in 1949 to over 1,500 in 1957. By the middle of 1958 over 10,000 nurses had got on the Roll in this way. But the number who had been admitted to the Roll as experienced nurses without ever having been 'assessed' was much larger—over 50,000. The new additions to the Roll were not sufficient to replace those who were retiring. At the end of 1949 there were about 12,000 whole-time and about 4,000 part-time enrolled assistant nurses at work in the hospitals. By the end of September 1958 there were only about 9,500 whole-timers in the hospitals, though the number of part-timers had increased to over 6,000.[1] The total contribution of assistant nurses to the hospital service was no larger than it had been at the start of the National Health Service, though a much higher proportion of those working in the grade had received formal training. At the end of 1956, the General Nursing Council started a re-assessment of the whole position of nurse training. The relative failure of the assistant nurse grade was attributed to a number of causes. First, the pay offered was not sufficiently attractive to make it worth while to take the training. Secondly, matrons of assistant nurse training schools were paid less than matrons of training schools for the Register.[2] Thirdly, the adjective 'assistant' was thought a deterrent to recruitment. The Council appreciated that the omission of the word 'assistant' would 'not at present be unanimously accepted by the nursing profession'. It stated, however, that it would itself 'raise no objection to this step, provided that it was appreciated that a change in title would not imply a change in the conditions laid down for the training of nurses for admission to the Roll and that it would still be envisaged that a person so trained would work under the supervision of registered nurses or doctors'.

The introduction of training had increased the quality but not the number of assistant nurses at work in the hospitals, and the improvements in the training for registration had failed to attract enough candidates to complete the course and stay on to

[1] *Ministry of Health Annual Report 1957*, pp. 172–3.
[2] This was remedied by the salary scales which took effect from 1 March 1959.

work in the hospitals. Thus the granting of a legal status to existing experienced nurses by the 1943 Act and the changes introduced by the 1949 Act did not have the effect of 'closing the nursing profession'. After the sudden departure of nursing auxiliaries at the end of the war, hospitals found they could not manage without them and started recruiting unqualified women again.

In most of the acute and semi-acute hospitals, women who were unqualified and had failed to be enrolled under the 1943 Act could be given clearly defined domestic duties; there were other staff available to do the basic nursing. In the chronic hospitals either the basic nursing was done by unqualified staff or it was not done at all: matrons had to make use of such staff as was available. As had been the practice before the 1943 Nurses Act, matrons recruited locally anyone who was suitable, and willing to do the work. Some were new immigrants over the age of 21 who were unwilling to subsist for two or three years on the low pay which they would have received had they started training, but the majority were married women employed on a full-time or part-time basis. Indeed, the whole system was very similar to that which had been in use before formal training had been started in the middle of the nineteenth century. As Mrs Bennett, the Chief Nursing Officer of the Ministry of Labour and National Service, said in the middle of 1949 of hospitals for old people, 'patients are being nursed by unskilled workers with a minimum of supervision'. The nursing services of this country were being maintained 'by the harassed efforts of trained nurses, a comparatively small group of qualified practical or assistant nurses, and an ever-increasing number of partially qualified or unqualified personnel'.[1]

The number of unqualified 'nurses' increased rapidly. By the end of 1949 'other nursing staff' amounted to about 12,000 whole-time and about 5,500 part-time; by the end of September 1958 the total had increased to about 14,500 whole-time and 12,500 part-time. Indeed by 1958 the number of 'other nursing staff' in the hospitals was 50 per cent larger than the number of enrolled assistant nurses.[2] In terms of whole-time equivalents 'other nursing staff' amounted to about a quarter of the total

[1] *NT*, 2 July 1949, p. 532.
[2] These figures do not include mental and mental deficiency hospitals and are taken from the *Ministry of Health Annual Report 1958*, pp. 282–3.

hospital nursing staff, excluding persons in training.[1] There were many more untrained nurses at work in the hospitals than before the war.

The untrained nurses filled up the gaps left by the shortage of trained staff. Only very rarely were they deliberately recruited to create a 'balanced nursing team'. At the end of March 1958, for every hundred beds, the acute hospitals controlled by Regional Hospital Boards had 5 'other nursing staff', the provincial teaching hospitals had 2 'other nursing staff' and the London undergraduate teaching hospitals had 1 'other nursing staff'.[2] In the chronic sick hospitals controlled by Regional Hospital Boards, the staff per hundred beds consisted of $6\frac{1}{2}$ trained nurses, $6\frac{1}{2}$ assistant nurses, and nearly 14 'other nursing staff'.[3] The untrained nurses made up almost half the nursing establishment.

The category 'other nursing staff' was an embarrassing anomaly. The Whitley Councils laid down the rates of pay for every grade of staff employed in the hospital service, but what was the right scale for these unrecognized persons doing nursing work? In practice some hospitals were paying them at rates laid down for orderlies by the Ancillary Staffs Whitley Council. But this could not be allowed to continue for two reasons. First, it was held to be wrong for the pay of persons doing nursing work to be laid down by a different Whitley Council from that which managed the affairs of the nurses. Secondly, the male orderly scale provided a higher rate of pay than trained nurses received, and even women could earn more than trained nurses if they worked overtime or at week-ends. Moreover, there were a few hospitals which were paying 'other nursing staff' at a rate of pay which they had fixed themselves. This was out of line with the arrangements made for all the other staff of the hospital service.

As it became clear that the recruitment of assistant nurses was not increasing rapidly enough to make it possible to manage without the services of 'other nursing staff', the management side of the Nurses and Midwives Whitley Council decided to face up to the issue. There was a heated debate in the Council. The staff side believed that management was attempting to lower the wages of these ancillary workers, and the professional associations wanted to keep the word 'nurse' in any form out of

[1] Counting two part-timers as one whole-timer.
[2] *National Consultative Council Report*, p. 5. [3] *Ibid.*, p. 5.

the title of any new proposed grade. Eventually, with the approval of the Ministers concerned, a salary scale was laid down for a new grade of 'nursing auxiliary', defined as 'a person who is engaged wholly or mainly on nursing duties in a hospital other than a mental hospital or a mental deficiency institution who has no recognized nursing or midwifery qualifications and who is not a student nurse, a pupil midwife or a pupil assistant nurse'.[1]

There were thus four different rates of pay for persons doing 'nursing work' in the hospital service who had never been 'examined' or 'assessed' under arrangements made by the General Nursing Council. Those who had been registered as existing nurses under the 1919 Act were paid as 'state-registered nurses'. Those who had been enrolled under the 1943 Act were paid as 'assistant nurses'. Some of the remainder were paid as 'nursing auxiliaries', others were paid as 'ward orderlies'.

A vigorous protest was made by Miss Gladys Goodchild, the Matron of a Manchester hospital, against the establishment of the nursing auxiliary grade. She protested to the Prime Minister, the Minister of Health, and the Royal College of Nursing.

This circular [she wrote] is a contravention of the Nurses Act of Parliament 1943, one of the main objects of which was to ensure that the public should be protected from unqualified persons, representing themselves as nurses. I solemnly declare to the nursing profession and to the public that this desperate gamble to cover a deficiency is leading us inevitably to a second 'black' age of nursing. . . . Wider and wider is becoming the entry into the profession through back-door channels. The lamp indeed needs trimming.[2]

The British Journal of Nursing was not slow to support her protest both in its editorials and correspondence columns. Letters were published under such headings as 'The Lamp is Flickering Out'.[3] It saw the solution to the whole nursing problem in higher salaries for state registered nurses. 'The "other ranks" would automatically become unnecessary', it continued, 'and once again Matrons would enjoy the pleasure of being able to choose the best applicants from an ever-increasing flow of would-be nurses.'[4]

Though the other journals published letters of indignation[5]

---

[1] NMC (Whitley Council) Circular No. 44, p. 1.

[2] BJN, February 1955, p. 69.

[3] Ibid., July 1955, p. 79.   [4] Ibid., December 1955, pp. 129–30.

[5] 'When we find ourselves bracketed in the same category as very un-

the editorials took a more moderate line. The *Nursing Mirror* wrote:

The plain truth is that the vital qualifications for *nursing*—basic nursing—are personal qualities—such as compassion, devotion, and common sense, however much the highly skilled and highly trained brain is demanded for the more complicated flights of medical and surgical techniques and the administrative aspects of hospital management. Let us, therefore, keep our highly trained and skilled nurses for the type of work requiring their special qualifications, and let us recognize invaluable and sterling qualities which many people who are not SRN, or even SEAN, may well bring to the service of the patient. . . . To recognize the various skills, to allocate the various duties and not to seek to restrict the whole expanding field of nursing to a single type of worker is not necessarily lowering nursing standards.[1]

The *Nursing Times* was also prepared to accept the nursing auxiliary:

It is a fact that in this country there is a great army of between 20,000 and 30,000 people who are willing and able to carry a great part of the burden of work entailed. Some hospitals which are nurse training schools or assistant nurse training schools have not needed to employ auxiliary grades. But many others and particularly the special hospitals and those for the long-term cases have had to rely on auxiliary help. Each of these hospitals has endeavoured to solve its own problem of shortage of workers by employing a variety of people—described variously as nursing auxiliaries, nursing orderlies, nursing attendants, or nursing aides. With these members of the staff carrying out the basic duties, the relatively few trained staff have been able to use their professional skill and service more widely than if they had had to perform themselves the manifold tasks entailed. . . . If nursing is the total care of the patients then nursing duties in hospital must include many tasks of a simple nature, which if the patient were in his own home would be performed by his relatives.[2]

In this last sentence, the *Nursing Times* drew attention to a point which the leaders of the profession had failed to face over the seventy years' history of professional organization. Most of

skilled amateurs, whose only object in obtaining hospital employment is in being placed in possession of a "nice, clean, cushy indoor job" and who possess no sense of vocation whatsoever, surely we must seriously consider whether it has been worthwhile sacrificing so much to achieve what we always considered a most honourable status.' *NM*, 1 July 1955, p. 936.

[1] *Ibid.*, 10 June 1955, p. 720.   [2] *NT*, 17 June 1955, p. 659.

the basic nursing of the patient at home is done by relatives. The district nurse may undertake the technical nursing, the injections and the dressings and also some of the basic nursing, but in practice much nursing work gets left for the family. If the basic nursing of chronic sick patients could be done by totally unskilled persons in the home, could it not also be done under supervision by untrained persons in the hospital? Would it be an affront to the dignity of the nursing profession for the simpler duties to be taught in short courses lasting a few weeks or a few months? At least it would be better for the patient to be looked after by an orderly with some organized training than by a nursing auxiliary with only such casual introduction to her work as matrons felt it essential to provide.

The position of the nursing auxiliary became accepted by the profession just as other facts had in time become accepted. In a report published in 1956, the Royal College of Nursing referred to auxiliaries in the following terms:

The war-time use in hospitals of workers without recognized nursing qualifications to supplement trained staff was a measure of expediency. Shortage of qualified nurses has made it necessary to continue the practice in certain types of hospitals, with the result that there is now a large body of these subsidiary workers who have become essential to the service.[1]

[They were] valuable in relieving the trained nurse of routine tasks not requiring professional knowledge, and thus enabling her to concentrate her skill where most needed and on duties which should never be delegated. Such helpers should therefore be regarded, and taught to regard themselves, as members whose efficiency is vital to the team.[2]

Beyond this brief mention of the attitude of mind which should be taught to the auxiliary there is no reference to any other form of instruction.

In earlier statements of policy, the profession had emphasized the importance of student nurses undertaking repetitive tasks. It was an essential part of their training to learn how to perform such duties for different kinds of patient. The profession did not seem to think it necessary for these duties to be taught in any systematic way to the 24,000 auxiliaries who were undertaking them in the hospitals. Short courses of training had been laid

[1] Royal College of Nursing: *Observations and Objectives*, p. 4.
[2] *Ibid.*, pp. 4–5.

down for auxiliaries working in the wartime Voluntary Aid Detachments; even in peacetime first-aid training was given to those whose services would be needed in a possible war, and in the army itself basic nursing continued to be taught in brief courses to nursing orderlies. Some matrons working in the National Health Service were deliberately trying to recruit as auxiliaries women who could produce evidence of training in first-aid during or after the war. Others were rather self-consciously providing some classroom instruction for their auxiliaries. But no lead in these matters came from the professional associations or the Ministry of Health, though the latter had recommended courses of training for the equivalent grade in mental hospitals (nursing assistants). Schemes of training in the National Health Service extended from the administrators to the stokers; there were no formal courses for nursing auxiliaries.

The shortage of 'nurses' was caused by the unrealistic policies of the profession. Either the profession had to delegate part of the care of the patient to less skilled persons provided with such training as they would absorb, or else it had to alter the requirements for state registration. The refusal of the profession to recognize the problem and to choose which course it would adopt until too late had a sad and paradoxical consequence. It led to unsatisfactory care of many hospital patients—the very people whom the profession wished most to serve.

CHAPTER XVI

Conclusion

FACTS do not speak for themselves. By their selection and presentation the reader is influenced to accept the viewpoint of the writer. For this reason an author should at some point come into the open and expose his values to the criticism of the reader. This is the purpose of this final chapter.

The changes which have occurred in the organization and, to some extent, the practice of nursing, have been set out in earlier chapters. The story has been told with a minimum of interpretation. At this stage it seems appropriate to attempt a summary, a tentative explanation and modest evaluation of the events which have been described. Lessons may be learnt which will be of value when new policies for the nursing profession come to be formed in the future. And if it is ever possible for the young to learn from the mistakes of the old, newer professions may find a message in the history of the nurses. They may learn that to seek too much too soon does not always render the best service to the public.

The policies of professional groups are matters which concern the community as a whole. At its very least a profession represents a quasi-monopoly of labour services and as such the terms of admission to it raise questions of the public interest. When a profession is given powers by statute, Parliament must watch to see that these powers are not used to the harm of other people. When the major employer of the profession is the state itself, government is inevitably involved in wider questions of policy. For each of these three reasons, government must concern itself with the affairs of the nursing profession.

Parallels to many of the incidents in the history of the nursing profession can be found in that of other professional groups. The delicate relations between the 'lady' nurses and the old types of nurse are similar to those between certified and uncertified teachers, and between qualified and unqualified social workers.

And in the field of health services there are many similar points of tension—between the ophthalmologists and the opticians, the dental surgeons and the dentists, and between the osteopaths and the specialists in physical medicine. The group which regards itself as superior has attempted to be restrictive—to draw a firm line between themselves and their inferiors. And in nearly every case the standards laid down for entry to the profession have resulted in a shortage of personnel. There is little in the history of nursing which is peculiar to that occupation.

What is exceptional in nursing is the nature of the work: the continuous and intimate association with pain and not infrequent contact with death. While the doctor transfers his attention from one case to another, the hospital nurse spends her time in the company of the same group of patients. Exposed to human contacts of this kind, the risk of emotional involvement becomes the greater with the consequential psychological stress. The setting in which nurses work may well account for some of the features of the profession—the tendency to withdraw to the protective solidarity of a uniformed group, the search for perfectionism and the attempt to achieve it by discipline, and last but not least, the widespread public admiration for those who take on nursing work. Not every man or woman would feel themselves able to undertake the duties of a nurse. In this sense, nursing is a vocation.

The history of nursing during the past hundred years is not hard to summarize. At the beginning of the nineteenth century hospital nursing was done by mature women of the domestic servant class. Hardened by their experience of life, and often reinforced with gin, they were able to face the confusion and stench of the hospital wards. When Miss Nightingale sought her first recruits, it was mature and respectable women used to hard work whom she hoped to attract. She also recruited some young ladies, but she never intended that the occupation should be restricted to women of that class. Indeed, when her 'best and dearest pupil' took over the Brownlow Hill Workhouse Infirmary, an attempt was made to train pauper women to act as a second grade of nurse.

Almost unintentionally, Miss Nightingale popularized nursing as an occupation for ladies. Many rushed in to take brief and privileged courses of instruction as a prelude to appointment in their middle-20's to the key positions of the nursing world. These ladies wrested control over the destiny of the profession from Miss Nightingale's hands. She favoured reform by example, but they sought to impose it by regulation. Armed with a ruthless leader, a Royal Charter and a Princess, they kicked down the ladder up which they had climbed by imposing a stiff three-year training on new entrants and tried to forbid the practice of nursing to anyone who had not been admitted in this way.

The restrictive attitudes of the profession reached a climax when an Act of Registration was obtained in 1919. A statutory body composed largely of nurses was set up to govern the affairs of the profession. This body attempted to make training a necessary condition for admission to the Register of existing nurses and to impose stiff educational tests upon new entrants. The plans of the profession were overruled by Parliament and modifications were made both in the rules for the admission of existing nurses and in the syllabus of training. But the educational standards actually adopted were too strict to yield enough nurses to meet all demands. Such was the toll exacted from society by the professionally-conscious lady nurses.

What were the motives, conscious or unconscious, for their actions? The fact that nursing consisted largely in manual work and had previously been so closely associated with domestic service made it particularly important that it should be distinguished from it. The fact that many women of the domestic servants' class were still entering nursing, in the workhouse infirmaries, if not in the voluntary hospitals, made the ladies who entered nursing insecure. Had they lost social caste in their choice of a career? The fact that nursing was the only exclusively female profession (or nearly so), in an age when feminine emancipation was on everyone's lips, was a good reason for showing the men how high the women could climb. The fact that nurses worked in such close proximity to the doctors, whose social origin was not always of the highest, provided a status target. The fact that most of the duties performed by the nurses looked to the casual observer so close to those performed by the housewife in her daily round may have led to exaggerated attempts to differentiate the work and expand the duration and content of the training syllabus. Finally, the highly skilled nurses knew better than anyone else the damage which could be done by an incompetent nurse. They were genuinely seeking to serve their patients.

The training of the nurse at the beginning of the twentieth century was long and arduous. It needs to be asked of the apprenticeship of the nurse, as of the apprenticeship of many skilled workers in industry, how much of it was really necessary. Over the past seventy years there has been an immense expansion in the technical procedures and theoretical knowledge which can be taught to the nurse. If three years of training were needed in 1890, the period of training must now be too short. If three years are adequate now, three years must have been too long sixty years ago. The very choice of the word 'probationer' for the trainee suggested initiation into a religious order rather than apprenticeship for a profession. And the emphasis on the repetition of menial domestic services was of the same character. The status of the profession was thought to be enhanced by narrowing the eye of the needle—by demanding not only knowledge but humility. But the routine character of the training served also a rational purpose. Faced with a crisis, the reaction of the nurse was to do and not to think. It served also to protect her from self-criticism if her efforts did not produce the required results. It was at least comforting to know that a recognized procedure had been perfectly performed even though it had been ineptly chosen.

Thus the development of nursing as a profession led to the introduction of a standard training of three years for general nursing. Only in wartime were short intensive courses for work in the hospitals tolerated at all. The long training and stiff examinations led to a shortage of recruits and trained nurses; it also involved a major change in the system of providing bedside care in the acute hospitals. The basic nursing had previously been in the hands of working-class married women who tended to stay for long periods on one ward and to provide a sense of stability for the long-stay patients. Working for longer periods under the same sister, and often the same doctors, they knew what was expected of them and could develop secure relationships with the senior hospital staff and with the patients. With the introduction of training the bulk of bedside work became the responsibility of young single women of a somewhat higher social origin and even higher social aspiration than the typical patient in their care.

The new probationers brought with them to the wards the vitality and enthusiasm of youth, somewhat dimmed by the

authoritarian and consciously dedicated atmosphere of the
hospital community in which they lived and worked. They
brought with them a kindliness and candour which may have
served as a substitute for that deeper sympathy of those of
maturer years. They brought with them knowledge and intelligence, though this equipment was inadequately used during
their harsh apprenticeship. They moved from ward to ward to
get a variety of experience. And as medical specialities developed,
movement became more frequent. No longer was it possible for
stable relationships to grow. Every few months the ward sister
had a new staff whose capacities and temperaments she had still
to gauge. Feeling unable to delegate with safety, she often tried
to run everything herself with curt orders and stern reprimands.
How often was the stress of the student communicated to the
patient? How many patients of mature years resented the cold
professional authority of the 'mere slip of a girl'?

The profession developed its language, its ritual, and its
uniform—its own body of traditions which were drawn from the
army, from the religious orders, and possibly also from the new
girls' public schools. As nurses lived apart from the rest of the
community so their thinking also drew apart. Living-in had
developed for the convenience of providing a cheap twenty-four-
hour service. It had become entrenched when training schools
started, partly because suitable accommodation for young ladies
was seldom available near the hospitals and partly because the
discipline required of the nurse was better taught and enforced
when she was permanently under the control of the matron.
In a well-supervised nurses' home it was hoped that the young
women could not be preyed upon by the younger members of
the medical staff during their off-duty periods: matrons could
protect them from moral corruption and male dominance. The
old nurses had come daily from the community outside to look
after those who were segregated from it. The new nurses were
permanently on the hospital premises. There were 'petty
quarrels and jealousies';[1] but from the solidarity fostered by
common uniform and rituals, and by constant contact with one
another, they found the reserves, physical and emotional, to
face their responsibilities on the wards. While the old nurses had
refreshed themselves with diverse external contacts, the new
nurses drew their strength from loyalty to the group. But they

[1] COHSE: *The Hospital Services*, p. 17.

tended to regard patients as persons living in an institution rather than as members of a family group temporarily segregated from it.

One effect on the community of professional policies was a shortage of nurses; a shortage accentuated by a variety of factors which arose from inside and outside the nursing world. The conditions under which nurses worked were not such as to attract the type of recruit the profession wanted, and the relative isolation of the hospital from the community made it slow to adjust itself to changes which were occurring outside. While young women were being emancipated in their own homes, nurses continued to be treated with Victorian authority.

Although the hours, the pay, and the attitude of management were out of line with the standards set by the world outside, nurses were deterred from vehement protest. They were restrained by the discipline which matrons had imposed on them, by their loyalty to their group and to their hospital, and by the spirit of uncomplaining service which was taken to be the heritage of their profession. Underfed, overworked, and underpaid, they struggled on rather than break a 'professional' code of honour. Activism was unprofessional, worse still it would have undermined the cherished spirit of vocation: it smelt of hard bargaining and the pursuit of selfish material interests. It was also unfeminine.

Even if there had been more protest from the nurses themselves, there remained many barriers to the improvement of their lot. The voluntary hospitals were in continuous economic difficulties; money was not available to improve the position of the nurses. Only some fundamental change in the system of financing medical care, such as came after the war, could have solved that problem. But even if it had been solved, the number of girls capable of taking the training was limited. They needed to have the 'right educational background' and they needed physical resilience. Enough recruits could not have been found with this equipment. Either the educational requirements for the basic training had to be lowered, or the care of patients had to be divided between different grades of staff, or patients had to be neglected or put on a waiting list.

The profession failed to grapple with the problem. Standards were resolutely maintained; indeed there was constant pressure to raise them, despite the ever-increasing demand for nurses.

The result was a continuous and growing shortage. Hospitals reacted by lowering the age of recruitment until girls as young as 15 were admitted to work in the wards. But even such drastic measures failed to solve the problem. Too few of the new nurses entered the hospitals by the front door, so the old nurses crept in continually by the back door.

It is in this context that the growth of trade union activity among nurses must be seen. The leading professional organization, the Royal College of Nursing, did not admit all those men and women who were engaged in nursing work. Trade unions recruited those whom the professional associations would not accept. They also enrolled some trained nurses who were greatly dissatisfied with their terms and conditions of service and disappointed that the College would not press their claims with vehemence. It was this challenge to its own position that led the Royal College to press for the appointment of a departmental committee to inquire into the problems of nursing.

The solution of introducing a second grade of nurse which that committee proposed in 1939 was at first unpalatable to the profession, but in time it became accepted in return for legislation which restricted the use of the title 'nurse' to the two grades with recognized qualifications. It seemed possible that once again patients would receive their basic nursing from nurses who stayed on the same wards. But once again what the profession demanded for the second grade was too restrictive to bring forward enough nurses of both grades to meet all needs. Indeed, the training required of the assistant nurse limited the progress that could otherwise have been made in improving the training for state registration.

After the second world war the care of the patients and the training of nurses were still frequently carried out against a background of a total shortage of staff. While before the war economy had been imposed upon the hospitals by the limitations of private beneficence and an antiquated system of financing local government, after the war, although nurses were granted much higher salaries, the expenditure of hospital management was closely confined to serve wider causes such as the stability of the pound and the balance of payments. These restrictions often account for nurses in unattractive living conditions, limited establishments of domestic staff, a lack of labour-saving equipment, and the continued use of buildings designed for an earlier era of medical care. Thus public parsimony, coupled with the un-willingness of some senior nurses to delegate tasks which had once been done by nurses, served to perpetuate those character-istics of staff relationships, of student training and nursing care which were now widely recognized to be undesirable. The needs of the students' training could not always be paramount. The students continued to supply substantial services to the hospitals, which could not have managed without them. Patients were faced with constant changes in the staff looking after them. Many of the staff under the sister's control were so newly assigned to her that she had little time to judge their capacities; in any case she had too few working under her. In such circumstances, sisters tended to direct rather than to delegate and to have less time than was needed to give the students practical instruction, let alone meet their psychological needs.

Matrons were also in difficulties. The hospital had to be staffed and training programmes had to be constantly re-organized. There was no pool of reserves. Faced with sickness, absenteeism or resignations, the planning of a rota of duties long in advance was impossible. And as the matron failed to plan ahead, likewise the nurses. They were not told their next assignments, or their next off-duty periods. This reinforced the isolation of the living-in system and frustrated the purpose of living-out. The student or nurse who could not plan ahead was less able to make friends outside the hospital. Constant change increased the feelings of insecurity of all grades of staff. It also encouraged resignations.

Though married nurses were brought in to work in the hospitals on a part-time and full-time basis, and though formal discrimination against male nurses was removed, much still remained of the isolation of the hospital community. Many single nurses continued to live in. At the start of the National Health Service, the Whitley Council had intended to make it easier for nurses to live out. In practice it did the opposite. The nurse who lived in continued to be financially better off than the nurse who lived out. Superficially, this policy was cheaper in the short-run for the National Health Service. And as the new Service was believed to be extravagant, economy, however short-sighted, became the guiding principle of the administration.

The basic training for the Register and the Roll remained focused in the hospitals because they could not manage without the services of the trainees. Students continued to see patients as individuals and as 'cases'; they had little or no contact with the family in its natural setting. What was basic to understanding the emotional problems of the patient had no place in the formal training for the Register. The policy of treating in the home as much sickness as possible was not reflected in the basic training of nurses. No effective bridge was created between the thinking of the nurse and the thinking of the almoner.

The introduction of training for a second grade of nurse failed to solve the problems of training for the Register and failed to provide much of a stable element in the wards. The standard demanded was too high and the period on pupil pay too long, to attract enough recruits. Unqualified nurses continued to work in the hospitals; they actually increased in number and became formally recognized under the title of 'nursing auxiliaries'. Here was the third portal to nursing work—a portal through which came many Irish girls, refugees from Europe, and immigrants from overseas.

However much the true character of the problem of nursing was recognized by Ministers and their advisers, they took no resolute course of action in the late forties and fifties. When the community took over responsibility for its hospitals in 1948, the entrenched power and privileges of professional interests became matters in which government had a direct interest. But Ministers did not dare to challenge a profession which had by now too high a standing in the eyes of public opinion. The devoted service given by nurses to the nation was recognized and admired, and rightly so. The profession enjoyed royal patronage and even royal participation. Its ruling bodies were well entrenched. Ministers were not prepared to risk an open quarrel on a major professional issue. In his minority report of the Working Party published in 1948, Dr Cohen bravely affirmed that 'the functions of the General Nursing Council are patterned on the privileges enjoyed by older professional organizations with traditions dating from the Middle Ages. It might be in the national interest to transfer some at least of their privileges to authorities directly or indirectly representing the community at large.'[1] But it seemed too late for such drastic measures.

[1] Ministry of Health, Department of Health for Scotland and Ministry of Labour and National Service: *Working Party on the Recruitment and Training of Nurses (Minority Report)*, p. 45: HMSO, 1948.

The course adopted by the Departments concerned was to persuade, infiltrate, and manipulate old committees and new committees created for the purpose. The British Civil Service is not unskilled at such operations, but the results inevitably are slow. Legislation was introduced which enabled changes to be made: the General Nursing Council was unobtrusively divested of its older members and strengthened with lay persons appointed by Ministers on a number of plausible pretexts. The profession moved in the desired direction—but not with haste.

The experiments conducted by the General Nursing Council in England and Wales have been narrow and cautious. And the wave of research into the fundamental problems of the nursing profession conducted between 1943 and 1947 has not been followed up with further studies. There are of course notable exceptions, such as the job analysis sponsored by the Nuffield Provincial Hospitals Trust.[1] But, compared to the United States, extremely little is known about the men and women who take up nursing work in Britain, or indeed, about the work which needs to be done in all the different types of hospital. Until such studies are undertaken, it would be absurd to make prophecies or recommendations for the future.

Superficially the prospects of recruitment of students in the coming years appear to be good. The larger number of girls born in the war are reaching the age of 18 and a higher proportion of children are staying at school beyond the compulsory school-leaving age. Nursing is an occupation which offers many intrinsic attractions. Compared to many others, it is so obviously worth while. The improvements in nurses' pay and hours have done much to reduce the opposition of parents and school teachers to nursing as a career. But more could be done to improve the working environment, to make it less restrictive, less status-ridden and to make spells of work shorter. In the late 1950's, the restrictions imposed upon nurses were vigorously criticized in the press as they had been twenty years earlier.[2] Improvements in this direction might lead to a larger number of recruits and a smaller number leaving during training; but it would be absurd to imagine that all 'wastage' could be prevented.

[1] Nuffield Provincial Hospitals Trust: *The Work of Nurses in Hospital Wards*: London, 1954.

[2] See, for example, the *Observer*, 23 June 1957; the *Manchester Guardian*, 30 March 1959.

Indeed, the use by the profession of the word 'wastage' represents an attitude which is not necessarily far-sighted. Training as a nurse, even if incomplete, has some value as a preparation for motherhood and the profession might be as well advised to draw attention to this aspect of it as to imply that it is a preparation for a lifelong career. Nurse training is also a preparation for citizenship received by about one girl in twenty. She can gain from it something analogous to what young men gain from national service: some discipline, some corporate life and some sense of responsibility to the community. It is not necessarily wasteful for so many families to have a mother or aunt equipped with some knowledge of nursing.

More students may come forward to take the training for state registration and a higher proportion might complete the course. But there is no *guarantee* that nursing would attract a higher proportion of better-educated girls even if substantial improvements were made in the system of training and terms and conditions of employment. The range of opportunities open to grammar school girls is constantly widening. There is a demand for such girls in the other para-medical professions and in social work, quite apart from posts as secretaries, computers, journalists, and in the growing fields associated with advertising and television. And even if more recruits were attracted to nursing, it should not be forgotten that marriage is becoming earlier and more frequent.

Training for the State Register demands some aptitude for theoretical work, and for this reason can only be taken by a selected group of school-leavers. Already the number of highly qualified nurses in Britain per head of population is as high as in any country in the world. It must be questioned whether the community is making the best use of well-educated girls when it employs them on basic nursing duties. Will such girls be willing to undertake them? They may prefer to find work which gives them greater opportunity to use the technical knowledge which they have acquired. If they continue to adopt the attitudes of those who work in the acute hospitals, nursing the chronic sick would not appeal to them. If this were the case, not all the shortage of nurses could be solved by increased recruitment and training of registered nurses. There would still be a need for a second grade. It may prove possible to increase the number of assistant nurses so that there are not only enough to replace those leaving work but even a greater number at work in the hospitals. But this would take time.

One logical solution to the problem of recruitment might be to simplify the requirements for registration so that enough candidates were forthcoming. At first sight it might seem acceptable to the profession to restore the principle of 'one portal' entry and encourage those who are able to reach the theoretical standard of present registered nurses by 'post-graduate courses'. For there is no doubt that doctors require a limited number of nurses for tasks which require knowledge and skill of an extremely high order. While this solution might attract to nursing more of the not-so-well-educated girls who are put off by the prospect of becoming a permanent 'second grade', the first year of practical nursing might discourage some of the better-educated from entering the profession. At least it can be said that this solution would not be popular with the profession. Less might have to be demanded of the new nurses than is at present required of assistant nurses, as recruitment to *both* grades is at present insufficient to meet all needs. While registered nurses are prepared to apply the word 'basic' to the assistant nurse grade, they do not wish to be taken literally.

If the Register and the Roll were to remain as at present, nursing auxiliaries would continue to work in the hospitals for many years to come. The question of providing some form of training would have to be faced, and the present 'training' of mental assistants might prove a useful precedent. The acceptance of the auxiliary with limited training 'on the job', and the employment of this grade in every type of hospital, could make possible dramatic changes in the training for state registration. Indeed it would once again become important to ask what the training is for and to design it for the tasks the nurse is expected to undertake.

In nursing, as in other professions, the work upon which training is centred does not closely correspond with the work which nurses actually do once their training is complete. If, for example, the main tasks of the registered nurse of the future will be to do the technical nursing, to administer the nursing team in the hospital, to administer the domiciliary team under the control of the general practitioner, to explain the whole treatment to the patient, and in general to play an ever-increasing part in preventive work, this must surely affect the course of training.

Where should it be conducted? Should it be based on the universities, the hospitals, the local health services, or on separate training schools? Should the student do her practical work only in hospitals which employ all members of the nursing team she is learning to lead? How far should the curriculum include personnel management, social science, psychology, and administration? Could any of the existing syllabus be omitted?

Throughout the world different solutions have been found to all these problems. Many countries which first modelled their nurse training on the British pattern have evolved different systems in recent years. For example, the shorter training recommended by the Wood Committee has been adopted in Finland and Sweden while it has not even been tried in England and Wales. But it is somewhat unrealistic to consider in any detail the ideal development of nurse training in Britain while there remain too few nurses to undertake the work they are expected to do. Until the problems of salaries, conditions of service, standards of training, and delegation of duties are resolved in such a way that there are no longer unfilled vacancies, and beds closed through lack of staff, there remain great obstacles to any dramatic improvements in the training of nurses in Britain.

The Censuses of Population 1901–51

In this appendix, statistics taken from the Censuses of Population showing the age, sex, and marital status of nurses are related to similar figures for the total population. In addition, some figures are presented which indicate the educational background of nurses in 1951.

During this century the same occupational classification of the population has not been used in different censuses. Care is needed, therefore, when comparisons are made of figures for one census year with those for another. In the case of nurses, the same classification was used for the 1921 and 1931 censuses, a different classification for the 1901 and 1911 censuses and a different one again for the 1951 census. Before 1901 nurses cannot be separately identified in the census tables.

An attempt is made here to show changes in the total number of nurses and in their age, sex, and marital status over a period of fifty years. It is, therefore, important that the definition of a 'nurse' used for different years should be as comparable as possible. The definition selected in this appendix is based upon the occupational classification used in the 1921 and 1931 censuses. An explanation is given where this diverges from that used in the 1951 census. An estimate is also presented for 1901 corresponding to the definition used for the later years.

The categories taken from the censuses of 1921 and 1931 are 'Midwives', 'Sick Nurses', and 'Mental Attendants'.[1] They correspond to three different categories used in the 1951 census ('Trained Nurses and Midwives', 'Assistant Nurses', and 'Student Nurses and Probationer Assistant Nurses')[2] except in two respects. First, 'mental attendants' are in these categories for 1921 and 1931 but excluded in the categories chosen for 1951. By 1951, the occupation of mental attendant had ceased to exist in the public services. The designation

---

[1] These were categories 843, 844, and 845 in 1921; and 793, 794, and 795 in 1931. See *Census of England and Wales 1921—Occupations Classifications and Tables*, p. 81: HMSO, 1924; and *Census of England and Wales 1931—Occupations Classifications and Tables*, p. 93: HMSO, 1934, respectively.

[2] These were categories 770, 771, and 772. See *Census of England and Wales 1951—Occupations Classifications and Tables*, p. 105: HMSO, 1956.

'nurse' was applied by this year to persons who would have described themselves as 'mental attendants' at the earlier censuses. It is of course possible that some persons working under the National Health Service described themselves incorrectly to the census enumerators, and there were probably a very few persons working outside the national service who still chose to use the old terminology. Those who did so would have been classified as 'Hospital or Ward Orderlies and Attendants'[1] in the 1951 census. Such cases must be few.

Secondly, health visitors and tuberculosis visitors are counted as trained nurses in the 1951 census. In 1921 and 1931 they were classified under 'Subordinate Medical Service'.[2] In this respect, therefore, the categories chosen for 1951 overstate the number of nurses compared with those which have been chosen for the earlier years. It is not known how large this overstatement is. On 31 December 1953, there were 7,624 health visitors and tuberculosis visitors in England and Wales.[3] Of this total only 1,586 were exclusively engaged on visiting work, and 937 were solely employed as school nurses. The remaining 5,101 combined health visiting or tuberculosis visiting with school nursing, home nursing, midwifery, and mental deficiency visiting. It is not clear how this latter group would have described themselves to the census enumerators.

One further factor needs to be taken into account when comparing the figures for 1921 and 1931 with those for 1951. The census for the latter year collected information about nurses engaged in part-time employment. Information of this kind is not available for the earlier years. However, in 1921 and 1931, the role of part-time employment in hospitals but not domiciliary service was very small. Moreover, in 1951 the majority of part-timers were married women and the number of such women who were nurses was certainly much smaller in the two earlier years than it was in 1951. Nevertheless there obviously were some nurses, particularly in private practice, who were not working whole-time in 1921 and 1931. In the tables two part-timers are counted as one full-time equivalent for the year 1951. As no adjustment on these lines can be made for the earlier years, the figures for 1921 and 1931 are slightly overstated in this respect.

In short, the comparison between 1951 and the two earlier censuses is subject to three inaccuracies. The 1951 figures include health visitors, while the earlier figures do not. On the other hand, two part-timers are treated as one whole-timer in the 1951 figures but

---

[1] This was category 871. *Census of England and Wales 1951—Occupations Classifications and Tables*, p. 114: HMSO, 1956.

[2] In 1921 this was category 849, *Occupations Classifications* (1921), p. 81; and in 1931 category 799, *Occupations Classifications* (1931), p. 93.

[3] Ministry of Health, Department of Health for Scotland and Ministry of Education: *An Inquiry into Health Visiting*, p. 162: HMSO, 1956.

not in the 1921 and 1931 figures. Thirdly, mental attendants are excluded from the 1951 figures but included in the earlier figures. All these points need to be borne in mind when interpreting the figures that follow.

In the 1901 and 1911 censuses, there were two categories, 'Midwives' and 'Sick Nurses and Invalid Attendants',[1] which taken together seem at first sight to correspond to the categories selected from the 1921 and 1931 censuses. But the field covered by these categories was in some respects too wide and in other respects too narrow for correct comparisons to be made with the later figures. The figures from the census of 1901 were carefully examined by Burdett in his evidence to the Select Committee on the Registration of Nurses,[2] and it is possible to use his evidence and other information to produce a total which roughly corresponds to the figures for later years. As information is not available from which the 1911 census figures can be adjusted, hardly any use is therefore made of the figures for this year.

Under the categories named above from the 1901 census, 68,361 persons were enumerated. This total consisted of 3,055 midwives (female); 64,214 female nurses and invalid attendants; and 1,092 male nurses and invalid attendants. The total included a number of persons not really engaged in nursing the sick and excluded employees of poor law authorities who were enumerated under the heading of 'local government employees'.

Estimates can be made of these omissions. First, it appears that there were over 3,000 paid nurses and about 2,000 probationers in the workhouses in 1901.[3] Secondly, the number of 'nurses' in the mental hospitals can be estimated from the *Fifty-ninth Report of the Commission on Lunacy.*[4] On 1 January 1905, there were 40,155 male patients and 46,936 female patients in the County and County Borough mental hospitals. Day attendants were provided at a ratio of 1 for 10 female patients and 1 for 9.7 male patients. Thus there were about 4,700 female attendants and 3,900 male attendants.[5] In addition there were about 600 night attendants of each sex. An allowance has also to be made for the staff needed to look after the 5,689 'imbeciles' under the care of the Metropolitan Asylums Board. From all the information, it seems reasonable to guess that there were 5,500 females and 4,700 males working as nurses under local authority employment who were excluded from the census figures.

---

[1] In 1911 these were categories 3 : 3 : 4 and 3 : 3 : 5, *Census of England and Wales*, Vol. X, Appendix *Classified and Alphabetical Lists of Occupations.* For 1901, see the Summary Tables, p. 93: HMSO, 1903.

[2] *Registration of Nurses, Select Committee Report, 1905*, (170) vii, p. 102.

[3] See p. 51 above.   [4] P. 265.

[5] It was the normal practice for patients to be looked after by persons of their own sex.

On the other hand, under the heading 'Sick Nurses and Invalid Attendants' many women were included in the total of 64,214 who were not really engaged in nursing the sick. First there were 'aspirants' —members of religious orders. Secondly there were 'wet nurses' and 'tender nurses' who were not sick nurses. Thirdly, many of the older women who called themselves nurses were not engaged whole-time in the occupation. In particular, there were 6,014 women over the age of 65 enumerated in this category. Burdett took the view that there were 60,000 *bona fide* nurses in Great Britain from his wide knowledge of the real position at the time. This figure included the 5,000 nurses in workhouses mentioned above, but excluded male nurses and mental nurses. By applying his proportions to the England and Wales figure, it can be calculated that there were about 55,000 female nurses.

Including the 3,000 midwives, the 5,500 females and 4,700 males working in asylums mentioned above, it seems that there were in 1901 about 63,500 females and 5,700 males corresponding to the definition used for later years.

Table 1 shows in full-time equivalents the increase in the number of nurses throughout the century and relates this to the population of England and Wales.

TABLE I

Total Number of Nurses (Male and Female) in Full-time Equivalents and the Total Population

(England and Wales 1901, 1921, 1931, and 1951)

	1901	1921	1931	1951*
Total population (thousands)	32,528	37,887	39,952	43,745
Nurses in full-time equivalents	(69,200)	122,804	153,843	224,616
Number of nurses per thousand	(2·13)	3·24	3·85	5·13

* Two part-time nurses are counted as equivalent to one whole-time nurse.

The number of nurses increased from about 69,000 in 1901 to about 225,000 in 1951. The increase was fairly steady throughout the century. In absolute numbers the rate of increase in every ten years tended to increase slightly, but while between 1901 and 1921 the total increased by 77½ per cent, between 1931 and 1951 the total increased by 46 per cent. It appears that while there were 2·13 nurses to every 1,000 persons in 1901, there were about 5·1 nurses to every 1,000 persons in 1951. The ratio of nurses per head increased by about two and one-half.

Table 2 shows separately the increase in male nurses and the increase in female nurses—again in full-time equivalents.

TABLE 2

Female and Male Nurses in Full-time Equivalents
(England and Wales 1901, 1921, 1931, and 1951)

	1901	*1921*	*1931*	*1951**
Females	(63,500)	111,501	138,670	199,089
Males	(5700)	11,303	15,173	25,527
Total	(69,200)	122,804	153,843	224,616

* Two part-time nurses are counted as equivalent to one whole-time nurse.

Between 1901 and 1951 the number of female nurses increased just over threefold from about 63,500 to about 199,000. The number of male nurses increased more than fourfold—from about 6,000 to about 25,500. Men played an increasing role in the nursing profession. Between 1931 and 1951 female nurses increased by about 44 per cent and male nurses by about 68 per cent.

In Table 3, the total of male and female nurses in 1951 is broken down into trained nurses, students, and assistant nurses.

TABLE 3

Female and Male Nurses in Different Categories
(England and Wales 1951)

	Females		*Males*	
	Number	*Percentage*	*Number*	*Percentage*
Trained nurses	136,953	68·7	19,144	75·0
Student nurses	45,723	23·0	4028	15·8
Assistant nurses	16,413	8·3	2355	9·2
Total	199,089	100·0	25,527	100·0

While 69 per cent of female nurses were trained, 75 per cent of males were trained. While 23 per cent of females were students, only about 16 per cent of male nurses were students. Males, once trained, were less likely than females to leave the profession. Nevertheless in

1951, females still represented 88½ per cent of the occupation. For this reason the rest of the analysis is confined to female nurses. Out of the total of 199,089, there were 16,547 part-timers who were counted in the preceding total as 8,274 full-time equivalents. Out of the part-time female nurses 84 per cent were married women and 7 per cent were widowed or divorced. Only 9 per cent of the part-timers were single.

Table 4 shows the marital state of the full-time female nurses.

TABLE 4

Female Nurses by Marital State

(England and Wales 1901, 1911, 1921, 1931, and 1951)

Year	Number			Percentage		
	Single	Married	Widowed and divorced	Single	Married	Widowed and divorced
1901	(37,213)	(30,056)		(55·3)	(44·7)	
1911	(55,288)	(11,867)	(16,507)	(66·1)	(14·2)	(19·7)
1921	93,760	7429	10,312	84·1	6·7	9·2
1931	121,990	6652	10,028	88·0	4·8	7·2
1951	141,162	41,232	8421	74·0	21·6	4·4

In this table and only in this table figures are shown unadjusted, in the form in which they appear in the censuses of 1901 and 1911. As mentioned above, these figures are not comparable with those for later years because they include a number of persons not really engaged in sick nursing and they exclude mental nurses and nurses working in poor law establishments. Nevertheless it is likely that the trends in the marital status of nurses have been broadly, though probably somewhat less strikingly, as indicated by the table. It shows that the proportion of single nurses was only 55 per cent in 1901 and 66 per cent in 1911. Taking midwives alone, who were separately enumerated, out of a total of 6,602 in 1911, only 1,085 (16 per cent) were single. By far the majority of mothers who got specialist help at confinement had the services of midwives who had probably been at some time confined themselves.

Between 1901 and 1931, the proportion of nurses who were single increased continuously—from 55 per cent in the first year to 88 per cent in 1931. The role of married women declined slightly faster than the role of widowed and divorced women. Between 1931 and 1951, however, the trend was reversed. The proportion of single women decreased from 88 per cent to 74 per cent and the role of widows and divorced women continued its regular decline, but the role of married women increased sharply. They made up only 5 per cent of female nurses in 1931: by 1951 married women were nearly 22 per cent of the total.

In Table 5, the total of married women in 1951 is divided into trained nurses, student nurses, and assistant nurses.

TABLE 5

Married Female Nurses in Different Categories
(England and Wales 1951)

	Number	Percentage
Trained nurses	34,013	82·5
Student nurses	1058	2·6
Assistant nurses	6161	14·9
Total	41,232	100·0

The table shows that $82\frac{1}{2}$ per cent of the married women were trained nurses and 15 per cent were assistant nurses: only $2\frac{1}{2}$ per cent of the married women were students. Thus the majority of married women engaged in nursing were presumably trained before marriage. The next largest group was working as assistant nurses. Very few married women undergo training. No doubt the low pay and the normal requirement to be resident in the hospital (quite apart from any age factor) discouraged married women from taking training.

Table 6 shows for 1951 a break-down of the total of widowed and divorced nurses on the same basis.

TABLE 6

Widowed and Divorced Nurses in Different Categories
(England and Wales 1951)

	Number	Percentage
Trained nurses	7067	83·9
Student nurses	307	3·6
Assistant nurses	1047	12·5
Total	8421	100·0

The proportions are very similar to those found for married women. While 84 per cent were trained and $12\frac{1}{2}$ per cent were assistant nurses, only $3\frac{1}{2}$ per cent (a slightly higher proportion) were students. No doubt low salaries and family responsibilities were the main factors discouraging widows from taking training.

Out of the total nursing staff in full-time equivalents of 224,616 in 1951, 141,162 (63 per cent) were single women engaged in full-time employment. As this is the largest group, the changes in the age structure of single nurses is examined against a wide demographic background.

Table 7 shows the number of females in each age group from 15 to 64 for each of the census years of this century.

TABLE 7

All Females by Age Groups 15–64

(*England and Wales 1901, 1911, 1921, 1931, and 1951*)

(*Thousands*)

Age group	1901	1911	1921	1931	1951
15–19	1639	1682	1775	1725	1369
20–24	1648	1673	1703	1795	1500
25–34	2770	3125	3140	3350	3219
35–44	2064	2509	2850	2954	3398
45–54	1506	1834	2287	2633	3122
55–64	1035	1213	1530	1960	2538
Total	10,662	12,036	13,285	14,417	15,146

The total of females aged 16–64 increased by 42 per cent between 1901 and 1951—from about 10·7 million to about 15·1 million. While the number in the older age groups increased proportionately more than the total, the number in the younger age groups actually diminished. Thus while the number of women aged 55–64 *increased* by 145 per cent, the number aged 15–19 *decreased* by 16½ per cent because of the declining birth rate. The highest number of women aged 15–19 enumerated in the census was in the year 1921. After 1921 there were less young women in the population.

Table 8 shows the percentage of women who were single in each age group.

Among women over 45 there was a somewhat higher proportion of single women in 1951 than at the beginning of the century, but the proportion of single women under the age of 45 declined dramatically. In other words marriage rates increased sharply after 1931. While in 1931, 74 per cent of women aged 20–24 were single, only 52 per cent of this age group were single in 1951; in the age group 25–34 single women declined from 33 per cent of the total to 18 per cent of the total between these two years.

Table 9 shows the absolute numbers of single women in each age group.

TABLE 8

Percentage of Females who were Single by Age Groups
(England and Wales 1901, 1911, 1921, 1931, and 1951)

(Percentages)

Age group	1901	1911	1921	1931	1951
15–19	98·4	98·8	98·3	98·2	95·6
20–24	72·6	75·7	72·6	74·2	51·8
25–34	34·0	35·5	33·7	33·0	18·2
35–44	18·5	19·6	19·2	19·4	13·7
45–54	13·6	15·8	16·4	16·4	15·1
55–64	11·7	13·2	15·3	15·6	15·5

TABLE 9

Single Females by Age Groups
(England and Wales 1901, 1911, 1921, 1931, and 1951)

(Thousands)

Age groups	1901	1911	1921	1931	1951
15–19	1613	1662	1745	1694	1309
20–24	1197	1267	1237	1332	777
25–34	941	1110	1059	1105	587
35–44	382	493	548	573	467
45–54	205	289	375	431	471
55–64	121	160	234	306	394
Total	4459	4981	5198	5441	4005

While the total number of women aged 15–64 increased by 42 per cent between 1901 and 1951, the number of *single* women aged 15–64 actually declined by 10 per cent from about 4·5 million to 4 million. The peak of the census years was 1931 when there were 5·4 million single women. Thus between 1931 and 1951 the number of single women aged 25–34 decreased from about 1·1 million to under 0·6 million.

This unfavourable development for the recruitment of unmarried young nurses was somewhat counteracted by an increase in the proportion of women who went out to work. These proportions are shown for the different years in Table 10.

TABLE 10

Percentage of Single Females who were Occupied by Age Groups
(England and Wales 1901, 1911, 1921, 1931, and 1951)

(Percentages)

Age groups	1901	1911	1921	1931	1951
15–19	66·7	69·4	—*	—*	80·5
20–24	73·4	77·7	80·5	—*	91·1
25–34	70·2	74·0	76·3	80·5	86·9
35–44	64·1	66·1	68·1	72·8	81·2
45–54	57·1	58·8	60·3	64·5	74·9
55–64	44·6	45·6	49·1	51·0	50·3

* The census does not give information in these exact age groups.

With only one exception, the proportion of single women going out to work increased in each age group between each census year. Table 11 shows the absolute numbers of occupied single women in each age group.

TABLE 11

Occupied Single Females by Age Groups
(England and Wales 1901, 1911, 1921, 1931, and 1951)

(Thousands)

Age groups	1901	1911	1921	1931	1951
15–19	1076	1154	—*	—*	1054
20–24	879	984	996	—*	708
25–34	661	821	808	890	510
35–44	245	326	373	417	379
45–54	117	170	226	278	353
55–64	54	73	115	156	198
	3032	3528			3202

* The census does not give information in these exact age groups.

While the total number of single females aged 16–64 decreased by 10 per cent between 1901 and 1951, the number of occupied single women increased by 5½ per cent between these years—from about 3 million to about 3·2 million. In the age group 25–34, which plays a large role in the provision of nurses, the number of occupied single women declined from 890,000 to 510,000 (by 43 per cent) between 1931 and 1951.

The number of single nurses is next related to the figures of the number of occupied single women in each age group. The table covers only the period 1921 to 1951 as it is not possible to divide into age groups the estimate of the number of nurses in 1901. Table 12 shows the proportion of occupied single women who were nurses.

TABLE 12

Percentage of Occupied Single Women who were Nurses by Age Groups
(England and Wales 1921, 1931, and 1951)

(*Percentages*)

Age groups	1921	1931	1951
15–19	—	—	2·56
20–24	2·07	—	4·91
25–34	4·12	3·96	6·26
35–44	4·98	4·73	5·75
45–54	4·82	4·82	4·45
55–64	3·72	4·51	4·19

This table deserves careful examination. Between 1921 and 1931, the proportion of occupied single women aged 25–44 who were nurses declined very slightly, while in the age group 55–64 the proportion of occupied single women engaged in nursing increased noticeably from 3·7 per cent to 4·5 per cent. Between 1931 and 1951 these trends were reversed. In the age group 25–34 the proportion of single occupied women who were nurses increased from about 4 per cent to about 6¼ per cent; in the age group 35–44 the increase was from about 4¾ per cent to 5¾ per cent; but in the older age groups nursing played a slightly smaller role among occupations for women in 1951 than in 1931. It is also possible to compare the role of nursing in the age group 20–24 between the years 1921 and 1951. The proportion of occupied single women who were nurses increased between these years from about 2·1 per cent to 4·9 per cent. The earlier age of admission to nursing in 1951 than in 1921 was one major reason for this change.

Table 13 shows the absolute numbers of single nurses in each age group.

Between 1921 and 1951, the number of single nurses of all ages increased from about 94,000 to about 141,000—an increase of about 50 per cent. In the age group 25–44 the change in numbers was small: the increase in the proportion of single occupied women engaged in nursing roughly offset the decline in the number of single occupied women aged 25–34 caused by the decline in the birth rate and the

TABLE 13

Female Single Nurses by Age Group
(England and Wales 1921, 1931, and 1951)

1921		1931		1951	
Age group	Number	Age group	Number	Age group	Number
−19*	5162	−21	18,174	15–19	27,015
20–24	20,617	21–24	26,595	20–24	34,750
25–34	33,187	25–34	35,262	25–34	31,950
35–44	18,563	35–44	19,713	35–44	21,780
45–54	10,902	45–54	13,399	45–54	15,719
55–64	4274	55–64	7033	55–64	8301
65 +	1055	65 +	1814	65 +	1647
Total	93,760		121,990		141,162

* In 1921 and 1931 it is not possible to separate the age group 14–15. However, there were only 78 and 99 nurses in this age group in 1921 and 1931 respectively.

increase in the incidence of marriage. The increase in the proportionate contribution of the age group 45–54 to nursing was roughly equivalent to that of all age groups: there were about 5,000 more nurses in this age group in 1951 than 1921. The number of nurses over age 55 increased between 1921 and 1931 and then remained fairly constant with about 4,500 more nurses in 1951 than in 1921. Both absolutely and relatively the largest increase in the number of nurses came from single women under the age of 25. In 1921 there were under 26,000; by 1931 there were about 45,000; by 1951 the number was increased to 62,000. Taking the age group under 20 by itself, the number of nurses in this group increased from about 5,000 in 1921 to about 27,000 in 1951.

Table 14 shows more closely these changes in the recruitment of nurses under the age of 20.

Taking the age group 16–17, the table shows that between 1921 and 1951, the total number of single girls decreased from about 700,000 to about 530,000—a fall of about 25 per cent. But an increasing proportion of these girls were occupied. Thus the number of occupied girls fell by only 14 per cent, compared to the fall of 25 per cent in the number of girls in this age group. But while only about 0·1 per cent of occupied girls in this age group were nurses in 1921, by 1951 1·9 per cent were nurses. Thus the contribution to the nursing profession increased from less than 700 in 1921 to over 8,000 in 1951.

TABLE 14

Single Women, Occupied Women, and Nurses under the Age of 20

(England and Wales 1921 and 1951)

	Age group 16–17		Age group 18–19	
	1921	1951	1921	1951
1. Single women	708,774	530,387	676,230	506,633
2. Occupied single women	503,403	434,632	533,420	476,978
3. (2 as percentage of 1)	71·0	81·9	78·9	94·1
4. Nurses	668	8285	4416	18,061
5. (4 as percentage of 2)	0·13	1·91	0·83	3·79

Similar trends were at work among girls aged 18–19. Between 1921 and 1951, the number in the age group fell, but the number occupied fell somewhat less. But while in 1921 only about 0·8 per cent of occupied girls aged 18–19 were nurses, by 1951 nearly 3·8 per cent were in the nursing profession. The total number of nurses in this age group increased from about 4,400 to about 18,000 between these two years.

The educational background of nurses in 1951

The census of 1951 obtained information showing the age at which persons in different occupations left school. In the case of nurses a table was published covering only trained nurses, midwives, and student nurses. Thus the coverage of this data is different from that shown in the other tables in this appendix for 1951. Assistant nurses and student assistant nurses are excluded from this section.

Table 15 summarizes the information collected in this way.

TABLE 15

Terminal Education Ages for Trained Nurses, Midwives, and Student Nurses

(England and Wales 1951)

Age group	Percentage of nurses replying	Percentage of those who replied who left school at:					
		Under 15	15	16	17–19	20 or over	Total
Under 20	93·5	19·2	27·9	29·7	23·2	—	100·0
20–24	94·9	25·7	13·0	25·3	34·7	1·3	100·0
25–44	93·3	35·1	13·2	23·9	25·5	2·3	100·0
45–64	87·5	47·5	13·3	19·1	18·2	1·9	100·0
65 and over	65·8	46·6	13·2	16·6	21·4	2·2	100·0

The response to the question asked was good from the younger nurses. Over 93 per cent of the nurses under the age of 44 answered the question, and 87½ per cent of nurses aged 45–64. Only in the cases of nurses over 65 years of age was the response rather poor: only about two-thirds of this age group answered the question.

In general, the table shows that on average the younger a nurse was in 1951, the longer had been her schooling. Only the figures for nurses who had continued their education beyond the age of 20 fail to indicate this trend, but the figures involved are very small. Thus about 18 per cent of nurses aged 45–64, 25½ per cent of nurses aged 25–44, and nearly 35 per cent of nurses aged 20–24 completed their education between the ages of 17 and 19.[1] And about 25 per cent of nurses aged 20–24 left school at age 16.

This table suggests, though it does not prove conclusively, that entrants to the nursing profession have been increasingly better educated since the second decade of this century. For example most of the age group 45–64 which had a low proportion of the late school leavers were presumably recruited between 1911 and 1931, as it has been rare in this century for nurse training to be taken by women who are over the age of 30. This conclusion can only be avoided if an unduly high proportion of the better educated women leave the profession at early ages. Were the better educated women more likely to marry, to take jobs outside the field of nursing, or retire at a very early age? If not, nursing had been continuously recruiting better educated women. Indeed one might expect nursing to share in the improving general standard of education during this century.

In Table 16, the same information is presented in another form. The number of nurses finishing their education at different ages is compared with the total of women occupied in 1951 finishing their education at these ages. Out of the total of occupied women in 1951 who left school at the age of 16, nursing had just under 8 per cent in each age group. But out of the total of occupied women in 1951 who finished their education between the ages of 17 and 19, nursing had a higher proportion in the younger age groups than in the older age groups. Thus about 7 per cent of occupied women with this educational background were nurses in the age group 45–64, about 12 per cent in the age group 25–44, and 15 per cent in the age group 20–24. Unless the better educated left the profession earlier than the less educated, not only had nursing been continuously recruiting better educated women, it had also been obtaining an increasing proportion of such women.

In Table 17, the share that nursing takes of the better educated

---

[1] The figures for nurses under 20 are not really comparable with the rest of the table in the sense that a nurse leaving school at the age of 19 had little time to enter nursing before she would fail to qualify for the age group.

women is compared with that of the two other occupational groups which take a high proportion of better educated women—'teachers (excluding music)'[1] and 'shorthand typists, secretaries'.[2]

TABLE 16

Percentage of Occupied Women Finishing Education at Different Ages who were Nurses

(*England and Wales*)

Age group	Total occupied women	Nurses	Nurses as percentage of total occupied women
Leaving school at age 16			
20–24	110,500	8588	7·8
25–44	216,135	16,756	7·8
45–64	79,370	6093	7·7
Leaving school at ages 17–19			
20–24	76,283	11,766	15·4
25–44	150,239	17,878	11·9
45–64	78,686	5798	7·4
Finishing education at age 20 or over			
25–44	81,472	1609	2·0
45–64	49,959	615	1·2

TABLE 17

Percentage of Occupied Women Classified by Age Groups and Terminal Education Ages Engaged in Different Occupations

(*England and Wales 1951*)

Age group	Nurses	Teachers	Shorthand typists, secretaries
Leaving school at age 16			
20–24	7·8	1·3	26·4
25–44	7·8	2·7	18·9
45–64	7·7	4·4	12·1
Leaving school at ages 17–19			
20–24	15·4	10·1	24·0
25–44	11·9	10·8	19·9
45–64	7·4	21·2	10·8
Finishing education at age 20 or over			
25–44	2·0	62·2	3·4
45–64	1·2	71·5	2·2

---

[1] Category 785 in the Occupational Classification for the 1951 census.
[2] Category 891 in the Occupational Classification for the 1951 census.

The teaching profession was the main occupation of women who continued their education beyond the age of 20. Among women who finished their education between the ages of 17 and 19, teaching had a much smaller proportion of occupied women under the age of 45 than above that age. Teaching took a lower proportion of women with this educational background than nursing and the secretarial group of occupations. Both the latter occupations seem to have been increasing their shares to roughly the same extent. In the age group 20–24 these three occupational groups had about half the employed women who left school between the ages of 17 and 19.

Teaching took very few women who left school at the age of 16. But while nursing had a constant proportion of just under 8 per cent of occupied women in each age group, the secretarial occupations had many more in the age group 20–24 than in the older age groups. While just under 8 per cent of occupied women aged 20–24 were nurses, over 26 per cent were in the secretarial occupations.

The evidence, therefore, seems to suggest that nursing was recruiting not only more better educated women but a higher proportion of such women. The main occupational groups which competed with nursing for the better educated girl were teaching and secretarial work.

Hospital Nurses in 1937

In this appendix we are publishing for the first time the results of the statistical inquiry conducted by the Athlone Committee at the end of 1937. The Committee suspended its activities at the outbreak of war and for this reason no final report was ever issued. However, the questionnaire which had been dispatched 'to all hospitals and institutions asking for statistical information on various points'[1] had been completed and the returns had been entered in large ledgers before the work came to an end.

These ledgers have been traced in the records of the Ministry of Health. Unfortunately it has not been possible to trace either the completed questionnaires themselves or the files concerned with them.[2] Consequently this report on the results of the inquiry is not as detailed as could be wished. The tables that follow have been carefully pieced together from the data that have survived, and the appropriate calculations have been made.[3] They are published here with the kind permission of the Ministry of Health, in the belief that they make a substantial contribution to knowledge about the position of hospital nursing before the war.

The response to the inquiry was good. Returns were received from nearly 2,200 hospitals and institutions containing nearly 440,000 beds. The details are shown in Table 1.

Hospitals were asked how many nursing staff they were employing in 1933 and 1937. About 8 per cent more hospitals returned information for 1937 than for 1933. Some new hospitals were built between these dates, but most of the difference must have arisen because some of the hospitals did not or could not make as full a return for 1933 as for 1937. If the returns were accepted at their face value, it would appear that the number of nursing staff increased by 22·4 per cent between these years. This figure exaggerates the increase. The figures for hospitals making complete returns in the two years are shown in Table 2.

---

[1] *Athlone Committee Report*, p. 5.
[2] Not all the records of the Ministry of Health have survived the war.
[3] Not all the ledgers were clearly labelled.

TABLE 1

Hospitals Replying to the Questionnaire and Stating the Number of Beds Provided

(England and Wales 1937)

	Voluntary hospitals	Local authority hospitals	Mental hospitals*
Number of hospitals	865	1145	188
Number of beds provided	76,577	189,086	173,083
Number of beds occupied	(61,870)†	138,579	168,129
Percentage occupied	(80·5)†	73·3	97·1

* England only.

† Estimates have been made of the number of occupied beds in ten hospitals with incomplete returns.

TABLE 2

Male and Female Nursing Staff Employed in Hospitals giving Complete Returns

(England and Wales 1933 and 1937)

	Voluntary hospitals	Local authority hospitals	Mental hospitals*
Number of hospitals	795	825	96
Nursing staff in 1933	26,839	29,975	19,688
Nursing staff in 1937	30,165	35,480	20,830
1937 as percentage of 1933	112·4	118·4	106·0

* England only.

In hospitals making complete returns for both years, there was a total increase in nursing staff of 13 per cent between 1933 and 1937. The staff of local authority hospitals increased by 18 per cent and of voluntary hospitals by 12 per cent. Mental hospitals developed more slowly: the nursing staff increased by 6 per cent. The rate of growth was almost identical in training and non-training local authority institutions. In the voluntary hospitals, on the other hand, non-training hospitals increased their nursing staff 2½ per cent more than training hospitals. The increase came largely from more untrained staff. The number of assistant nurses on ward duty in the voluntary hospitals doubled according to the figures actually returned.[1] The figures in Table 2 almost certainly underestimate the actual expansion, but the figure of an 18 per cent increase in staff in four years seems more consistent with the estimate of increase in establishments made by the Society of Medical Officers of 52 per cent between 1928–29 and 1938.[2]

The full return of nursing staff is shown in Table 3.

---

[1] See Table 3.   [2] See p. 122 above.

TABLE 3

Male and Female Nursing Staff Employed by Hospitals (England and Wales 1933 and 1937)

Date	Type of hospital	Number of hospitals	Sex	Administrative staff*	Ward sisters†	Deputy charge nurses	Staff nurses on ward duty‡	Probationers§ 1st year	2nd year	3rd year	Others	4th year nurses on ward duty	Assistant nurses on ward duty‖	Ward orderlies	Special departments** Sisters	Staff nurses	Assistant nurses¶	Other nursing staff	Total
1933	Voluntary	786	F	2011	2489	—	2133	4576	4032	3362	930	626	3121	605	952	706	132	567	26242
			M	—	1	—	2	7	10	2	—	—	10	61	7	2	6	20	128
	Municipal	1128	F	2216	3170	—	3531	4828	3962	2622	599	522	10125	494	304	297	173	317	33160
	Mental††	161	M	17	43	—	76	16	20	20	—	—	659	251	5	8	18	29	1162
		161	F	758	2321	1009	1648	3147	1969	1323	930	—	628	—	32	34	28	119	13946
		142	M	491	1855	866	3847	736	582	508	636	—	1062	—	31	59	61	64	10798
1937	Voluntary	856	F	2494	2896	—	2989	5046	4381	3623	992	743	6221	696	1184	987	172	720	33144
			M	1	1	—	6	6	12	2	—	—	10	88	6	2	13	20	167
	Municipal	1201	F	2645	3783	—	4517	5067	4244	2826	913	789	12500	1163	417	591	216	454	40125
	Mental††	173	M	25	54	—	164	46	29	20	15	1	995	356	6	39	19	54	1823
		173	F	895	2498	1219	1902	3527	2226	1300	987	—	746	—	52	63	40	154	15609
		158	M	560	2041	993	4760	1038	731	657	711	—	911	—	42	113	52	77	12686

* All female administrative nurses: matron, assistant matron, home sister, sister housekeeper, sister tutor, night superintendent (or night sister).

† This column includes charge nurses in mental hospitals.

‡ Staff nurses who are not State Registered are not included in this column. RMPA qualified male nurses are included.

§ In the case of voluntary and municipal hospitals probationers are persons who are receiving training in the hospital with the object of passing, during the time they are in the hospital, the examinations of the General Nursing Council for admission to the State Register, General or Supplementary.

‖ This column is for nurses who remain in the hospital for a year after passing the final examinations of the General Nursing Council.

¶ This includes all persons carrying out any nursing duties who cannot be entered under any other heading in the table. In the case of mental hospitals it includes other established nurses with five years' service, no qualifications.

** This heading includes X-ray departments, out-patient departments, theatre staff, etc.

†† England only.

A number of interesting points emerge from this table. The first is the share of work done by trained staff, untrained staff, and students. This is summarized in Table 4.

TABLE 4

The Proportion of Work Done by Different Grades of Nurses

(England and Wales 1933 and 1937)

(Percentages)

Year	Staff	Voluntary hospitals	Local authority hospitals	Mental hospitals	All hospitals
1933	Trained	34·7	30·3	52·4	38·2
	Untrained	15·0	33·7	7·9	20·4
	Students	50·3	36·0	39·7	41·4
	Total	100·0	100·0	100·0	100·0
1937	Trained	34·8	32·2	53·5	39·0
	Untrained	22·0	35·2	7·0	23·1
	Students	43·2	32·6	39·5	37·9
	Total	100·0	100·0	100·0	100·0

As a whole nearly 1 per cent more of the nursing work was done by trained staff in 1937 than in 1933. The local authority hospitals had 2 per cent more trained staff, the mental hospitals had 1 per cent more, and the voluntary hospitals had the same proportion as before. The share of the work done by students decreased by 3½ per cent between these two years. As a result, 2½ per cent more of the work was done by untrained staff. The position in mental hospitals changed little in this respect, but the local authority hospitals had 1½ per cent more untrained staff in 1937 than in 1933. The change in the voluntary hospitals was dramatic between the two years—they had 7 per cent less students and 7 per cent more untrained staff.

About 6½ per cent of the trained nursing staff of the hospitals in both years was engaged in administration, and 5·4 per cent worked in special departments in 1937 (compared to 4·7 per cent in 1933). As a result, the proportion of trained staff at work on the wards was low. In all hospitals, 31 per cent of ward staff was trained, but in the voluntary hospitals only 18 per cent of ward staff (including sisters) was trained.

Hospitals were asked whether they were finding increasing difficulty in obtaining staff. The replies are shown in Table 5.

TABLE 5

Percentage of Hospitals Finding Increasing Difficulty in Obtaining Nursing Staff

(*England and Wales 1937*)

	Voluntary hospitals		Local authority hospitals		Mental hospitals*	
	Number of hospitals replying	Percentage finding increasing difficulty	Number of hospitals replying	Percentage finding increasing difficulty	Number of hospitals replying	Percentage finding increasing difficulty
Fully trained nurses:						
Female	676	76	896	76	128	57
Male	28	4	262	12	110	6
Probationers:						
Female	699	57	536	71	158	74
Male	—	—	—	—	137	9
Assistant nurses	299	62	844	70	—	—
Orderlies	41	12	90	4	—	—
Ward maids	469	60	619	53	—	—

* England only

In non-mental hospitals, the shortage was worse for trained nurses than for probationers. Voluntary and local authority hospitals were in relatively the same position in their search for trained personnel. About three-quarters of the hospitals reported that they were having increasing difficulty in recruiting staff. But while 71 per cent of local authority hospitals reported increasing difficulty in obtaining probationers, only 57 per cent of the voluntary hospitals were in this position. This was true despite the substantially larger pay provided by the local authority hospitals.[1] Assistant nurses were almost as hard to get as trained nurses. There was, however, virtually no difficulty in obtaining male nurses. Only 9 per cent of mental hospitals found increasing difficulty in obtaining male probationers and 6 per cent in obtaining male trained nurses.

Table 6 shows the number of hospitals reporting that they admitted probationers before the age of 18.

---

[1] See p. 276 below.

TABLE 6

Hospitals Admitting Probationers to Ward Duty Before the Age of 18

(England and Wales 1929 and 1937)

	Voluntary hospitals	Local authority hospitals	Mental hospitals*
1929	30	22	13
1937	94	69	28

* England only.

The table indicates that three times the number of hospitals admitted probationers before the age of 18 in 1937 than in 1929. The increase was less in mental hospitals than in other types of hospital.

The inquiry provided some interesting information on the educational origin of probationers which is shown in Table 7.

TABLE 7

The Proportion of Probationers who were Educated at an Elementary School Only

(England and Wales 1929, 1933, and 1937)

	Voluntary hospitals			Local authority hospitals			Mental hospitals*		
	1929	1933	1937	1929	1933	1937	1929	1933	1937
Number of hospitals replying	293	293	293	153	153	153	82	82	82
Number of probationers admitted	4807	5856	6058	3146	3738	2984	3205	2911	3488
Probationers with elementary education only	829	1062	1513	2067	2157	2131	3025	2704	3221
Percentage with elementary education only	17	18	25	66	58	71	94	93	92

* England only.

Between 1929 and 1937, the voluntary hospitals recruited a steadily decreasing proportion of probationers with secondary education. In 1929, 83 per cent of their recruits were secondary school girls compared with 75 per cent in 1937. The local authorities did not obtain anything like this proportion of secondary school girls. They admitted 34 per cent in 1929 and 29 per cent in 1937. In 1933, on the other hand, possibly owing to the depression, 42 per cent of the recruits had secondary education. In the mental hospitals secondary school girls were very rare. The proportion admitted increased from 6 per cent in 1929 to 8 per cent in 1937. About 16½ per cent of girls and 16½ per cent of boys in this age group in the whole country were provided with secondary education.[1] Mental hospital probationers were by this criterion less well educated than the average population of their age group.

Table 8 shows the arrangements made for accommodating the nursing staff of mental hospitals.

TABLE 8

Accommodation of Mental Nurses in 179 Mental Hospitals
(England 1937)

	Females		Males	
	Number	*Percentage*	*Number*	*Percentage*
Separate homes or hostels	7657	50·1	282	2·7
Rooms adjoining wards	3894	25·4	2179	20·6
Elsewhere in hospital	1938	12·7	415	3·9
Estate cottages	168	1·1	1688	16·0
Outside	1634	10·7	5998	56·8
Total	15,291	100·0	10,562	100·0

A quarter of the female nurses in mental hospitals lived in rooms adjoining the wards, and a further eighth lived elsewhere in the hospital but not in separate homes or hostels. Male nurses were in a more favourable position. A fifth of them lived in rooms adjoining the wards and 3·9 per cent lived elsewhere within the hospital.

Table 9 shows the average of salaries reported for nurses in voluntary and local authority hospitals.

In round figures the voluntary hospitals paid probationers £21, £25, £30, and £40 in their first, second, third, and fourth years respectively. The local authority scales were substantially higher— £34, £38, £41, and £45 10s. in the four years. The salaries paid to probationers by the voluntary hospitals were slightly higher in London than in the rest of the country. Regional differences were much wider for local authority hospitals. In London, the first-year probationer was paid about £39, in the provinces £33 10s., and in

---

[1] D. V. Glass: *Social Mobility in Britain*, p. 128: London, 1954. The figures apply to those born between 1910 and 1919 inclusive.

TABLE 9

The Average Salaries* of Nurses

(England and Wales 1937)

Grade	Voluntary hospitals		Local authority hospitals	
	Commencing	Maximum	Commencing	Maximum
	£ s.	£ s.	£ s.	£ s.
Matron	158 14	211 18	137 18	173 6
Ward sister	81 8	96 6	90 16	109 4
Staff nurse	66 16	75 4	71 15	80 18
Assistant nurse	48 3	58 3	53 15‡	63 17
Nurse without previous experience	25 0	†	36 4	—
Ward orderly (non-resident)	†	†	136 5	147 18

Grade	1st year	2nd year	3rd year	4th year	1st year	2nd year	3rd year	4th year
	£ s.	£ s.	£ s.	£ s.	£ s.	£ s.	£ s.	£ s.
Probationer	20 11	25 3	29 11	40 4	33 6	38 4	41 8	45 10

* Receipts in cash (i.e. excluding the value of emoluments in kind).
† Insufficient sample.
‡ Non-resident £122 10s.

Wales £27. These regional differences were preserved throughout the three or four years of training.

The local authorities paid higher salaries than the voluntary hospitals to all grades of nursing staff.[1] They paid staff nurses about £5 more than the voluntary hospitals, and ward sisters about £10 more. The untrained grades were also better paid.

The position with regard to superannuation is shown in Table 10.

In 1937, 84 per cent of the local authority hospitals and only 63 per cent of voluntary hospitals insisted on the nurses making provision for their old age.

The longest hours were worked by probationers in voluntary hospitals. They were on duty 129 hours per fortnight when on night duty, and 111 hours per fortnight when on day duty. In local authority hospitals, the probationer worked 108 hours per fortnight on day duty and 119 hours on night duty. Hours worked in mental

---

[1] The figures shown for matrons in the table are of very limited value. The salary of the matron varied according to the size of the hospital.

TABLE 10

Percentage of Hospitals with a Compulsory Superannuation Scheme
(England and Wales 1937)

	Voluntary hospitals	Local authority hospitals	Mental hospitals*
Number of hospitals replying	913	1081	12
Number with a compulsory super-annuation scheme	576	911	5
Percentage with a compulsory superannuation scheme	63·0	84·3	41·7

* England only.

TABLE 11

Average Hours Worked by Nurses
(England and Wales 1937)

	Voluntary hospitals, females	Local authority hospitals, females	Mental hospitals*	
			females	males
Hours worked per fortnight				
1st-year probationer:				
day duty†	111·2	107·7	105·3	104·8
night duty†	128·6	118·9	106·6	105·5
State registered nurse‡				
day duty§	103·7	104·0	104·4	103·8
night duty§	124·2	117·2	105·3	103·9
Hours worked during longest day				
1st-year probationer:				
day duty†	9·5	9·4	11·2	11·1
night duty†	10·7	11·0	10·7	10·6
State registered nurse‡				
day duty§	8·9	9·2	11·0	11·0
night duty§	9·9	10·7	10·5	10·3

* England only.
† Excluding meal times but including time spent at compulsory lectures.
‡ Other than the ward sister.
§ Ward duty only.

hospitals were shorter. In all types of hospital trained nurses worked about 104 hours per fortnight on day duty. On night duty the voluntary hospital nurse worked 124 hours per fortnight. These are average figures. A 140-hour fortnight was worked in some hospitals in 1937.

Table 12 shows the proportion of hospitals operating a 96-hour fortnight.

TABLE 12

Percentage of Hospitals Operating a 96-hour Fortnight
(England and Wales 1937)

	Voluntary hospitals	Local authority hospitals	Mental* hospitals
Number of hospitals replying	802	771	183
Number operating a 96-hour fortnight	100	162	43
Percentage operating a 96-hour fortnight	12	21	23

* England only.

In 1937 12 per cent of voluntary hospitals, 21 per cent of local authority hospitals, and 23 per cent of mental hospitals operated a 96-hour fortnight.

Nurses' Pay

In this appendix information is presented showing the remuneration of the nursing profession during the past hundred and fifty years. Data for the last century are inevitably very patchy, but from 1930 onwards it is possible to provide a more complete picture. The appendix concludes with a brief description of the negotiations conducted in the Nurses and Midwives Whitley Council in the 1950's.

In the first half of the nineteenth century there were wide variations in the pay provided for nurses. One reason for these variations was the different practices of the hospitals with regard to what was provided in kind. At some hospitals, food, drink, and clothing represented a considerable part of the remuneration. Thus in 1838, nurses at St Thomas's Hospital were paid 9s. 7d. a week and beer, while at Guy's in the same year nurses received £30 a year. At St George's, the nurses received £16 per year and in addition 'six pounds of bread per week, two pints of table beer daily, and one shilling a day for board wages'.[1] At St Bartholomew's, the nurses received 7s. a week, two gowns and one cap per annum, half a loaf and a pint of beer daily, the meat from the hospital broth, and dinner on Sundays. Nurses on night duty received 8s. 9d. a week.[2] In one provincial hospital in 1843 nurses were paid either ten or twelve guineas.[3] In 1858 the maximum for day nurses was fixed at £18 at St Mary's; the night nurses were to have a maximum of £20 per annum.[4] This figure of £20 was also the maximum pay of a nurse at All Saints Home with all found in 1862.[5] However, the charge for the hire of these nurses for work in private families was one guinea per week. At this

---

[1] Saunders: *The Middlesex Hospital 1745–1948*, pp. 23–24.

[2] *Lancet Commission on Nursing*, pp. 18–19.

[3] F. H. Jacob: *A History of the General Hospital near Nottingham*, p. 134: Bristol and London, 1951.

[4] Cope: *A Hundred Years of Nursing at St Mary's Paddington*, p. 44. St Mary's raised the maximum pay of nurses to £22 in 1865 and to £25 in 1876; the maximum for sisters went up to £30 in 1865 and £40 in 1879 with all found.

[5] From a contemporary circular in the British Museum (BM Tract 1862–1890 CUP 401 g⁵).

time private nursing could be very rewarding. Five guineas a week was paid to one private ladies' nurse in 1854, who apparently alternated nursing with prostitution.[1]

The hospitals paid the sisters more than the nurses. In 1838 sisters received £50 per year at Guy's, £37 a year at St Thomas's and £20 at St Mary's[2] and St George's. However, in the last case, the sisters also received the same items in kind as the nurses which are mentioned above.[3] In 1837, St Bartholomew's paid sisters between 14s. 6d. and £1 a week, rather more for senior sisters plus one cap and one gown per annum and dinner on Sundays.[4]

The first probationers were paid £10 per year at St Thomas's in 1860 and the same figure was adopted at St Mary's in 1876. At this latter date, £16 to £18 was thought suitable pay for respectable ward maids, with board, lodging, uniform, and partial washing.[5] In 1890 Burdett reported that 'probationers' salaries are usually £10 the first year, £15 the second, and £20 the third; increasing afterwards £1 yearly up to £26. Sisters, or head nurses who have charge of the large wards, receive from £30 to £60 a year.'[6] When the secretary of St Mary's Hospital examined the wages paid to probationers in other hospitals in 1893, he reported in much the same terms. 'The wages of probationers under training average about £14 during the three years.'[7] In 1897 a similar study of eleven London hospitals showed the salaries paid to nurses in the three years after qualification averaged just over £26 10s.[8] Burdett's statement seems reliable—at least for the larger London hospitals.

Nurses received more in kind than they received in cash. If the expenditure on nursing salaries in thirteen hospitals in 1902 is divided by the numbers of nurses, the average salary of a nurse works out at about £19. The cost of maintenance, laundry, and uniforms for nurses in these same hospitals amounted to over £25 a head.[9] Allowing for all costs attributable to board and lodging nurses, £30 a head might be a more realistic figure.

Table 1 shows the pay of nurses in the poor law service at the turn of the century. The information is taken from the *Departmental Committee on Workhouse Nursing* (1902).[10]

---

[1] Letter from Mrs Gaskell, 1854. See Woodham-Smith: *op. cit.*, p. 51.
[2] Cope: *op. cit.*, p. 44.   [3] Saunders: *op. cit.*, pp. 23–24.
[4] *Lancet Commission Report*, p. 19.   [5] Cope: *op. cit.*, pp. 45–46, 60, 69.
[6] *Burdett's Annual 1890*, p. lxxxvii.   [7] *Ibid.*, p. lxxxvi.
[8] These figures are taken from *Burdett's Annual* for this year.
[9] Cope: *op. cit.*, pp. 98–99. See also *Select Committee on Registration 1905*, p. 22. The matron of the London Hospital confirms the figures collected by St Mary's.
[10] Departmental Committee on Workhouse Nursing: *Minutes of Evidence taken before the Departmental Committee appointed by the President of the Local*

TABLE 1

The Pay of Nurses in the Poor Law Service
(England and Wales 1896 and 1901)

Year	Grade	Separate infirmaries	Town workhouses	Country workhouses*
		£ s.	£ s.	£ s.
1896	Nurses	25 2 (950)†	25 16 (1310)	24 14 (459)
	Probationer nurses	13 6 (588)	10 16 (340)	10 4 (8)
1901	Superintendent nurses	—	39 8 (164)	38 0 (63)
	Nurses	27 10 (1032)	26 14 (1338)	26 14 (557)
	Probationer nurses	13 8 (1119)	13 6 (875)	13 0 (79)

* A workhouse situated in a Parish which is part of a Rural District or which constitutes or forms part of an Urban District of less than 5,000 inhabitants is, for the purposes of this statement, called a 'Country workhouse'.

† The figures in brackets show the number of nurses.

The workhouse probationers received on average slightly less than the probationers in voluntary hospitals. At Bath probationers received only £5 in the first year.[1] Nurses on the other hand were paid about the same as their voluntary hospital equivalents. The pay in separate infirmaries tended to be higher than in the workhouses.

Much higher pay could be earned in domiciliary work than institutional work. In Bournemouth, a nurse from the Victoria and Bournemouth Nursing Institute and Home Hospital would get 31s. 6d. per week for ordinary cases and two guineas for infectious and mental cases. If she chose to go on a salaried basis, she would receive £35 per year plus 5 or 10 per cent of her takings.[2] In London two or three guineas would be paid for a nurse. At the London Hospital a nurse on private work earned £30 to £50.

The estimates of nurses' pay in 1930 are shown in Table 2. They are calculated from information collected by the Lancet Commission on Nursing.

Among the complete training schools, the municipal hospitals paid probationers and staff nurses about £10 more per annum than the voluntary hospitals. They were nevertheless still very short of staff. Work in children's hospitals was the most popular and the worst

Government Board to enquire into the Nursing of the Sick Poor in Workhouses, Part II, Cmd. 1367, p. 157: HMSO, 1902.

[1] Committee on Workhouse Nursing 1902, p. 89.

[2] Select Committee on Registration 1905, p. 3.

TABLE 2

The Average Pay of Nurses in 1930*

Type of hospital	Probationers			Staff nurses (minimum)	Sisters (minimum)
	1st year	2nd year	3rd year		
	£ s.	£ s.	£ s.	£ s.	£ s.
Approved for complete training:					
London Voluntary	20 13	24 11	29 18	51 14	75 0
Provincial Voluntary	20 5	24 13	30 11	55 4	72 19
Municipal	28 13	33 3	40 9	60 13	78 11
Approved for partial training	22 13	26 0	34 6	61 11	74 1
Approved for special training:					
Children	19 12	23 6	29 13	51 14	74 9
Fever	32 1	37 12	†	57 15	79 19
Tuberculosis (not approved)	29 8	33 5	40 13	56 15	79 4
All in inquiry	24 14	28 16	34 9	57 5	76 2

* This table is based on figures taken from the *Lancet Commission on Nursing 1932*, p. 235. The information from which this table has been calculated shows the number of hospitals paying salaries within certain ranges. We have assumed an average salary for each range which seems to fit the data.

† Insufficient sample reporting.

paid. Fever and tuberculosis hospitals tended to give the highest remuneration.

The salaries of female nurses at various dates between 1937 and 1959 are shown in Table 3. The information for 1937 is taken from data collected by the Athlone Committee (see Appendix II, p. 269). As so few hospital nurses were non-resident in this year, insufficient information was available to form the basis of an estimate of the value attributed to emoluments (board, lodging, and other services). Thus no estimate of the total salary can be made. The figures for later years are taken from the recommendations of the Nurses' Salaries Committee for 1943 and 1947[1] and the decisions of the Nurses and Midwives Whitley Council for later years.[2] The rates quoted are for female nurses in general hospitals. The rates for staff nurses and sisters apply to nurses on the General Register. For the rates before 1948, the net salary shown is salary exclusive of emoluments: the value of emoluments is shown as the residence charge. The table

[1] Ministry of Health: *First Report of Nurses' Salaries Committee* (HMSO, 1943), Cmd. 6424; and Ministry of Health: *Nurses' Salaries Committee Notes No. 15*, 1947.   [2] NMC (*Whitley Council*) Circulars 30, 55, and 74.

TABLE 3.—The Salaries of Nurses (1937–1959) (£ per annum)

	1937 Voluntary hospitals	1937 Municipal hospitals	1943	Dec. 1946	Feb. 1949	June 1952	Dec. 1954	April 1956	March 1959
Total salary									
1st-year student	—	—	115	130*	200†	225	240	260	285
2nd-year student	—	—	120	140*	210†	235	250	270	300
3rd-year student	—	—	125	150*	225†	250	265	285	320
Staff nurse Minimum	—	—	190	220*	315	360	385	417	496
Maximum	—	—	230	280*	415	460	485	522	621
Ward sister Minimum	—	—	230	280*	375	425	450	487	620
Maximum	—	—	300	380*	500	550	575	615	800
Assistant nurse Minimum	—	—	165‡	210	285	325	345	374	425
Maximum	—	—	185‡	270	385	425	445	479	545
Net salary of resident									
1st-year student	20·55	33·3	40	55*	100†	117	127	141	157
2nd-year student	25·15	38·2	45	65*	110†	127	137	151	172
3rd-year student	29·55	41·4	50	75*	125†	142	152	166	192
Staff nurse Minimum	66·8	71·75	100	120*	195	225	242	264	316
Maximum	75·2	80·9	140	180*	295	325	342	369	441
Ward sister Minimum	81·4	90·8	130	160*	245	280	297	323	415
Maximum	96·3	109·2	200	260*	370	405	422	451	595
Assistant nurse Minimum	48·15‡	53·75‡	75‡	110	165	193	207	228	260
Maximum	58·15‡	63·85‡	95‡	170	265	293	307	333	380
Residence charge									
Student	—	—	75	75*	100†	108	113	119	128
Staff nurse	—	—	90	100*	120	135	143	153	180
Ward sister	—	—	100	120*	130	145	153	164	205
Assistant nurse	—	—	90‡	100	120	132	138	146	165

* 1 January 1946.   † 1 January 1949.

‡ In 1937 the rates apply to an experienced assistant nurse and in 1943 to an assistant nurse holding a certificate of training.

omits the revised salary scales introduced in October 1947, July 1948, and July 1957.

The first general review of nurses' salaries by the Whitley Council is described in Chapter XIII. The second claim from the staff side came in March 1952. It asked for a flat £100 for all grades from the staff nurse upwards. The management side refused to give the same amount to all nurses and after some delay, caused by government appeals for wage restraint, offered increases varying from £35 for an enrolled assistant nurse to £85 for a matron. The staff side repeated its request for a flat rate increase, but eventually accepted in September 1952 'a gently graduated increase from £40 to £60 "with reluctance" and without prejudice to a number of outstanding claims for various grades'.[1] Relative differentials were narrowed.

The next general claim came in August 1954. The staff argued that the increase of 1952 did not fully compensate for the increased cost of living since 1948. They therefore asked for all grades sufficient to compensate for half the fall in the value in their real salaries from February 1949 to June 1952, and complete compensation from that date. . . . The management side refused to consider changes in the cost of living before 1952 as relevant and, in November, offered £15 for students and £25 for staff nurses and higher grades. The staff expressed profound disappointment, and arbitration was asked and conceded. In February 1955 the Industrial Court awarded in favour of the management's offer.[2]

There was thus a further reduction of relative differentials for trained nurses.

In nursing, as in many other fields of employment, men had traditionally been paid more than women. This tradition had become enshrined in the wage structure of the National Health Service though the premium for men was not large. For many years, governments had been under pressure to introduce equal pay in the public services, and in the spring of 1955 the Government decided to act. Equal pay was to be introduced in seven stages spread over six years and the management side of the Whitley Council agreed to apply government policy to nurses. Pressure from the staff side for swifter action was firmly resisted.

Early in 1956, the staff side put in a new and substantial claim for all grades, arguing that nurses had had a relatively bad deal under the National Health Service; the administrative and clerical grades in particular had done much better than nurses. The management side rejected the claim but made an offer which would have provided increases for all grades broadly on a proportionate basis. Students were offered £15 more per year, staff nurses £25 at the minimum

---

[1] Clegg and Chester: *Wage Policy and the Health Service*, p. 43.
[2] *Ibid.*, pp. 44–45.

and £30 at the maximum, while the highest paid matrons would have received £75 at the maximum of their scale. After a suitably prolonged debate, the staff side agreed to accept the offer providing nobody received less than a £20 rise. This the management side eventually accepted; students gained therefore the largest relative increase.

In the spring of 1957, the staff side presented a further claim. In the general field, it asked for increases for students of between 15 and 23 per cent. If granted, the claim would have cost the hospital service £16 million for Great Britain. The management side refused to consider these proposals, stating that there had been a complete review of all salaries only a year before. All it would do would be to look at the salaries agreed in April 1956 in the light of any relevant changes which had taken place since that date. The staff side eventually agreed to negotiate on this basis, and agreement was reached for a 5 per cent increase for all grades to take effect from 1 July 1957.

In July 1958, the staff side submitted a substantial claim for mental nurses, and it was made clear during negotiations that a claim for higher salaries in other nursing fields was under consideration. The management side stated that it could not deal with the claim for mental nurses in isolation and asked to see the whole picture. The staff side reacted by submitting in November 1958 a claim for a 5 per cent increase for all grades which was made without prejudice to the proposals for a general revision which were still to come. The management side, rather than deal with this claim, decided to submit proposals itself for a complete review of nurses' salaries. An offer for the main grades of the hospital service was made in March 1959 consisting of increases of between 4½ per cent and 7 per cent for student and assistant nurses, of about 12½ per cent for staff nurses, and of about 20 per cent for ward sisters. The staff side pressed for another £15 for the lower grades and another £25 for the maximum of the ward sister scale. Ward sisters were granted the extra £25, and with this amendment the management side's offer was accepted.

Index